Level 1

Vocabulary Power

TEACHER'S MANUAL

Vocabulary Power

TEACHER'S MANUAL

Lessons for Students Who Use African American Vernacular English

by

Latrice M. Seals,
Sharolyn D. Pollard-Durodola,
Barbara R. Foorman,
and
Ashley M. Bradley

·PAUL·H·
BROOKES
PUBLISHING Co.®

Baltimore • London • Sydney

Paul H. Brookes Publishing Co.
Post Office Box 10624
Baltimore, Maryland 21285-0624

www.brookespublishing.com

Typeset by Barton Matheson Willse & Worthington, Baltimore, Maryland.
Manufactured in the United States of America by
Versa Press, Inc., East Peoria, Illinois.

For information on purchasing books used in this curriculum, see http://www.brookespublishing.com/seals.

Week 1 is based on *Richard Wright and the Library Card.* Text © 1997 by William Miller; illustrations © 1997 by Gregory Christie. Permission arranged with Lee & Low Books Inc, New York, New York 10016.

Weeks 2, 3, and 4 are based on *The Stories Julian Tells* by Ann Cameron, illustrated by Ann Strugnell. Permission arranged with Random House, Inc.

Weeks 6 and 7 are based on *The Hundred Penny Box* by Sharon Bell Mathis, illustrated by Leo and Diane Dillon. Permission arranged with Penguin Putnam Books for Young Readers.

Weeks 8, 9, and 11 are based on *Donavan's Word Jar* by Monalisa DeGross, illustrated by Cheryl Hanna. Text copyright © 1994 by Monalisa DeGross, illustrations copyright © 1994 by Cheryl Hanna. Permission arranged with HarperCollins Publishers Inc.

Week 12 is based on *More Stories Huey Tells* by Ann Cameron, illustrated by Lis Toft. Permission arranged with Farrar, Straus, and Giroux.

Weeks 13 and 14 are based on *Five Notable Inventors* by Wade Hudson, illustrated by Ron Garnett. Permission arranged with Scholastic Inc.

Weeks 16, 17, and 18 are based on *Justin and the Best Biscuits in the World* by Mildred Pitts Walter, illustrated by Catherine Stock. Permission arranged with Alfred A. Knopf.

Week 19 is based on THE BAT BOY AND HIS VIOLIN, by Gavin Curtis. Text copyright © 1998 Gavin Curtis. Reprinted with the permission of Simon & Schuster Books for Young Readers, an imprint of Simon & Schuster Children's Publishing Division.

Library of Congress Cataloging-in-Publication Data

Seals, Latrice M.
   Vocabulary power teacher's manual: lessons for students who use African American Vernacular English / by Latrice M. Seals . . . [et al.]
      p.   cm.
   Includes index.
   ISBN-13: 978-1-5766-680-2 (Teacher's manual: Level 1)
   ISBN-10: 1-55766-680-6 (Teacher's manual: Level 1)
   ISBN-13: 978-1-5766-681-9 (Teacher's manual: Level 2)
   ISBN-10: 1-55766-681-4 (Teacher's manual: Level 2)
   1. Vocabulary—Study and teaching (Elementary)   2. African Americans—Education   I. Title
LB1574.5.S43 2007
372.61—dc22
                                                2007002043

British Library Cataloguing in Publication data are available from the British Library.

Contents

About the Authors

Latrice M. Seals, M.Ed., is a doctoral candidate and lecturer at the University of Houston and an educational consultant for the Houston Independent School District. Ms. Seals is former Research Director of Reading Rockets. Prior to joining Reading Rockets, she was with the University of Texas's Center for Academic and Reading Skills in Houston, which is headed by Dr. Barbara R. Foorman. She was Lead Coordinator on a secondary study, the Vocabulary Enrichment Program, within the NIH-funded grant titled Early Interventions for Children with Reading Problems. She was also responsible for conducting preservice and in-service teacher training, as well as providing in-classroom support and mentoring to teachers at research sites in Houston, Texas, and Washington, D.C. Ms. Seals has co-authored several articles and book chapters on vocabulary and scientific-based reading research.

Sharolyn D. Pollard-Durodola, Ed.D., is Assistant Professor in the Special and Bilingual Education Program at Texas A&M University. Her research interests are in the area of early literacy in Spanish and English, with an emphasis on vocabulary acquisition and early interventions. She specifically focuses on developing intervention curricula that build on empirically validated instructional design principles and evaluating their impact on the language and reading development of second language learners by attending to both oral language (vocabulary) and comprehension needs. Dr. Pollard-Durodola is Co-principal Investigator on a project funded by the U.S. Department of Education, Institute of Education Sciences, that investigates the acceleration of vocabulary and listening comprehension skills in preschool children through a shared-book reading intervention. Her scholarship and publications are focused on a range of learners from preschool to fourth grade. Dr. Pollard-Durodola worked for 14 years as a public school teacher and school administrator.

Barbara R. Foorman, Ph.D., is the Francis Eppes Professor of Education and Associate Director of the Florida Center for Reading Research at Florida State University. During 2005, she served as the Commissioner of Education Research in the Institute of Education Sciences in the U.S. Department of Education. From 1978 to 1996, Dr. Foorman was Professor of Educational Psychology at the University of Houston, and, from 1996 to 2006, she was Professor of Pediatrics and Director of the Center for Academic and Reading Skills at the University of Texas Health Science Center at Houston. Dr. Foorman has more than 100 publications in the area of reading and language development. She serves on editorial boards of several journals, national advisory committees, and national consensus committees on reading and has been principal investigator of several federally funded grants concerning early reading interventions, scaling assessment-driven instruction, and literacy development in Spanish-speaking children. In addition, her centers have provided professional development and technical assistance to school districts in Texas, Florida, and the eastern seaboard that are receiving Reading First funds. Dr. Foorman has been actively involved in outreach to the schools and to the general public, having chaired Houston Independent School District's Committee on a Balanced Approach to Reading and having worked to revise and validate the Texas Primary Reading Inventory, used in 96% of the school districts in Texas and in several other states.

Ashley M. Bradley lives in Longmont, Colorado, and teaches German to students in kindergarten through fifth grade as part of a world cultures curriculum at Rocky Mountain School for the Gifted and Creative in Boulder, Colorado. She spent several years teaching English and German at Bellaire High School, a foreign language magnet school in Houston, Texas. She was head of the language department while at Bellaire High School. Later, while staying at home with her preschool children, Mrs. Bradley did independent study of linguistics and language acquisition and volunteered her time teaching English as a second language at the Literacy Council of Tyler, Texas.

Foreword

The existence of large and persistent gaps between the reading performance of African American children and white children represents an educational challenge. While fourth-grade performance between African American and white children on the National Assessment of Educational Progress reading test has narrowed since the 1970s, there is still a 26-point advantage for white students (National Center for Education Statistics, 2005). Gaining access to the information taught in middle and secondary school content area classes requires that all children exit the elementary grades with good reading comprehension capacity. Without this capacity, access to grade-appropriate content knowledge, entry to challenging courses in secondary school, success on the tests increasingly being required for promotion and graduation, and entry to tertiary education or employability in a knowledge-based economy are all unlikely. Thus, closing this gap has high priority because failing to do so will generate social and economic problems.

The intellectual challenge posed by the gap involves isolating its root cause. Considerable research suggests that one major determinant of poor reading comprehension is low vocabulary (Beech & Keys, 1997; Carlisle, Beeman, Davis, & Spharim, 1999; Carlisle, Beeman, & Shah, 1996; García, 1991; Verhoeven, 1990). In our own work, we have replicated this relationship, showing the robust relation of word knowledge to reading comprehension outcomes, in combination with word reading efficiency and listening comprehension (Proctor, Carlo, August, & Snow, 2005a, 2005b). Lack of knowledge of many of the words encountered in middle and secondary school texts impedes comprehension of those texts, which in turn impedes the natural process of learning new word meanings from exposure during reading—a problem Stanovich (1986) has famously called "the Matthew effect."

The factors that predict vocabulary acquisition are well researched. For example, it has been demonstrated that frequency of exposure to a word predicts its likelihood of acquisition (Hart, 1991), that cumulative number of words heard predicts total vocabulary size (Hart & Risley, 1995), that exposure to words in rich semantic contexts increases their likelihood of acquisition (Weizman & Snow, 2001), and that exposure to contexts like book-reading and focused play increase vocabulary learning (see De Temple & Snow, 2003, for a review).

Based on the existing research, several researchers have called for a comprehensive approach to vocabulary instruction that includes four components (Graves, 2006; Nagy & Stahl, 2006). One method of building word knowledge is to expose children to a rich assortment of language experiences. For younger children, the experiences will tend to be oral and include such things as read-alouds and discussion. As children become older, the read-alouds are replaced by the students' own reading of text, but discussion remains an important venue for vocabulary development. A second method to help students gain vocabulary is through direct instruction of individual words. Research indicates that vocabulary instruction is most effective when learners are given both definitional and contextual information, actively process the new word meanings, and experience multiple encounters with the words. A third approach is to provide students with strategies they can use to learn words. Strategies include using context to figure out word meanings (Baumann, Edwards, Boland, Olejnik, & Kame'enui, 2003); using affixes; learning root words; using dictionaries or peers; and, in the case of second language learners whose native languages share cognates with English, using cognate knowledge (Carlo et al., 2004). Finally, a fourth strategy entails building word consciousness that involves metacognition about words, motivation to learn words, and interest in words.

This multifaceted approach to developing vocabulary recommended by research has been systematically and effectively incorporated into the Vocabulary Power program. Vocabulary Power consists of 20 weeks of vocabulary lessons that are based on storybooks. Thus, children learn word meanings in the context of read-alouds of rich children's literature. The program provides direct instruction in individual words through a variety of engaging activities, including developing personalized flashcards, completing crossword puzzles, solving word riddles, using context clues, and using vocabulary words to talk about personal experiences. Through multiple engagements with the vocabulary words in different contexts, the program builds depth of word meaning as well as breadth of word knowledge. A third component of the program teaches word-learning strategies such as the use of affixes and roots. Finally, the program builds word consciousness through the use of activities like Word Wizard in which students are encouraged to listen outside of class for the words they are learning during vocabulary instruction.

The well-designed, research-based Vocabulary Power program will be a very welcome addition to any classroom where vocabulary and comprehension are considered important educational outcomes and where student engagement and enthusiasm for learning are valued.

Diane August, Ph.D.
Senior Research Scientist
Center for Applied Linguistics

References

Baumann, J.F., Edwards, E.C., Boland, E., Olejnik, S., & Kame'enui, E.J. (2003). Vocabulary tricks: Effects of instruction in morphology and context on fifth-grade students' ability to derive and infer word meanings. *American Educational Research Journal, 40,* 447–494.

Beech, J.R., & Keys, A. (1997). Reading, vocabulary and language preference in 7- to 8-year-old bilingual Asian children. *British Journal of Educational Psychology, 67*(4), 405–414.

Carlisle, J.F., Beeman, M.M., Davis, L.-H., & Spharim, G. (1999). Relationship of metalinguistic capabilities and reading achievement for children who are becoming bilingual. *Applied Psycholinguistics, 20*(4), 459–478.

Carlisle, J.F, Beeman, M.B., & Shah, P.P. (1996). The metalinguistic capabilities and English literacy of Hispanic high school students: An exploratory study. *Yearbook of the National Reading Conference, 45,* 306–316.

Carlo, M., August, D., McLaughlin, B., Snow, C., Dressler, D., Lippman, D., et al. (2004). Closing the gap: Addressing the vocabulary needs of English language learners in bilingual and mainstream classrooms. *Reading Research Quarterly, 39,* 188–206.

De Temple, J. & Snow, C.E. (2003). Learning words from books. In A. van Kleeck, S.A. Stahl, & E.B. Bauer (Eds.), *On reading books to children: Teachers and parents* (pp. 16–36). Mahwah, NJ: Lawrence Erlbaum Associates.

García, G.E. (1991). Factors influencing the English reading test performance of Spanish-speaking Hispanic children. *Reading Research Quarterly, 26*(4), 371–392.

Graves, M.F. (2006). *The vocabulary book: Learning and instruction.* New York: Teachers College Press.

Hart, B. (1991). Input frequency and children's first words. *First Language, 11,* 289–300.

Hart, B., & Risley, T.R. (1995). *Meaningful differences in the everyday experience of young American children.* Baltimore: Paul H. Brookes Publishing Co.

Nagy, W.E., & Stahl, S.A. (2006). *Teaching word meanings.* Mahwah, NJ: Lawrence Erlbaum Associates.

National Center for Education Statistics. (2005). *Trends in average reading scale scores by race/ethnicity: White-black gap.* Retrieved January 18, 2007, from http://nces.ed.gov/nationsreportcard/ltt/results2004/sub-reading-race.asp

Proctor, C.P., Carlo, M., August, D., & Snow, C. (2005a). *The intriguing role of Spanish language vocabulary knowledge in predicting English reading comprehension.* Manuscript submitted for publication.

Proctor, C.P., Carlo, M., August, D., & Snow, C.E. (2005b). Native Spanish-speaking children reading in English: Towards a model of comprehension. *Journal of Educational Psychology, 97*(2), 246–256.

Stanovich, K.E. (1986). Matthew effects in reading: Some consequences of individual differences in the acquisition of literacy. *Reading Research Quarterly, 21,* 360–407

Verhoeven, L.T. (1990). Acquisition of reading in a second language. *Reading Research Quarterly, 25*(2), 90–114.

Weizman, Z., & Snow, C.E. (2001). Lexical input as related to children's vocabulary acquisition: Effects of sophisticated exposure and support for meaning. *Developmental Psychology, 37,* 265–279.

Books Used in Vocabulary Power

Level 1 (in order of use)

Richard Wright and the Library Card by William Miller, illustrated by Gregory Christie

The Stories Julian Tells by Ann Cameron, illustrated by Ann Strugnell

"Shoe Talk" from *Falling Up,* poems and drawings by Shel Silverstein

The Hundred Penny Box by Sharon Bell Mathis, illustrated by Leo and Diane Dillon

Donavan's Word Jar by Monalisa DeGross, illustrated by Cheryl Hanna

More Stories Huey Tells by Ann Cameron, illustrated by Lis Toft

Five Notable Inventors by Wade Hudson, illustrated by Ron Garnett

Justin and the Best Biscuits in the World by Mildred Pitts Walter, illustrated by Catherine Stock

The Bat Boy and His Violin by Gavin Curtis, illustrated by E.B. Lewis.

Level 2 (in order of use)

The Gold Cadillac by Mildred D. Taylor, illustrated by Michael Hays

The Watsons Go to Birmingham—1963 by Christopher Paul Curtis

Phillip Hall Likes Me. I Reckon Maybe. by Bette Greene, illustrated by Charles Lilly

At Her Majesty's Request: An African Princess in Victorian England by Walter Dean Myers

Circle of Gold by Candy Dawson Boyd

Journey to Jo'Burg: A South African Story by Beverley Naidoo, illustrated by Eric Velasquez

Acknowledgments

We would like to acknowledge those teachers in the Houston and Washington, D.C., schools who so graciously implemented the intervention with enthusiasm and dedication throughout our study. In addition, we would like to acknowledge the many children, speakers of African American Vernacular English, who participated in our daily lessons. We hope the selected storybooks infused in them a greater love for literature, their own language, and the power of words!

I am eternally grateful that I am able to incorporate two of my greatest passions—writing and teaching—but I would not have this opportunity without the support of so many wonderful people. First and foremost, my family: my late grandmother, Mrs. Mineola White; my mother, Mrs. Doris Seals Nichols; my sisters, Chanteryl L. Jasper and Demetria Martin; my late stepfather, Mr. Tillman H. Nichols; my brother-in-law, Hubert (Mickey) Martin; my aunt, Ms. Viola Seals; and my uncles, Mr. Rinzley C. Phillips and Mr. Horace Nelson. Thank you for your unwavering support, and encouragement.

I would like to thank the educators who changed my life by challenging me to be a better student, researcher, writer, and instructor. They include Mr. Donnee C. Hill, Dr. Philip Gough, Dr. Barbara R. Foorman, Dr. John Gaa, Dr. Louisa C. Moats, Dr. Reid Lyon, Dr. Bill Labov, Dr. Hollis Scarborough, Ms. Darion Griffin, Dr. Shirley Yu, Dr. Jackie Hawkins, Dr. David Francis, Dr. Jason Anthony, Dr. Nita Copley, and Dr. Robert (Bob) McPherson. Thank you for giving me the gift of pursuing academic excellence, while maintaining academic integrity, which is priceless. It is a gift that I continue to share with students everywhere.

I would also like to thank my godchildren: Clarissa Robinson; Jacolby and Brandon Jasper; Jalen, Jaia, and Jarin Martin; Matthew Wharton; and Britney and Brinae' Batiste. Thank you for your unwavering support and for pushing me to pursue my dreams.

I wish to thank my friends and support system, Ms. Rhonda L. Coleman, Pastor Byron and Mrs. Bernadette Wyatt, Mr. Vernon and Mrs. LaGatha Wharton, Mr. John and Mrs. Vera Dawkins, Dr. Ann Voss, Dr. Ernestine Gardner, Mrs. Torie and Gary Rubin, and the members of Galilee Baptist Church (Houston, Texas). In addition, Vocabulary Power would not be possible without the guidance, support, and hard work of the staff of Paul H. Brookes Publishing Co. Many thanks to Janet Betten, Senior Production Editor; Jessica Allan, Senior Acquisitions Editor; Sarah Shepke, Associate Editor; and Susannah Ray, Professional Development Coordinator/Rights and Permissions Coordinator.

Last, but not least, I am eternally grateful to the administrators, teachers, and students in Houston Independent School District and the District of Columbia Public Schools who graciously piloted this program. Your feedback and dedication to this curriculum remains invaluable.

—LMS

To my beloved grandmother, Mrs. Mineola White

Granny, thank you for teaching me to love language. You taught me to love my native speech—African American Vernacular English—while insisting that I gain proficiency in Standard American English. You remain my greatest inspiration, and not a day goes by without me thinking about you. Thank you for giving me roots to keep me grounded and wings with which to fly.

—LMS

Introduction

Students who speak African American Vernacular English (AAVE), like those who speak a foreign language, must gain proficiency in oral and written Standard American English (SAE) in order to be successful in school (Labov, 1972; Wolfram & Schilling-Estes, 1998). Vocabulary Power is a research-based vocabulary program for AAVE speakers that builds skills during the process of reading books (Foorman, Seals, Anthony, & Pollard-Durodola, 2003). We tested and designed Vocabulary Power Levels 1 and 2 for third- and fourth-grade AAVE speakers, respectively, but the curriculum can be useful for AAVE speakers of other ages, as well.

Features of African American Vernacular English

Some of the phonological, semantic, and grammatical features of AAVE are inconsistent with SAE (Labov, 1972; Wolfram & Schilling-Estes, 1998). The following are the most common phonological characteristics of AAVE (Labov, 1995):

- Reduction of final consonants (*suit = sue, beat = be, seed = see*)

- Reduction of consonant clusters (*ask = as, hold = hole, wasp = was*)

- *R*-lessness (*guard = god, sore = so, four = foe*)

- *L*-lessness (*toll = toe, fault = fought, tool = to*)

- Turning /th/ into /f/ at the end of words (*mouth = mouf, south = souf, breath = breaf*)

- Turning /th/ into /d/ at the beginning of words (*them = dem, than = dan, this = dis*)

- Dropping forms of "to be" from sentences (*He is with us. = He with us.*)

   To illustrate, in AAVE *tore* is pronounced as *toe.* AAVE speakers must learn that when they hear the word *toe,* it refers to the appendage on one's foot and not to a synonym of *ripped.* They must add the word *tore* to their mental lexicons and modify the definition of the word *toe* to delete the synonym for *ripped.*

   Teaching students how their home language differs from SAE can motivate them to become bidialectal and help them to restructure their vocabulary to lessen the divergence between words spoken in AAVE and written in SAE (Wheeler & Swords, 2006). Those AAVE speakers who are able to incorporate the rules of SAE into their vocabularies are more likely to become successful readers (Labov, 1995). Some of the books in this vocabulary program include AAVE in the dialogue to provide the opportunity for AAVE speakers to contrast their home language with that of SAE. To motivate AAVE speakers to become bidialectal, the majority of books feature African American heroes and heroines.

Research-Based Practices for Vocabulary Instruction

Building an effective vocabulary program requires a number of instructional practices that have been supported by research. The theoretical framework for this program is based on the following research-based practices: 1) integration, frequent encounters, and meaningful use; 2) primed background knowledge; 3) explicit teaching of high-utility words; 4) depth of word knowledge; 5) judicious review; and 6) extended rich instruction.

Integration, Frequent Encounters, and Meaningful Use

Integration, frequent encounters, and meaningful use, or *deep processing,* are crucial elements in effective vocabulary instruction (Nagy, 1988). Because words are integrated with knowledge, they must be taught within the *broader context* of concepts. Knowledge, however, is *structured* and built on sets of *relationships* so that effective vocabulary instruction assists children in understanding new information by *relating* it to what they already know. Frequent encounters with a new word are necessary if vocabulary instruction is to have a measurable effect on comprehension.

Vocabulary Power includes a Deep Processing activity that encourages students to use the vocabulary words to talk about their lives and the world in general. The activity is open-ended and lends itself to discussion, allowing students to obtain a deeper and richer understanding of a word's meaning and to discover relationships between words. There are other opportunities throughout the week that provide students with frequent, meaningful encounters with the vocabulary words.

Primed Background Knowledge

Hirsch (2006) suggested that broad knowledge in the realm of culture and nature is a prerequisite to gaining deeper understanding while listening to or reading text. Thus, background knowledge provides a conceptual foundation for learning new information (Gunn, Simmons, & Kame'enui, 1998) and helps the reader make connections between the text and the world (Coyne, Simmons, & Kame'enui, 2004). Effective vocabulary instruction primes or activates relevant knowledge in students prior to reading text.

Vocabulary Power includes an activity called Predict the Storyline that helps students to anticipate and explore the topic of the week's story prior to reading the text. Students use illustrations in the book or the story's title to make inferences about what the characters might experience and to make connections to world concepts. Weekly Semantic Webs are tools that provide opportunities for dialogues on book-related topics within the context of real life.

Explicit Teaching of High-Utility Words

The words selected in our lessons are high-utility words that can be employed in multiple contexts. Beck, McKeown, and Kucan (2002) refer to these as Tier 2 words. Tier 2 words go beyond the basic vocabulary known by students at their grade (Tier 1) and are used frequently by mature language users. Some examples of Tier 2 words are *coincidence, absurd, industrious,* and *fortunate.* These are words that enrich students' vocabulary by allowing them to describe familiar situations with greater specificity, using complex forms of familiar words (e.g., employing the word *virtuous* vs. *good*).

Tier 2 words are explicitly taught in Vocabulary Power. Explicit teaching refers to preteaching of vocabulary word meanings and modeling correct syntactic use of words while discussing what was learned or when making real-life connections. We strategically selected Tier 2 words because they would enable students to associate new words with familiar life experiences and generalize vocabulary across contexts.

Because several of the storybooks and informational texts elaborate on science or social studies concepts, some of the words in Vocabulary Power are actually Tier 3 words. These words are driven by specialized knowledge (e.g., science: *gravity,* social studies: *oligarchy*) and are usually taught when learners need to understand technical concepts.

Depth of Word Knowledge

Considering levels of word knowledge is also important in vocabulary development (Baker, Simmons, & Kame'enui, 1998). There are three levels of word knowledge that reflect depth of understanding. For example, students develop *associative knowledge* when they are able to link a definition or context to a new word. In the next level, *comprehension knowledge,* students demonstrate broad knowledge of the word and are able to identify an antonym or classify words into categories. *Generative knowledge* is evident when students can paraphrase the word or utilize it in a novel sentence.

Specifically, Vocabulary Power helps students develop associative knowledge through activities that require solving riddles, associating word clues with the target word, choosing words that can be substituted for a vocabulary term, and employing words beyond the context of the story. Students develop comprehensive knowledge through activities such as Same and Different, which asks students to select which word does not belong with others in the group and to explain why, and Synonyms and Antonyms, which explores words that are the same or opposite in meaning. Vocabulary Power encourages students to develop generative knowledge through activities such as Paraphrasing Vocabulary in Text. When creating flashcards, students are asked to write the definition for the vocabulary word using their own words.

Judicious Review

Effective instruction provides opportunities for students to apply knowledge that they have learned (Gunn et al., 1998). Judicious review suggests that reviews must be frequent, purposeful, and accompanied with meaningful practice. Weekly discussions and cumulative review units every 5 weeks provide opportunities for students to review word knowledge and to deeply study relationships between words (e.g., Semantic Feature Analysis: Heating Systems). Judicious review implies daily opportunities in which teachers check for understanding prior to moving on to subsequent activities to ensure that students have grasped the "big ideas," or important concepts (Hall, 2002).

Extended Rich Instruction

Extended rich instruction (Beck, McKeown, & Omanson, 1987) extends learning beyond the classroom in a Word Wizard activity in which students are asked to describe any occasions for hearing or using the target words at home or in school. Students write their descriptions of these occasions in a weekly log and share their information in class. This extension of instruction allows students to make connections between classroom learning and the world in which they live and may provide opportunities for family and community members to participate in the students' learning.

How to Use This Program

Vocabulary Power consists of 20 weeks of lessons based on storybooks. We chose paperback book-club books that should be readily available (see Books Used in Vocabulary Power for a complete list of books for both levels). Fifteen new words selected from the stories the students are reading will be taught each week. Every fifth week of instruction is a cumulative review unit, covering 25 words selected from the previous 4 weeks.

Day 1

In a regular week (as opposed to a review unit, which will be explained on page 5), Day 1 serves as a preview. The objective of Day 1 is to introduce students to the 15 new words they will be learning and using all week. First, the teacher reads the words and helps the students with their pronunciation. Sounds that are often pronounced differently in AAVE are presented in boldface, so the teacher should pay special attention to helping students pronounce these sounds. The second activity on Day 1 is to read the definitions and relevant sentences containing the target words.

The At-Home assignment on Day 1 is a Riddle Page and Matching Activity, which assists the students in reviewing the words at home and encourages them to think about the salient features of the words, instead of committing to a rote memorization of definitions. Second, students create their own flashcards for the target words, using their own phrasing when defining the words. In general, the flashcards are employed throughout the 20 weeks to help students study the words at home. All At-Home activities can be found in the Student Workbook.

Day 2

Day 2 begins with a quick review of the 15 words that were introduced the previous day. Then, the teacher goes over the Day 1 At-Home assignment with students, checking their work and providing them with correct answers and clarification as necessary. Answers to At-Home and in-class assignments can be found in the Answer Key at the back of this book. Next, the reading selection is introduced with a Predict the Storyline activity, which primes students' background knowledge and promotes student engagement. Students write down a question that they think the story will answer. Then, the teacher reads the story aloud as the students follow along silently in their own copies of the book. The students are instructed to keep their eyes open for vocabulary words and to show a "thumbs up" sign each time the teacher reads one of the vocabulary words in the text. The teacher also discusses the predictions students made. After the reading, the teacher guides the students in paraphrasing the vocabulary in a few select passages from the text they just read.

The At-Home assignment on Day 2 instructs students to study the flashcards they made the previous night, then to complete Word Substitution and Same and Different activities. These activities assist students in making associations and seeing relationships between words.

Day 3

The focus of Day 3 is using the vocabulary words in context. Just as in Day 2, this day begins with a rapid review of the vocabulary words and a review of the previous day's At-Home assignment. Day 3 then proceeds with a Using Context Clues activity. This activity provides two or three sentences of context with several clues for each vocabulary word, which assists students in discovering the word that most appropriately completes the sentence. Then, students describe the most important clues that helped them select the appropriate target word, thus developing students' metacognitive knowledge of how to utilize context to understand the meanings of future unknown words.

Day 3 also presents a Word Wizard Journal in which students are encouraged to record instances when target words are heard or utilized in conversations at home, in the community, or at school. Students are divided into Word Wizard Groups and share with each other and the class the context in which vocabulary knowledge was used beyond the classroom. The Word Wizard activity has a game format in which groups record the number of sentences they heard. The At-Home assignment on Day 3 focuses on reviewing vocabulary flashcards, completing a context clues assignment, and recording information in the Word Wizard Journal.

Day 4

The instructional objective of Day 4 is expanding meaning. After a quick review of vocabulary and the previous day's At-Home assignment, students do an activity designed to expand their vocabulary knowledge via one of the following tools:

- *Word Roots*—an activity that introduces students to the important role of Latin and Greek roots in deciphering unfamiliar words. For example, after learning that *fac* means to do or to make, students discuss possible meanings for *factory, satisfaction,* and *benefactor* within the context of meaningful sentences.

- *Multiple Meanings*—an activity that expands the students' understanding of the vocabulary by teaching secondary and tertiary definitions of some of the week's words.

- *Morphographic Elements*—an activity that focuses on how prefixes and suffixes can assist students in understanding the meaning of new words. In Word Cousins, students apply morphographic elements to base words and discuss possible word meanings.

- *Synonyms and Antonyms*—an activity that introduces students to words that are similar to or opposite in meaning of specific vocabulary words. This is accomplished by evaluating words in the context of meaningful sentences.

- *Deep Processing*—an activity that allows students to understand relationships between words and to integrate word knowledge with lived experiences. For example, after learning the words *inventor* and *patent*, a student might be asked, "Would an *inventor* apply for a *patent* when his product is not finished? Why or why not."

The Day 4 At-Home assignment is to study the flashcards and to complete a crossword puzzle. Other fun review activities, such as a scrambled word puzzle, may be included as well.

Day 5

The purpose of the fifth and final day of each week is multifold. It consists of review, further expansion of meaning, and assessment. A review of the previous day's At-Home assignment is followed by a Bingo game to help students review the words and definitions they have been learning all week, which is then followed by an activity similar to the Day 4 Expanding Meaning activities (e.g., Multiple Meanings, Deep Processing, Morphographic Elements, Synonyms and Antonyms).

Day 5 occasionally includes a writing activity that provides opportunities to integrate word knowledge with personal experiences and to communicate creatively in written form using SAE. For example, after learning about African American inventors and the words *inventor, treatment, product, common,* and *cure*, students are asked to write about their cure for the common cold, including the product, its ingredients, and the procedure for treatment. Students may also discuss and rewrite AAVE idiomatic expressions used in the story, with emphasis that we speak and write differently depending on the context and purpose of a task. All writing activities are designed to help students process and understand the vocabulary on a deeper level. Day 5 ends with a quick 15-question assessment. Assessments are only found in the Teacher's Manual and are photocopiable.

Review Unit

In a Review Unit (every fifth week of the curriculum), 25 words are selected from the previous 4 weeks. The entire week focuses on specific game-like activities that provide multiple exposures to words taught in previous lessons and reinforces the students' memory of these important vocabulary words. Some of the review games in the Review Units are "I Spy"; Tic-Tac-Toe; Find It, Say It; and Clueless. Some Review Units also contain context clues activities and word or semantic feature analysis to encourage deeper understanding of the language. The fifth day of each review unit is a multiple-choice assessment covering all 25 words.

Note to Teachers

Teachers will benefit from reading lessons prior to implementation as some activities require that instructional materials be prepared in advance. Throughout the curriculum, italics are used to indicate specific language of the teacher. Although teachers may find that their own phrasing of some concepts seems more natural and complements their teaching style, consistency in explanations and teacher modeling is crucial for student understanding of critical knowledge. For this reason, we have provided specified teacher language throughout the book to promote clarity and suggested scaffolding of complex skills (e.g., priming background knowledge).

References

Baker, S.K., Simmons, D.C., & Kame'enui, E.J. (1998). Vocabulary acquisition: Research bases. In D.C. Simmons & E.J. Kame'enui (Eds.), *What reading research tells us about children with diverse learning needs* (pp. 183–217). New York: Guilford.

Beck, I.L., McKeown, M.G., & Kucan, O. (2002). *Bringing words to life: Robust vocabulary instruction.* New York: Guilford.

Beck, I.L., McKeown, M.G., & Omanson, R.C. (1987). The effects and uses of diverse vocabulary instructional techniques. In M.G. McKeown & M.E. Curtis (Eds.), *The nature of vocabulary acquisition* (pp. 147–163). Mahah, NJ: Lawrence Erlbaum Associates.

Coyne, M.D., Simmons, D.C., & Kame'enui, E.J. (2004). Vocabulary for young children at-risk of experiencing reading difficulties: Teaching word meanings during shared storybook readings. In J.F. Baumann & E.J. Kame'enui (Eds.), *Vocabulary instruction: Research to practice* (pp. 41–58). New York: Guilford.

Foorman, B., Seals, L., Anthony, J., & Pollard-Durodola, S. (2003). Vocabulary enrichment program for third and fourth grade African American students: Description, implementation, and impact. In B. Foorman (Ed.), *Preventing and remediating reading difficulties: Bringing science to scale* (pp. 419–441). Austin, TX: PRO-ED.

Hall, T. (2002). *Explicit instruction.* Wakefield, MA: National Center on Accessing the General Curriculum.

Hirsch, E.D. (2006, Spring). Building knowledge: The case for bringing content into the language arts block and for a knowledge-rich curriculum core for all children [Electronic version]. *American Educator.* Retrieved September 25, 2006, from http://www.aft.org/pubs-reports/american_educator/issues/spring06/hirsch.htm

Gunn, B.K., Simmons, D.C., & Kame'enui, E.J. (1998). Emergent literacy: Instructional and curricular basics and implications. In B. Foorman (Ed.), *Preventing and remediating reading difficulties: Bringing science to scale* (pp. 419–441). Austin, TX: PRO-ED.

Labov, W. (1972). Some features of the English of Black Americans. In R.W. Bailey & J.L. Robinson (Eds.), *Varieties of present-day English* (pp. 236–255). New York: MacMillan.

Labov, W. (1995). Can reading failure be reversed? A linguistic approach to the question. In V. Gadsden & D. Wagner (Eds.), *Literacy among African-American youth* (pp. 39–68). Cresskill, NJ: Hampton Press.

Mehta, P., Foorman, B.R., Branum-Martin, L., & Taylor, W.P. (2005). Literacy as a unidimensional multilevel construct: Validation, sources of influence, and implications in a longitudinal study in grades 1–4. *Scientific Studies of Reading, 9*(2), 85–116.

Moats, L.C., Foorman, B.R., & Taylor, W.P. (2006). How quality of writing instruction impacts high-risk fourth graders' writing. *Reading and Writing: An Interdisciplinary Journal, 19,* 363–391.

Nagy, W.E. (1988). *Teaching vocabulary to improve reading comprehension.* Newark, DE: International Reading Association.

Wheeler, R.S., & Swords, R. (2006). *Code-switching: Teaching Standard English in urban classrooms.* Urbana, IL: National Council of Teachers of English.

Wolfram, W., & Schilling-Estes, N. (1998). *American English: Dialects and variation.* Oxford, UK: Blackwell.

Richard Wright and the Library Card
by William Miller

DAY 1 Preview of Lesson	DAY 2 Introduction	DAY 3 Using Words in Context	DAY 4 Expanding Meaning	DAY 5 Keys to Understanding
Read New Words Say and Write New Words Read Definitions Assign At-Home 1	Vocabulary Review Review At-Home 1 Predict the Storyline Story Reading (entire book) Identifying Vocabulary in Text Paraphrasing Vocabulary in Text Assign At-Home 2	Vocabulary Review Review At-Home 2 Using Context Clues Word Wizard Assign At-Home 3	Vocabulary Review Review At-Home 3 Multiple Meanings: *Master* and *Approach* Assign At-Home 4	Review At-Home 4 Bingo Game Morphographic Elements: *-ian* Assessment

Words and Definitions

The following are target words for this week. If the word has multiple meanings, we provide only the definition listed in the text. ***Please review the definitions prior to instruction.***

1. **bend**—a curving part

2. **master**—a man who rules over others

3. **rebel**—fighting against those in control or authority

4. **troop**—a group of soldiers

5. **wealthy**—rich with money or property

6. **borrow**—to be able to use something by agreeing to return it at a certain time

7. **optician**—a person who makes or sells eyeglasses and other products for the eye

8. **boardinghouse**—a house where meals and a place for stay are available for a certain amount of money

9. **ignore**—to pay no attention to someone or something

10. **approach**—to draw closer to someone

11. **roam**—to wander or travel about without a specific plan

12. **powerful**—strong, influential

13. **suspicious**—causing others to feel that one is guilty or wrong

14. **cautious**—careful not to make mistakes

15. **stacks**—a series of bookshelves in a library

Day 1: Preview of Lesson

Prepare for Lesson

☆ Materials: Student Workbooks, *Richard Wright and the Library Card* by William Miller, display copy of Week 1 Word List

☆ Read Teacher Tip: Reading New Words

☆ Read Teacher Tip: Making Flashcards

Teacher Tip: Reading New Words

It is important that students pronounce all ending sounds. Endings that AAVE speakers might overlook are in bold. Make sure that students enunciate these endings.

Pronounce words clearly.

One-syllable words can be sounded out by sweeping a finger from left to right under the word (e.g., b-e-n-d—*bend*).

Correction procedure—When students cannot *sound out* words, say: *Sound it out with me.* Then, sound out the word together with the class.

Correction procedure—When students cannot *say* the word, say: *The word is* <u>bend</u>. *Say* <u>bend</u>.

---

5 min.

Read New Words

☆ Say: *Today, we will begin a new story,* <u>Richard Wright and the Library Card</u>*. We will learn to read new words that you will study at home. The words we learn will help you to read this story better and will help you to express your thoughts on paper and when talking to others. Let's see if there are any words that you already know.*

☆ Display the Week 1 Word List. Cover the bottom box, leaving the word columns at the top of the page exposed. Say: *Which words do you already know?*

☆ Uncover the bottom box. Say: *Let's read these words. Sound out each syllable as I point to it. Be sure to say each sound clearly. Sound it out.*

☆ Students sound out each syllable. Say the word. Students repeat the word. Say: *Yes, the word is . . . .*

10 min.

Say and Write New Words

☆ Cover the bottom box, and use the word columns at the top of the page.

☆ Say: *Let's read the words together.* Point to each word and read one time.

☆ Say: *Take out your pencil and Student Workbook. Find the page that says Week 1: Say and Write New Words. Let's get ready to say and write each word.*

☆ Point to each word. Say: *What word?* Students say the word. *Write [the word].*

☆ Students write the word on the appropriate line. Continue until all words are written.

Week 1 Word List

ben**d**	bor**row**	roa**m**
mast**er**	opti**cian**	power**ful**
rebe**l**	board**ing**house	suspi**cious**
troo**p**	ig**n**ore	cau**tious**
wealth**y**	appro**ach**	stack**s**

1. ben**d**
2. mast **er**
3. reb e**l**
4. troo**p**
5. wealth
   wealth **y**
6. bor **row**
7. op tic
   op ti **cian**
8. board
   board **ing**
   board **ing** hou**se**

9. ig n**o**re
10. ap proa**ch**
11. roa**m**
12. pow **er**
    pow er **ful**
13. sus pi cion
    sus pi **cious**
14. cau tion
    cau **tious**
15. stack
    stack**s**

Read Definitions

☆ Say: *I will read the definitions so that we will understand what each word means. Some words have more than one meaning; however, these are the definitions that are used in the story.*

☆ Read the definitions out loud as students read silently. Choose a student to read each sentence.

Definitions

1. **bend** (a curving part)
   While canoeing, we could see ahead that there was a <u>bend</u> in the river.

2. **master** (a man who rules over others)
   The tiger in the circus did not seem willing to obey his <u>master</u>.

3. **rebel** (fighting against those in control or authority)
   The <u>rebel</u> army attacked the British because they wanted freedom for their country.

4. **troop** (a group of soldiers)
   The <u>troop</u> marched all night until it reached the bend in the river where the enemy had been spotted.

5. **wealthy** (rich with money or property)
   Howard Hughes was a <u>wealthy</u> man and movie producer who died during the 1970s.

6. **borrow** (to be able to use something by agreeing to return it at a certain time)
   My father taught me to never <u>borrow</u> money so that I would not become a debtor.

7. **optician** (a person who makes or sells eyeglasses and other products for the eye)
   After 2 weeks, we returned to the <u>optician</u> to see if Mom's contact lenses were ready.

8. **boardinghouse** (a house where meals and a place for stay are available for a certain amount of money)
   When Grandpa moved to Harlem in the early 1930s, he lived in a <u>boardinghouse</u>, where he paid $5.00 per week for a room and meals.

9. **ignore** (to pay no attention to someone or something)
   We tried to <u>ignore</u> the child's wild behavior, but after 10 minutes we could no longer withstand his loud screams.

10. **approach** (to draw closer to someone)
    As the storm <u>approach</u>ed, everyone in the town found a place to take shelter.

11. **roam** (to wander or travel about without a specific plan)
    When Rita arrived at the Prado museum in Spain, she <u>roam</u>ed from one collection of art to the other, enjoying the colors and display of famous artists.

12. **powerful** (strong, influential)
    W.E.B. DuBois became a <u>powerful</u> leader in the black community, and his advice was sought by all.

13. **suspicious** (causing others to feel that one is guilty or wrong)

    The man who approached the bank teller made us <u>suspicious</u> because he was nervously looking around.

14. **cautious** (careful not to make mistakes)

    The teacher warned the students to be <u>cautious</u> when walking on the damp floor in the cafeteria.

15. **stacks** (a series of bookshelves in a library)

    As a child, I remember walking through the <u>stacks</u> of the library, amazed that there were so many books.

Teacher Tip: Making Flashcards

Each time that students use vocabulary words after the initial "formal" definitions are introduced, it is crucial that students have an opportunity to write their own definitions. Therefore, students should write the definitions for the flashcards in their own words when possible. Model writing original definitions for some of the vocabulary words in class.

Depending on students' familiarity with the construction of flashcards, you may need to demonstrate how to cut paper into flashcard-size squares or rectangles.

Show students how to write a vocabulary word on one side of the flashcard and their original definition on the other side.

Explain and model for students how to study using flashcards. A parent or sibling may help quiz students using the flashcards.

Assign At-Home 1

Say: *Tonight you will . . .*

1. *Study the vocabulary words with definitions.*

2. *Complete the Riddle Page.*

3. *Do the Matching Activity.*

4. *Make flashcards.*

Day 2: Introduction

Prepare for Lesson

☆ Materials: Student Workbooks, *Richard Wright and the Library Card* by William Miller

Vocabulary Review
3 min.

☆ Rapid review of vocabulary words (Students use the Week 1 Word List in their Student Workbooks.)

Review At Home 1
7 min.

☆ Review the correct answers to At-Home 1.

☆ Review student work to confirm or clarify responses.

Predict the Storyline
8 min.

☆ Students look at the cover of *Richard Wright and the Library Card* by William Miller.

☆ Say: *Today, we will read the book <u>Richard Wright and the Library Card</u> by William Miller. What are some things that one does when visiting the library?* Call on individual students.

☆ Say: *Historically, African Americans were not permitted to check books out of the library. In the story that we will read today, the main character, Richard, loves to read and wants to check books out of the library. By getting a library card, Richard Wright checked out books illegally. By reading about authors who suffered and longed for freedom, Richard learns that he is just like them and that books can change his life because books are powerful! This book is a biography because it depicts true information about a real person's life.*

☆ Say: *Open your Student Workbook to Semantic Web: Library. What were Richard's experiences in the library? How can a trip to the library change one's life? Why do people go to the library?*

☆ Say: *Think of a question that you think the story will answer. Write the question at the bottom of Semantic Web: Library.*

Story Reading 1: Identifying Vocabulary in Text
8–10 min.

☆ Say: *As I read the story out loud, you will follow along silently. When you see a word from our vocabulary list, give a thumbs up.*

☆ Read the entire book.

☆ Discuss what students predicted would happen in the story.

Day 2: Introduction

 Story Reading 2: Paraphrasing Vocabulary in the Text

☆ Say: *As I read specific paragraphs of the story out loud again, let's paraphrase what the author has said by using our own words. Let's focus on the first paragraph on page 6. Follow along as I read out loud.* Read the paragraph ("Richard walked the hot streets . . .").

☆ Say: *What's another way of saying, "He was looking for his ticket to freedom?" We might say, "Richard was looking for a job that would change his life by giving him more choices. He wanted to live differently."*

☆ Help students to paraphrase the remaining paragraphs on the page.

Assign At-Home 2

Say: *Tonight you will . . .*

1. *Study your flashcards.*

2. *Complete Word Substitutions.*

3. *Complete Same and Different.*

Day 3: Using Words in Context

Prepare for Lesson

☆ Materials: Student Workbooks

☆ Read Teacher Tip: Word Wizard

Teacher Tip: Word Wizard

For At-Home 3, students will use a Word Wizard Journal to record instances when they hear their vocabulary words used. These journals can be spiral notebooks or books created in class.

If students do not hear target words used in sentences, they should write sentences using these words. During the week, employ vocabulary words in daily conversations. Create opportunities for students to hear and use the words.

Students will be assigned Word Wizard Groups.

On Day 3 of the following week, each group member will share sentences from his or her journal with the other group members. Then, each group will read/share two sentences with the class.

Keep track of how many sentences each group has written. Record the total number of sentences on a special Word Wizard Chart.

---

 3 min. ## Vocabulary Review

☆ Rapid review of vocabulary words (Students use the Week 1 Word List in their Student Workbooks.)

 7 min. ## Review At-Home 2

☆ Review the correct answers to At-Home 2.

☆ Review student work to confirm or clarify responses.

 15 min. ## Using Context Clues

☆ Say: *Open your Student Workbook to Week 1: Using Context Clues. Today, we will use context clues to help us choose the word that fits in the blank by using the clues from other words and information in the sentence or sentences. I will read the sentences out loud. Raise your hand when you know which word best completes the sentence. Write the word in the blank. Sometimes the word might require an ending such as -ed, -s, or -ing. Each word will be used only one time.*

☆ Choose individual students to give answers. Have students point out context clues that helped them to choose the correct answer.

☆ Say: *Cross out words in the vocabulary box as we use them. Write your answers in the blank, and write the context clues you used in the space below.*

Word Wizard

☆ Say: *As Word Wizards this week, you must always be on the lookout for opportunities to use and demonstrate your word knowledge. Use your Word Wizard Journals to keep track of each time you hear one of this week's vocabulary words used in a sentence at home, school, or even on television. Remember, write the sentence as best as you can remember it in your Wizard Journal.*

☆ Say: *If you don't hear the words used in a sentence, be creative and write original sentences using your new vocabulary knowledge.*

☆ Divide the students into groups of three or four. Say: *Next week, each group will read their favorite two sentences to the class!*

Assign At-Home 3

Say: *Tonight you will . . .*

1. *Study your flashcards.*

2. *Complete the Word Wizard Journal.*

3. *Complete the Context Clues Activity.*

Day 4: Expanding Meaning

Prepare for Lesson

☆ Materials: Student Workbooks

 Vocabulary Review *(3 min.)*

☆ Rapid review of vocabulary words (Students use the Week 1 Word List in their Student Workbooks.)

 Review At-Home 3 *(7 min.)*

☆ Review the correct answers to At-Home 3.

☆ Review student work to confirm or clarify responses.

 Multiple Meanings: *Master* **and** *Approach* *(20 min.)*

☆ Say: *Sometimes words have several meanings. For example, the word* <u>depression</u> *may mean feeling sad or it could refer to an era or time of unemployment.*

☆ Say: *Some of the words in this week's story also have multiple meanings. Let's look at two of these words:* <u>master</u> *and* <u>approach</u>*. Open your Student Workbook to Multiple Meanings:* <u>Master</u> *and* <u>Approach</u>*. Let's read the definitions for these words.*

☆ Say: *Let's read sentences using these words and look for context clues that can help us to choose the correct definition.*

☆ Read the first sentence out loud. Say: *Which definition for* <u>master</u> *are we using in this sentence?* The answer is f, a college degree showing that one has studied at least 1 year beyond a bachelor's degree.

☆ Say: *What context clues helped us to understand the meaning of the word?* Answers include degree, go back to school, and engineering.

☆ Say: *I will read each sentence out loud, and you will choose the letter of the definition that describes how the word is used in the sentence.*

Assign At-Home 4

Say: *Tonight you will . . .*

1. *Study your flashcards.*

2. *Complete the Crossword Puzzle.*

3. *Do Get Ready to Read!* (optional)

Day 5: Keys to Understanding

Prepare for Lesson

 Materials: Student Workbooks, photocopies of Assessment 1

 Read Teacher Tip: Morphographic Elements

Teacher Tip: Morphographic Elements

Morphographic elements are affixes that are added to the beginning and ending of words (e.g., prefixes, suffixes).

On Day 4 or Day 5, morphographic elements may be studied as a tool to help students understand the meaning of new words.

It is important that activities are completed orally and are followed by oral discussions so that students understand how morphographic elements can add to the meaning of a base word.

---

7 min. ## Review At-Home 4

 Review the correct answers to At-Home 4.

 Review student work to confirm or clarify responses.

8 min. ## Bingo Game

 Say: *Choose nine words from the Week 1 Word List, and write them on the Bingo Card in your Student Workbook. When I read a definition, raise your hand to identify the word. If you have the word on your card, mark it with an X. The first person who has 3 Xs in a row (across, down, diagonally) wins the game.*

 Read the definitions. As students identify definitions, write the words on the board until someone wins the game.

8–10 min. ## Morphographic Elements: *-ian*

 Say: *Today we will look at a suffix that is present in this week's vocabulary list. Find Morphographic Elements: -ian in your Student Workbook.*

 Say: *Let's look at the information in the top box. Suffixes are word parts that can be added to the end of a word. Can you think of any suffixes that you have studied?* Briefly discuss. *Today, we will look at words that use the suffix -ian.*

 Read the definition for *-ian*. Say: *Let's look in the box and read words that use this suffix.* Read the word, definition, and sentence that corresponds with the word using the suffix *-ian*.

 Say: *Suffixes can help us to see relationships between words when we read. Let's read and discuss the word cousins that appear in Part A.* Read each word pair and discuss.

☆ Say: *Now, let's read the sentences in Part B and choose the best definition.*

☆ Say: *After we finish this activity, we will take the assessment.*

Assessment

☆ Distribute Assessment 1 to each student.

Name: _____ Date: _____

Assessment 1
Richard Wright and the Library Card

A. Match the word with the appropriate definition.

a) bend	d) troop	g) optician	j) approach	m) suspicious
b) master	e) wealthy	h) boardinghouse	k) roam	n) cautious
c) rebel	f) borrow	i) ignore	l) powerful	o) stacks

_____ 1.   a person who disagrees with those in control

_____ 2.   having a lot of money

_____ 3.   to use for a short period of time

_____ 4.   shelves of books in a library

_____ 5.   a place where one can eat and sleep

B. Circle the word that does not belong.

1.	ignore	overlook	notice	skip
2.	roam	sit	wander	walk
3.	cautious	unthinking	forgetful	careless
4.	suspicious	distrustful	comfortable	doubtful
5.	powerful	helpless	strong	forceful

Vocabulary Power, Level 1, by Latrice M. Seals, Sharolyn D. Pollard-Durodola, Barbara R. Foorman, and Ashley M. Bradley

C. Write the letter of the item in the blank that completes the sentences.

_____ 1. If a troop approaches a powerful enemy it might _____.

       a)   plan cautiously

       b)   ignore the problem

       c)   borrow money

_____ 2. In history, a wealthy master might own _____.

       a)   land

       b)   horses

       c)   all of the above

_____ 3. A rebellious troop might be suspicious of which of the following _____.

       a)   a wealthy boardinghouse

       b)   a bend in the road

       c)   a cautious optician

_____ 4. A suspicious king would not ignore which of the following _____.

       a)   a wealthy optician

       b)   a powerful rebel

       c)   all of the above

_____ 5. When roaming through the countryside, one might discover _____.

       a)   an approaching troop

       b)   a bend in the road

       c)   all of the above

The Stories Julian Tells
The Pudding Like a Night on the Sea
by Ann Cameron

DAY 1 Preview of Lesson	DAY 2 Introduction	DAY 3 Using Words in Context	DAY 4 Expanding Meaning	DAY 5 Keys to Understanding
Read New Words Say and Write New Words Read Definitions Assign At-Home 1	Vocabulary Review Review At-Home 1 Predict the Storyline Story Reading (pages 1–16) Identifying Vocabulary in Text Paraphrasing Vocabulary in Text Assign At-Home 2	Vocabulary Review Review At-Home 2 Using Context Clues Word Wizard Assign At-Home 3	Vocabulary Review Review At-Home 3 Deep Processing Assign At-Home 4	Review At-Home 4 Bingo Game Personification and Simile Assessment

Words and Definitions

The following are target words for this week. If the word has multiple meanings, we provide only the definition listed in the text. ***Please review the definitions prior to instruction.***

1. **pudding**—a kind of dessert that is soft and creamy

2. **whip**—to beat with a stick; to beat into a froth with a utensil (e.g., beater)

3. **loosen**—to untie, to release and set free

4. **beater**—a utensil used to mix or blend food (e.g., eggs)

5. **thick**—closely packed, crowded, dense

6. **straight**—without a bend or curve

7. **guard**—to protect, keep safe, shield

8. **crater**—large hole in the moon's or earth's surface; hole created by an explosion

9. **smooth**—having an even surface

10. **even**—to make a surface flat and level

11. **press**—to push against

12. **crack**—to break or split apart

13. **leave**—to discontinue association with; stop bothering someone or something

14. **booming**—a loud sound

15. **counter**—a level surface over which business is conducted or food is prepared

Day 1: Preview of Lesson

Prepare for Lesson

 Materials: Student Workbooks, *The Stories Julian Tells* by Ann Cameron, display copy of Week 2 Word List

 Read Teacher Tip: Reading New Words (Week 1, page 8)

Read New Words

5 min.

 Say: *Today, we will begin a new story. Let's read the title of this story together:* <u>The Stories Julian Tells</u>*. This week, we will read Chapter 1, "The Pudding Like a Night on the Sea." Remember, on Day 1 we learn to read new words that you will study at home. The words we learn will help you to read this story better and will help you to express your thoughts on paper and when talking to others. Let's see if there are any words that you already know.*

 Display the Week 2 Word List. Cover the bottom box, leaving the word columns at the top of the page exposed. Say: *Which words do you already know?*

 Uncover the bottom box. Say: *Let's read these words. Sound out each syllable as I point to it. Be sure to say each sound clearly. Sound it out.*

 Students sound out each syllable. Say the word. Students repeat the word. Say: *Yes, the word is . . . .*

Say and Write New Words

10 min.

 Cover the bottom box, and use the word columns at the top of the page.

 Say: *Let's read the words together.* Point to each word and read one time.

 Say: *Take out your pencil and Student Workbook. Find the page that says Week 2: Say and Write New Words. Let's get ready to say and write each word.*

 Point to each word. Say: *What word?* Students say the word. *Write [the word].*

 Students write the word on the appropriate line. Continue until all words are written.

Read Definitions

5 min.

 Say: *I will read the definitions so that we will understand what each word means. Some words have more than one meaning; however, these are the definitions that are used in the story.*

 Read the definitions out loud as students read silently. Choose a student to read each sentence.

Definitions

1. **pudding** (a kind of dessert that is soft and creamy)
   Julian's dad combined eggs and sugar to make a <u>pudding</u>.

2. **whip** (to beat with a stick; to beat into a froth with a utensil [e.g., beater])
   Mom <u>whipped</u> the eggs, sugar, flour, and milk with the electric blender.

Week 2 Word List

pudding	straight	press
whip	guard	crack
loosen	crater	leave
beater	smooth	booming
thick	even	counter

1. pud ding
2. whip
   whip ped
3. loose
   loos en
4. beat
   beat er
5. thick
   thick er
6. straight
7. guard
   guard ed

8. cra ter
   cra ters
9. smooth
10. e ven
    e ven ed
11. press
12. crack
13. leave
14. boom
    boom ing
15. coun ter

3. **loosen** (to untie, to release and set free)
   The seamstress <u>loosen</u>ed the skirt by removing the elastic band.

4. **beater** (a utensil used to mix or blend food [e.g., eggs])
   Julian's dad used the <u>beater</u> to whip the eggs for the omelet.

5. **thick** (closely packed, crowded, dense)
   The longer the Jello remained in the refrigerator, the <u>thick</u>er it became.

6. **straight** (without a bend or curve)
   Highway 52 is a <u>straight</u> and narrow road.

7. **guard** (to protect, keep safe, shield)
   Someone from the security office <u>guard</u>ed the diamonds at the jewelry store.

8. **crater** (large hole in the moon's or earth's surface; hole created by an explosion)
   NASA sent our science teacher pictures of <u>crater</u>s on the moon's surface.

9. **smooth** (having an even surface)
   I like to wear silk because it is soft and <u>smooth</u>.

10. **even** (to make a surface flat and level)
    Auntie Grace <u>even</u>ed the bedspread with the gentle movements of her hands.

11. **press** (to push against)
    At summer camp, we placed chocolate and marshmallows between two graham crackers and <u>press</u>ed all of the ingredients together.

12. **crack** (to break or split apart)
    We decided to <u>crack</u> three eggs for the ham and cheese omelet.

13. **leave** (to discontinue association with; stop bothering someone or something)
    If you want the cake to bake, please <u>leave</u> it in the oven for 45 minutes.

14. **booming** (a loud sound)
    The <u>booming</u> music filled the concert hall.

15. **counter** (a level surface over which business is conducted or food is prepared)
    Ramon left his dirty dishes on the clean kitchen <u>counter</u>.

Assign At-Home 1

Say: *Tonight you will . . .*

1. *Study the vocabulary words with definitions.*

2. *Complete the Riddle Page.*

3. *Do the Matching Activity.*

4. *Make flashcards.*

Day 2: Introduction

Prepare for Lesson

 Materials: Student Workbooks, *The Stories Julian Tells* by Ann Cameron

Vocabulary Review

3 min.

 Rapid review of vocabulary words (Students use the Week 2 Word List in their Student Workbooks.)

Review At-Home 1

7 min.

 Review the correct answers to At-Home 1.

 Review student work to confirm or clarify responses.

Predict the Storyline

8 min.

☆ Students look at the illustration on page 1 and on the front cover of *The Stories Julian Tells* by Ann Cameron.

☆ Say: *Today, we will begin to read a new book,* <u>The Stories Julian Tells</u>. *In fact, we will read three chapters from this book in the next 3 weeks. The first chapter that we will read is "The Pudding Like a Night on the Sea." What is pudding? Yes, it is a kind of dessert, and it is sweet and creamy. We could say that it is a special food that we might prepare for a special occasion. Let's talk about special foods and special occasions.*

☆ Say: *Open your Student Workbook to Semantic Web: Special Foods. What are some special foods that people prepare for special occasions? Where do people prepare special foods? What kinds of cooking utensils or instruments are used to prepare special foods?*

☆ Say: *Think of a question that you think the story will answer. Write the question at the bottom of Semantic Web: Special Foods.*

Story Reading 1: Identifying Vocabulary in Text

8–10 min.

 Say: *As I read the story out loud, you will follow along silently. When you see a word from our vocabulary list, give a thumbs up.*

 Read pages 1–16.

 Discuss what students predicted would happen in the story.

Story Reading 2: Paraphrasing Vocabulary in Text

6 min.

 Say: *As I read specific paragraphs of the story out loud again, let's paraphrase what the author has said by using our own words. Let's focus on the second paragraph on page 2. Follow along as I read out loud.* Read the paragraph ("My father is a big man . . .").

 Say: *What's another way of saying, "When he laughs, the sun laughs in the windowpanes"? We might say, "When he laughs, everyone laughs. He makes everyone feel like laughing."*

☆ Say: *In this story, the author uses special words to make comparisons. The author also makes objects and ideas have human qualities. We will learn more about this technique on Friday.*

☆ Help students to paraphrase the remaining sentences in the paragraph as appropriate.

Assign At-Home 2

Say: *Tonight you will . . .*

1. *Study your flashcards.*

2. *Complete Word Substitutions.*

3. *Complete Same and Different.*

Day 3: Using Words in Context

Prepare for Lesson

☆ Materials: Student Workbooks

☆ Read Teacher Tip: Word Wizard (Week 1, page 14)

Vocabulary Review

☆ Rapid review of vocabulary words (Students use the Week 2 Word List in their Student Workbooks.)

Review At-Home 2

☆ Review the correct answers to At-Home 2.

☆ Review student work to confirm or clarify responses.

Using Context Clues

☆ Say: *Open your Student Workbook to Week 2: Using Context Clues. Today, we will use context clues to help us choose the word that fits in the blank by using the clues from other words and information in the sentence or sentences. I will read the sentences out loud. Raise your hand when you know which word best completes the sentence. Write the word in the blank. Sometimes the word might require an ending such as -ed, -s, or -ing. Each word will be used only one time.*

☆ Choose individual students to give answers. Have students point out context clues that helped them to choose the correct answer.

☆ Say: *Cross out words in the box as we use them. Write your answers in the blank, and write the context clues you used in the space below.*

Word Wizard

☆ Say: *As Word Wizards this week, you must always be on the lookout for opportunities to use and demonstrate your word knowledge. Use your Word Wizard Journals to keep track of each time you hear one of this week's vocabulary words used in a sentence at home, school, or even on television. If you don't hear the words in a sentence, be creative and write original sentences using your new vocabulary knowledge. Next week, each group will read two of their sentences to the class!*

☆ Say: *Get in your Word Wizard Groups from last week, and share your best sentences.*

☆ Say: *Which group would like to read two of their sentences using the words from last week's story?* Tally the number of sentences per group, and record the amounts on the Word Wizard Chart.

Assign At-Home 3

Say: *Tonight you will . . .*

1. *Study your flashcards.*

2. *Complete the Word Wizard Journal.*

3. *Complete the Context Clues Activity.*

Day 4: Expanding Meaning

Prepare for Lesson

☆ Materials: Student Workbooks

☆ Read Teacher Tip: Deep Processing

Teacher Tip: Deep Processing

Deep Processing activities allow students to see deeper relationships between words that have been studied on Days 1–3.

These activities encourage students to use the vocabulary words to talk about their lives and the world in general. Students are able to obtain a deeper and richer understanding of a word's meaning.

Many Deep Processing activities are open-ended and lend themselves to discussion. Other activities that have a yes or no answer must be justified by logical explanations.

It is important that the teacher explain, "The answers come from your head and from your own thoughts." Answers for Deep Processing activities cannot be found in a book. This is the true test of vocabulary knowledge and usage.

---

3 min.

Vocabulary Review

☆ Rapid review of vocabulary words (Students use the Week 2 Word List in their Student Workbooks.)

7 min.

Review At-Home 3

☆ Review the correct answers to At-Home 3.

☆ Review student work to confirm or clarify responses.

15–20 min.

Deep Processing

☆ Say: *You have already learned the definitions for this week's vocabulary words. You have also learned many words that mean the same as or have the opposite meaning of the vocabulary words. It is great that you have learned so many words in such a short period of time. That proves that you are really smart; however, definitions don't really teach you everything you need to know to really understand word meanings. It is important to be able to use these words to describe your own experiences in life and to describe conditions in the world in general.*

☆ Say: *In today's activity, you will think about how words relate to each other. For example, you know that the word* cracked *can refer to breaking an object or making a very sharp, explosive sound, but can you tell which of the following can be cracked: a whip, a flower vase, thunder, a seashell, a person's voice, or water? Ask students to discuss why each possibility is likely or unlikely.*

Day 4: Expanding Meaning

☆ Say: *When you think about each of these possibilities, you ask yourself if each item could or could not produce a sharp sound or if the object has a hard texture and could split apart into pieces. This process makes you think more about the word <u>crack</u> and how it can be used to describe situations in your life. This is called <u>deep processing</u>.*

☆ Say: *Open your Student Workbook to Deep Processing: "The Pudding Like a Night on the Sea." We will work as a team to answer questions similar to the one we just talked about. Let's read each question together and decide what is a reasonable answer and why. The answers are not in the book we read but come from your own thinking. Think about the questions and what would be a reasonable response. Remember, you must be able to explain why you chose your answer.*

☆ Read each question out loud. Discuss and decide on possible answers.

Assign At-Home 4

Say: *Tonight you will . . .*

1. *Study your flashcards.*

2. *Complete the Crossword Puzzle.*

Day 5: Keys to Understanding

Prepare for Lesson

☆ Materials: Student Workbooks, "Shoe Talk" by Shel Silverstein, photocopies of Assessment 2

☆ Read Teacher Tip: Personification and Simile

Teacher Tip: Personification and Similes

Personification—describing animals, ideas, and things with human qualities.

Examples:

1. When father laughs, the sun laughs in the window–panes.

   (Julian's father's laughter is being compared with a laughing sun. The sun is personified or described with a human quality. His laughter is cheery and jovial.)

2. When father thinks, you can almost see his thoughts sitting on the tables and chairs.

   (Julian's father's thoughts are personified or described with human qualities. His thoughts are clear and apparent—it is easy to tell what he is thinking.)

Simile—comparing two things that are different by using the words *like* or *as*.

Examples:

1. The pudding tasted like a whole raft of lemons.

   (A simile is used to compare the taste of the pudding to the tart, bitter taste of lemons.)

2. The pudding tasted like floating at sea.

   (A simile is used to compare the taste of the pudding with floating—the pudding is light and airy.)

Review At-Home 4

☆ Review the correct answers to At-Home 4.

☆ Review student work to confirm or clarify responses.

Bingo Game

☆ Say: *Choose nine words from the Week 2 Word List, and write them on the Bingo Card in your Student Workbook. When I read a definition, raise your hand to identify the word. If you have the word on your card, mark it with an* X. *The first person who has 3* X*s in a row (across, down, diagonally) wins the game.*

☆ Read the definitions. As students identify definitions, write the words on the board until someone wins the game.

Day 5: Keys to Understanding

Personification and Simile

☆ Say: *Sometimes writers use special words to describe the common things of life.* Personification *is a technique in which special words are used to describe objects, ideas, and animals with human qualities.*

☆ Say: *Open you Student Workbook to Week 2: Personification and Simile. Listen as I read "Shoe Talk." We will talk about how the writer describes the shoe as a person.* Discuss the human qualities of shoe.

☆ Say: *Writers also use* similes *to make comparisons between two things that are different by using the words* like *or* as. *Let's look at some ways in which Ms. Cameron, writer of* The Stories Julian Tells, *makes comparisons in the story by using the techniques of personification and similes.* Have students read Student Tip: Making Comparisons.

☆ Say: *Let's look at Part A. We will identify the sentences as either personification or simile.* Call on individual students to read the sentences.

☆ Say: *Let's complete Part B. Which letter best describes the idea that the author tries to communicate when she makes comparisons by using personification and similes?* Call on individual students to read the sentences.

Description in poem	Human qualities	What we know about shoes
Tongue	For speaking	Tongue helps one to pull on a shoe
Inner soul	Inner spirit, heart	Inner part of shoe
Polished	Well dressed	Shoe polish
Straight laced	Prim, well groomed	Straight laces of shoes
Talks about nothing	Talks only about feet	Shoes don't talk

Assessment

☆ Distribute Assessment 2 to each student.

Name: _____ Date: _____

Assessment 2
The Stories Julian Tells
The Pudding Like a Night on the Sea

A. Match the word with the appropriate definition.

a) pudding	d) beater	g) guard	j) even	m) leave
b) whip	e) thick	h) crater	k) press	n) booming
c) loosen	f) straight	i) smooth	l) crack	o) counter

_____ 1. hole created by an explosion on the earth

_____ 2. a cooking utensil used to mix ingredients

_____ 3. a loud, rumbling sound

_____ 4. to beat into a creamy substance

_____ 5. to push against with force

B. Circle the word or phrase that does not belong.

1.	mashed potatoes	pudding	whipped cream	crackers
2.	chaperone	patrol	destroy	guard
3.	exit	enter	leave	walk away
4.	split	crack	even	fracture
5.	circular	straight	linear	unbent

C. Complete the sentence with the best answer.

_____ 1. The smooth, thick bathroom counter was made of _____.

      a) paper

      b) plastic

      c) marble

_____ 2. The carpenter loosened the straight nail with a _____.

      a) hammer

      b) saw

      c) beater

_____ 3. The suitcase was too thick to fit under the seat because it was _____.

      a) smooth and leathery

      b) straight and cracked

      c) stuffed and overpacked

_____ 4. Carter evened the sand in the sandbox with a _____.

      a) plastic knife

      b) bicycle wheel

      c) toy boat

_____ 5. We pressed the wild flowers between the book pages so that the petals would be _____.

      a) nice and cracked

      b) smooth and flat

      c) thick and loosened

The Stories Julian Tells
My Very Strange Teeth
by Ann Cameron

DAY 1 Preview of Lesson	DAY 2 Introduction	DAY 3 Using Words in Context	DAY 4 Expanding Meaning	DAY 5 Keys to Understanding
Read New Words Say and Write New Words Read Definitions Assign At-Home 1	Vocabulary Review Review At-Home 1 Predict the Storyline Story Reading (pages 46–57) Identifying Vocabulary in Text Paraphrasing Vocabulary in Text Assign At-Home 2	Vocabulary Review Review At-Home 2 Using Context Clues Word Wizard Assign At-Home 3	Vocabulary Review Review At-Home 3 Morphographic Elements: *Pre-, Un-, -ic,* and *-ly* Assign At-Home 4	Review At-Home 4 Bingo Game Synonyms and Antonyms Assessment

Words and Definitions

The following are target words for this week. If the word has multiple meanings, we provide only the definition listed in the text. ***Please review the definitions prior to instruction.***

1. **thread**—a string

2. **pliers**—small tools used for holding small objects or bending wire

3. **method**—a way or process of doing something

4. **prehistoric**—period of time before written history and during the early development of man

5. **mastodon**—an extinct animal known for its large teeth; ancestor of the elephant

6. **decide**—to make a decision, choice, or judgment; to make up one's mind

7. **twist**—to curve or bend

8. **saber-toothed tiger**—a prehistoric cat with long, curving teeth

9. **grunt**—a noise like the sound pigs make; groan

10. **suddenly**—quickly

11. **unusually**—not common, rare; out of the ordinary

12. **special**—unique, not common; having something extra

13. **either**—one or the other

14. **caveman**—a person who lived in caves during the Stone Age; prehistoric man

15. **strange**—different, unusual, not common

Day 1: Preview of Lesson

Prepare for Lesson

☆ Materials: Student Workbooks, *The Stories Julian Tells* by Ann Cameron, display copy of Week 3 Word List

☆ Read Teacher Tip: Reading New Words (Week 1, page 8)

Read New Words

☆ Say: *Today, we will begin a new story, "My Very Strange Teeth." Remember, on Day 1 we learn to read new words that you will study at home. The words we learn will help you to read this story better and will help you to express your thoughts on paper and when talking to others. Let's see if there are any words that you already know.*

☆ Display the Week 3 Word List. Cover the bottom box, leaving the word columns at the top of the page exposed. Say: *Which words do you already know?*

☆ Uncover the bottom box. Say: *Let's read these words. Sound out each syllable as I point to it. Be sure to say each sound clearly. Sound it out.*

☆ Students sound out each syllable. Say the word. Students repeat the word. Say: *Yes, the word is . . . .*

Say and Write New Words

☆ Cover the bottom box, and use the word columns at the top of the page.

☆ Say: *Let's read the words together.* Point to each word and read one time.

☆ Say: *Take out your pencil and Student Workbook. Find the page that says Week 3: Say and Write New Words. Let's get ready to say and write each word.*

☆ Point to each word. Say: *What word?* Students say the word. *Write [the word].*

☆ Students write the word on the appropriate line. Continue until all words are written.

Read Definitions

☆ Say: *I will read the definitions so that we will understand what each word means. Some words have more than one meaning; however, these are the definitions that are used in the story.*

☆ Read the definitions out loud as students read silently. Choose a student to read each sentence.

Definitions

1. **thread** (a string)
   The seamstress used a needle and <u>thread</u> to mend the hole in my pants.

2. **pliers** (small tools used for holding small objects or bending wire)
   The electrician used a small pair of <u>pliers</u> to bend the wires together.

Week 3 Word List

thread	decide	unusually
pliers	twist	special
method	saber-toothed tiger	either
prehistoric	grunt	caveman
mastodon	suddenly	strange

1. thread
2. pli ers
3. meth od
4. his tory
   pre his tor ic
5. mas to don
6. de cide
   de cided
7. twist
8. sa ber–tooth ed ti ger
9. gr unt
10. sud den
    sud den ly
11. us u al
    un us u al ly
12. sp e cial
13. ei ther
14. cave man
15. strange

3. **method** (a way or process of doing something)
   French chefs use cooking <u>method</u>s that have been passed down from generation to generation.

4. **prehistoric** (period of time before written history and during the early development of man)
   During <u>prehistoric</u> times, families prepared their food over an outdoor fire.

5. **mastodon** (an extinct animal known for its large teeth; ancestor of the elephant)
   We recognized the <u>mastodon</u> at the Museum of Natural History by its long ivory teeth.

6. **decide** (to make a decision, choice, or judgment: to make up one's mind)
   The judges <u>decide</u>d on a winner after observing each ice skater perform.

7. **twist** (to curve or bend)
   In Boy Scouts, we learned how to <u>twist</u> heavy ropes into decorative knots.

8. **saber-toothed tiger** (a prehistoric cat with long, curving teeth)
   On the cartoon *The Flintstones,* Fred wrestles with a <u>saber-toothed tiger</u>.

9. **grunt** (a noise like the sound pigs make; groan)
   Sammy <u>grunt</u>ed for attention because his tooth hurt too badly to be able to talk.

10. **suddenly** (quickly)
    <u>Suddenly</u>, the rain stopped and two rainbows appeared in the sky.

11. **unusually** (not common, rare; out of the ordinary)
    This past summer was <u>unusually</u> hot with temperatures soaring in the 100s.

12. **special** (unique, not common; having something extra)
    A blue diamond is <u>special</u> and not easily found when mining gems.

13. **either** (one or the other)
    <u>Either</u> homeroom 203 or 219 will win the ice cream party because they have sold over 500 tickets.

14. **caveman** (a person who lived in caves during the Stone Age; prehistoric man)
    The <u>caveman</u> hunted for food with tools made from animal bones.

15. **strange** (different, unusual, not common)
    In the movie *The Dinosaurs,* the monkeys find themselves lost in a <u>strange</u> land.

Assign At-Home 1

Say: *Tonight you will . . .*

1. *Study the vocabulary words with definitions.*

2. *Complete the Riddle Page.*

3. *Do the Matching Activity.*

4. *Make flashcards.*

Day 2: Introduction

Prepare for Lesson

 Materials: Student Workbooks, *The Stories Julian Tells* by Ann Cameron

 Vocabulary Review

3 min.

 Rapid review of vocabulary words (Students use the Week 3 Word List in their Student Workbooks.)

7 min. **Review At-Home 1**

 Review the correct answers to At-Home 1.

 Review student work to confirm or clarify responses.

8 min. **Predict the Storyline**

 Students look at illustrations on pages 46 and 50 of *The Stories Julian Tells* by Ann Cameron.

 Say: *Today we will begin reading a new story from <u>The Stories Julian Tells.</u> Last week, we read Chapter 1, "The Pudding Like a Night on the Sea." We were introduced to several characters: Julian; his brother, Huey; and their parents. Chapter 1 was about the special pudding that Julian's father made and how the boys couldn't leave the pudding alone. This week's story focuses on Julian and his loose tooth. How do you feel when have a loose tooth?*

 Say: *Open your Student Workbook to Semantic Web: Pulling Teeth. Let's talk about pulling teeth. How do people feel when a tooth is pulled? Who are some people who can pull a loose tooth?*

 Say: *What are some ways of pulling teeth? What do people do when their teeth are pulled?*

 Say: *Think of a question that you think the story will answer. Write the question at the bottom of Semantic Web: Pulling Teeth.*

8–10 min. **Story Reading 1: Identifying Vocabulary in Text**

 Say: *As I read the story out loud, you will follow along silently. When you see a word from our vocabulary list, give a thumbs up.*

 Read pages 46–57.

 Discuss what students predicted would happen in the story.

6 min. **Story Reading 2: Paraphrasing Vocabulary in Text**

 Say: *As I read specific paragraphs of the story out loud again, let's paraphrase what the author has said by using our own words. Let's focus on the third paragraph on page 54. Follow along as I read out loud.* Read the paragraph ("A cave bay with two teeth . . .").

 Say: *How could you summarize this paragraph in your words?*

Assign At-Home 2

Say: *Tonight you will . . .*

1.   *Study your flashcards.*

2.   *Complete Word Substitutions.*

3.   *Complete Same and Different.*

Day 3: Using Words in Context

Prepare for Lesson

☆ Materials: Student Workbooks

☆ Read Teacher Tip: Word Wizard (Week 1, page 14)

Vocabulary Review

☆ Rapid review of vocabulary words (Students use the Week 3 Word List in their Student Workbooks.)

Review At-Home 2

☆ Review the correct answers to At-Home 2.

☆ Review student work to confirm or clarify responses.

Using Context Clues

☆ Say: *Open your Student Workbook to Week 3: Using Context Clues. Today, we will use context clues to help us choose the word that fits in the blank by using the clues from other words and information in the sentence or sentences. I will read the sentences out loud. Raise your hand when you know which word best completes the sentence. Write the word in the blank. Sometimes the word might require an ending such as -ed, -s, or -ing. Each word will be used only one time.*

☆ Choose individual students to give answers. Have students point out context clues that helped them to choose the correct answer.

☆ Say: *Cross out words in the box as we use them. Write your answers in the blank, and write the context clues you used in the space below.*

Word Wizard

☆ Say: *As Word Wizards this week, you must always be on the lookout for opportunities to use and demonstrate your word knowledge. Use your Word Wizard Journals to keep track of each time you hear one of this week's vocabulary words used in a sentence at home, school, or even on television. If you don't hear the words in a sentence, be creative and write original sentences using your new vocabulary knowledge. Next week, each group will read two of their sentences to the class!*

☆ Say: *Get in your Word Wizard Groups from last week, and share your best sentences.*

☆ Say: *Which group would like to read two of their sentences using the words from last week's chapter?* Tally the number of sentences per group, and record the amounts on the Word Wizard Chart.

Assign At-Home 3

Say: *Tonight you will . . .*

1. *Study your flashcards.*

2. *Complete the Word Wizard Journal.*

3. *Complete the Context Clues Activity.*

Day 4: Expanding Meaning

Prepare for Lesson

☆ Materials: Student Workbooks

☆ Read Teacher Tip: Morphographic Elements (Week 1, page 17)

Vocabulary Review

☆ Rapid review of vocabulary words (Students use the Week 3 Word List in their Student Workbooks.)

Review At-Home 3

☆ Review the correct answers to At-Home 3.

☆ Review student work to confirm or clarify responses.

Morphographic Elements: *Pre-, Un-, -ic,* and *-ly*

☆ Say: *Today, we will look at prefixes and suffixes that are present in this week's vocabulary words. Find Morphographic Elements:* Pre-, Un-, -ic, *and* -ly *in your Student Workbook.*

☆ Say: *Let's look at the information in the top box. Prefixes are word parts that can be added to the front of a word. Can you think of any prefixes that you have studied?* Briefly discuss. *Today, we will look at words that use the prefixes* pre- *and* un-.

☆ Read the definition for *pre-.* Say: *Let's look in the box and read words that use this prefix.* Read the word, definition, and sentence that corresponds with the word using the prefix *pre-.*

☆ Read the definition for *un-.* Say: *Let's look in the box and read words that use this prefix.* Read the word, definition, and sentence that corresponds with the word using the prefix *un-.*

☆ Say: *Let's look at the information in the suffix box. Suffixes are word parts that can be added to the end of a word. Can you think of any suffixes that you have studied?*

☆ Read the definition for *-ic.* Say: *Let's look in the box and read words that use this suffix.* Read the word, definition, and sentence that corresponds with the word using the suffix *-ic.*

☆ Read the definition for *-ly.* Say: *Let's look in the box and read words that use this suffix.* Read the word, definition, and sentence that corresponds with the word using the suffix *-ly.*

☆ Say: *Prefixes and suffixes help us to see relationships between words when we read. Let's read and discuss the word cousins that appear in Part A.* Read each word pair and discuss.

☆ Say: *Let's look at Part B. Each underlined word is written with a suffix or prefix that we have studied today. We will read the word in a sentence and then use context clues and the meaning of the prefix or suffix to help us to select the best definition.*

Assign At-Home 4

Say: *Tonight you will . . .*

1. *Study your flashcards.*

2. *Complete the Crossword Puzzle.*

Day 5: Keys to Understanding

Prepare for Lesson

 Materials: Student Workbooks, photocopies of Assessment 3.

7 min.

Review At-Home 4

 Review the correct answers to At-Home 4.

 Review student work to confirm or clarify responses.

8 min.

Bingo Game

 Say: *Choose nine words from the Week 3 Word List, and write them on the Bingo Card in your Student Workbook. When I read a definition, raise your hand to identify the word. If you have the word on your card, mark it with an <u>X</u>. The first person who has 3 <u>X</u>s in a row (across, down, diagonally) wins the game.*

 Read the definitions. As students identify definitions, write the words on the board until someone wins the game.

20 min.

Synonyms and Antonyms

 Say: *You have learned many new words this week. When using context clues yesterday, we noticed that some words were the same and some words were opposite in meaning. Words that have the same meaning are called synonyms. Words that have the opposite meaning are called antonyms.*

 Say: *Think of the word <u>small</u>. What are some words that mean the same as <u>small</u>? Instead of saying, "The baby's feet are small," we could say, "The baby's feet are tiny." Think of a word that means the opposite of <u>small</u>. We can use an antonym to say, "The baby's feet are gigantic."*

 Say: *Today, we will learn to express ideas with words that are the same or opposite in meaning. We will concentrate on five words from our vocabulary list.*

 Say: *Open your Student Workbook to Week 3: Synonyms and Antonyms. This worksheet has sentences that you took home at the beginning of the week in the Student Study Guide. Let's look at how we can rewrite some of these sentences to express ideas that are the opposite or same in meaning.*

 Say: *I will read the original sentence with the underlined word and the definition. Then, we will read the synonym or antonym sentences together. Remember, not every word has a synonym or antonym. Read and discuss the examples.*

 Say: *Let's read a story about a boy named Sam. In the story, we will use synonyms and antonyms that we have learned today. First, I will read the story out loud. Then, I will read the story again. When you figure out what goes in the blank, raise your hand during the second reading of the story.*

10 min.

Assessment

 Distribute Assessment 3 to each student.

Name: _____ Date: _____

Assessment 3
The Stories Julian Tells
My Very Strange Teeth

A. Match the word with the appropriate definition.

a) thread	d) prehistoric	g) twist	j) special	m) either
b) pliers	e) mastodon	h) saber-toothed tiger	k) unusually	n) caveman
c) method	f) decide	i) suddenly	l) grunt	o) strange

_____ 1. a tool used for holding small objects

_____ 2. one or the other

_____ 3. a string

_____ 4. an ancestor of the elephant

_____ 5. groan

B. Circle the word or phrase that does not belong.

1.	unusual	strange	odd	common
2.	quickly	suddenly	slowly	rapidly
3.	sloppy	technique	organization	method
4.	modern	prehistoric	present day	current
5.	straighten	braid	twist	bend

C. Complete the sentence with the best answer.

_____ 1. During prehistoric times, it would be unusual to find _____.

   a) a brave caveman

   b) a house made of wood

   c) a mastodon

_____ 2. A caveman might decide to give _____ as a special gift.

   a) a television

   b) a hunting tool

   c) a video game

_____ 3. I would be surprised if I saw _____ because it is very unusual.

   a) a pig that grunts

   b) a thread that breaks

   c) a saber-toothed tiger that talks

_____ 4. We were surprised when _____ because it happened suddenly.

   a) a plate fell to the floor and broke

   b) a turtle won a race

   c) a flower grew

_____ 5. An example of something that can be twisted is _____.

   a) clean air

   b) red ribbons

   c) apple juice

Vocabulary Power, Level 1, by Latrice M. Seals, Sharolyn D. Pollard-Durodola, Barbara R. Foorman, and Ashley M. Bradley

The Stories Julian Tells

Gloria Who Might Be My Best Friend

by Ann Cameron

DAY 1 Preview of Lesson	DAY 2 Introduction	DAY 3 Using Words in Context	DAY 4 Expanding Meaning	DAY 5 Keys to Understanding
Read New Words Say and Write New Words Read Definitions Assign At-Home 1	Vocabulary Review Review At-Home 1 Predict the Storyline Story Reading (pages 58–71) Identifying Vocabulary in Text Paraphrasing Vocabulary in Text Assign At-Home 2	Vocabulary Review Review At-Home 2 Using Context Clues Word Wizard Assign At-Home 3	Vocabulary Review Review At-Home 3 Morphographic Elements: -tion Assign At-Home 4	Review At-Home 4 Bingo Game Deep Processing Assessment

Words and Definitions

The following are target words for this week. If the word has multiple meanings, we provide only the definition listed in the text. *Please review the definitions prior to instruction.*

1. **tease**—to make fun of someone

2. **field**—an open land area free of woods and buildings

3. **branch**—part of a tree

4. **braided**—twisted together

5. **cartwheel**—kind of somersault or handspring with arms and legs extended

6. **seriously**—not jokingly; in a sincere or thoughtful manner

7. **practice**—do again and again as a habit

8. **squawk**—to make a loud, harsh sound or scream

9. **mustache**—hair on the upper lip that is trimmed a specific style

10. **giggle**—to laugh in a silly way

11. **collection**—an accumulation or group of objects for enjoyment or display

12. **piece**—a bit or part

13. **knot**—hard lump formed from tying threads together

14. **catalog**—book that contains a list of items

15. **fasten**—to lock or pin down

Day 1: Preview of Lesson

Prepare for Lesson

☆ Materials: Student Workbooks, *The Stories Julian Tells* by Ann Cameron, display copy of Week 4 Word List

☆ Read Teacher Tip: Reading New Words (Week 1, page 8)

5 min.

Read New Words

☆ Say: *Today, we will begin a new chapter in* <u>The Stories Julian Tells</u>. *This week, we will read Chapter 6, "Gloria Who Might Be My Best Friend." Remember, on Day 1 we learn to read new words that you will study at home. The words we learn will help you to read this story better and will help you to express your thoughts on paper and when talking to others. Let's see if there are any words that you already know.*

☆ Display the Week 4 Word List. Cover the bottom box, leaving the word columns at the top of the page exposed. Say: *Which words do you already know?*

☆ Uncover the bottom box. Say: *Let's read these words. Sound out each syllable as I point to it. Be sure to say each sound clearly. Sound it out.*

☆ Students sound out each syllable. Say the word. Students repeat the word. Say: *Yes, the word is . . . .*

10 min.

Say and Write New Words

☆ Cover the bottom box, and use the word columns at the top of the page.

☆ Say: *Let's read the words together.* Point to each word and read one time.

☆ Say: *Take out your pencil and Student Workbook. Find the page that says Week 4: Say and Write New Words. Let's get ready to say and write each word.*

☆ Point to each word. Say: *What word?* Students say the word. *Write [the word].*

☆ Students write the word next to one that appears on Week 4: Say and Write New Words. Continue until all words are written.

5 min.

Read Definitions

☆ Say: *I will read the definitions so that we will understand what each word means. Some words have more than one meaning; however, these are the definitions that are used in the story.*

☆ Read the definitions out loud as students read silently. Choose a student to read each sentence.

Definitions

1. **tease** (to make fun of someone)
   People liked to <u>tease</u> Julian because he had a girl as a friend.

2. **field** (an open land area free of woods and buildings)
   Julian and Gloria flew their kites in an open <u>field</u>.

Week 4 Word List

tea**se**	serious**ly**	collec**tion**
fiel**d**	prac**tice**	pie**ce**
bran**ch**	squaw**k**	kno**t**
braid**ed**	musta**che**	catalo**g**
cartwhee**l**	giggle	faste**n**

1. tea**se**
2. fiel**d**
3. bran**ch**
4. brai**d**
   braid **ed**
5. cart whee**l**
6. ser ious
   ser i ous **ly**
7. prac **tice**

8. squaw**k**
9. mus ta**che**
10. gig gle
11. col lect
    col lec **tion**
12. pie**ce**
13. kno**t**
14. cat a lo**g**
15. fast e**n**

Vocabulary Power, Level 1, by Latrice M. Seals, Sharolyn D. Pollard-Durodola, Barbara R. Foorman, and Ashley M. Bradley

3. **branch** (part of a tree)
   The kite's tail was caught on a broken tree <u>branch</u>.

4. **braided** (twisted together by using three or more strands)
   The kite's tail was <u>braided</u> with red, white, and blue ribbons.

5. **cartwheel** (kind of somersault or handspring with arms and legs extended)
   In my gymnastics class, we learned how to do <u>cartwheel</u>s.

6. **seriously** (not jokingly; in a sincere or thoughtful manner)
   The news reporter <u>seriously</u> described what it was like to be caught in a hurricane.

7. **practice** (do again and again as a habit)
   Linda is a virtuoso because she <u>practice</u>s playing the cello on a daily basis.

8. **squawk** (to make a loud, harsh sound or scream)
   The mother bird <u>squawk</u>ed when she saw the little boy approach her nest.

9. **mustache** (hair on the upper lip that is trimmed in a specific style)
   The girls like Mr. Daily because he has a very curly <u>mustache</u>.

10. **giggle** (to laugh in a silly way)
    Julian felt embarrassed whenever Gloria <u>giggle</u>d in a high-pitched voice.

11. **collection** (an accumulation or group of objects for enjoyment or display as a hobby)
    Mom keeps her seashell <u>collection</u> in a glass case.

12. **piece** (a bit or part)
    We wrote our names on a <u>piece</u> of paper and put it in the drawing for the scooter.

13. **knot** (hard lump formed from tying threads together)
    My baby brother tied his shoestrings in a <u>knot</u>.

14. **catalog** (book that contains a list of items)
    Grandma buys our clothes from a mail-order <u>catalog</u> because she does not like to go to malls.

15. **fasten** (to lock or pin down)
    We <u>fasten</u>ed the baby's diaper with a huge safety pin.

Assign At-Home 1

Say: *Tonight you will . . .*

1. *Study the vocabulary words with definitions.*

2. *Complete the Riddle Page.*

3. *Do the Matching Activity.*

4. *Make flashcards.*

Day 2: Introduction

Prepare for Lesson

 Materials: Student Workbooks, *The Stories Julian Tells* by Ann Cameron

(3 min.) Vocabulary Review

 Rapid review of vocabulary words (Students use the Week 4 Word List in their Student Workbooks.)

(7 min.) Review At-Home 1

 Review the correct answers to At-Home 1.

 Review student work to confirm or clarify responses.

(8 min.) Predict the Storyline

 Students look at illustrations on pages 58 and 68 of *The Stories Julian Tells* by Ann Cameron.

 Say: *Today, we will read Chapter 6 of <u>The Stories Julian Tells</u>, which is called "Gloria Who Might Be My Best Friend." Last week, we read Chapter 5, "My Very Strange Teeth." Chapter 5 was about Julian having a loose tooth and about how it eventually fell out. This week's story focuses on a new friend that Julian makes. Her name is Gloria. Let's talk about some things that friends like to do together.*

 Say: *Open your Student Workbook to Semantic Web: Making Friends. What are some qualities of a good friend? What are some things that friends share? Describe some places you might make a new friend.*

 Say: *Why do you think Julian says that Gloria <u>might</u> be his best friend? Let's read and find out. In this chapter, Julian and his new friend, Gloria, do something special.*

 Say: *Think of a question that you think the story will answer. Write the question at the bottom of Semantic Web: Making Friends.*

(8–10 min.) Story Reading 1: Identifying Vocabulary in Text

 Say: *As I read the story out loud, you will follow along silently. When you see a word from our vocabulary list, give a thumbs up.*

 Read pages 58–71.

 Discuss what students predicted would happen in the story.

(6 min.) Story Reading 2: Paraphrasing Vocabulary in Text

 Say: *As I read specific paragraphs of the story out loud again, let's paraphrase what the author has said by using our own words. Let's focus on the first two paragraphs on page 69. Follow along as I read out loud.* Read the paragraphs ("We ran through the back yard . . .").

 Say: *How could you summarize these paragraphs in your own words?*

 Help students to paraphrase the remaining page as appropriate.

Assign At-Home 2

Say: *Tonight you will . . .*

1. *Study your flashcards.*
2. *Complete Word Substitutions.*
3. *Complete Same and Different.*

Day 3: Using Words in Context

Prepare for Lesson

 Materials: Student Workbooks

 Read Teacher Tip: Word Wizard (Week 1, page 14)

3 min. Vocabulary Review

 Rapid review of vocabulary words (Students use the Week 4 Word List in their Student Workbooks.)

7 min. Review At-Home 2

 Review the correct answers to At-Home 2.

 Review student work to confirm or clarify responses.

15 min. Using Context Clues

 Say: *Open your Student Workbook to Week 4: Using Context Clues. Today, we will use context clues to help us choose the word that fits in the blank by using the clues from other words and information in the sentence or sentences. I will read the sentences out loud. Raise your hand when you know which word best completes the sentence. Write the word in the blank. Sometimes the word might require an ending such as -ed, -s, or -ing. Each word will be used only one time.*

 Choose individual students to give answers. Have students point out context clues that helped them to choose the correct answer.

 Say: *Cross out words in the box as we use them. Write your answers in the blank, and write the context clues you used in the space below.*

5 min. Word Wizard

 Say: *As Word Wizards this week, you must always be on the lookout for opportunities to use and demonstrate your word knowledge. Use your Word Wizard Journals to keep track of each time you hear one of this week's vocabulary words used in a sentence at home, school, or even on television. If you don't hear the words in a sentence, be creative and write original sentences using your new vocabulary knowledge. Next week, each group will read two of their sentences to the class!*

 Say: *Get in your Word Wizard Groups from last week, and share your best sentences.*

 Say: *Which group would like to read two of their sentences using the words from last week's chapter?* Tally the number of sentences per group, and record the amounts on the Word Wizard Chart.

Assign At-Home 3

Say: *Tonight you will . . .*

1. *Study your flashcards.*

2. *Complete the Word Wizard Journal.*

3. *Complete the Context Clues Activity.*

Day 4: Expanding Meaning

Prepare for Lesson

☆ Materials: Student Workbooks

☆ Read Teacher Tip: Morphographic Elements (Week 1, page 17)

 Vocabulary Review

(3 min.)

☆ Rapid review of vocabulary words (Students use the Week 4 Word List in their Student Workbooks.)

 Review At-Home 3

(7 min.)

☆ Review the correct answers to At-Home 3.

☆ Review student work to confirm or clarify responses.

(8–10 min.) **Morphographic Elements: *-tion***

☆ Say: *Today we will look at a suffix that is present in one of this week's vocabulary words. Find Morphographic Elements: -tion in your Student Workbook.*

☆ Say: *Let's review the definition for suffix at the top of the page.* Briefly discuss. *Today, we will look at words that use the suffix -tion.*

☆ Read the definition for *-tion.* Say: *Let's look in the box and read words that use this suffix. Read the word, definition, and sentence that corresponds with the word using the suffix -tion.*

☆ Say: *Suffixes can help us to see relationships between words when we read. Let's read and discuss the word cousins that appear in Part A. Let's read these word cousins together.* Read each word pair and discuss.

☆ Say: *Now, let's read the sentences in Part B and choose the best definition.*

Assign At-Home 4

Say: *Tonight you will . . .*

1. *Study your flashcards.*

2. *Complete the Crossword Puzzle.*

Day 5: Keys to Understanding

Prepare for Lesson

☆ Materials: Student Workbooks, photocopies of Assessment 4

☆ Read Teacher Tip: Deep Processing (Week 2, page 28)

7 min.

Review At-Home 4

☆ Review the correct answers to At-Home 4.

☆ Review student work to confirm or clarify responses.

8 min.

Bingo Game

☆ Say: *Choose nine words from the Week 4 Word List, and write them on the Bingo Card in your Student Workbook. When I read a definition, raise your hand to identify the word. If you have the word on your card, mark it with an X. The first person who has 3 Xs in a row (across, down, diagonally) wins the game.*

☆ Read the definitions. As students identify definitions, write the words on the board until someone wins the game.

8–10 min.

Deep Processing

☆ Say: *Does anyone remember what is <u>deep processing</u>? It is thinking about how words relate to each other.*

☆ Say: *We have learned the definitions of this week's vocabulary words, but definitions do not really teach us everything you need to know to really understand the meaning of a word. Remember, it is important to be able to use these words to describe your own experiences in life and to describe conditions in the world in general.*

☆ Say: *Open your Student Workbook to Deep Processing: "Gloria Who Might Be My Best Friend." We will read each question together and decide what is a reasonable answer and why. The answers are not in the book we read but come from your own thinking. Think about the questions and what would be a reasonable response. Remember, you must be able to explain why you chose your answer.*

☆ Read each question out loud. Discuss and decide on possible answers. It is more important that students are able to defend their answers than that they choose the answer that seems to be right.

10 min.

Assessment

☆ Distribute Assessment 4 to each student.

Name: _____ Date: _____

Assessment 4
The Stories Julian Tells
Gloria Who Might Be My Best Friend

A. Match the word with the appropriate definition.

a) tease	d) braided	g) seriously	j) mustache	m) piece
b) field	e) fasten	h) practice	k) giggle	n) knot
c) branch	f) squawk	i) cartwheel	l) collection	o) catalog

_____ 1. a somersault or handspring

_____ 2. a hard lump

_____ 3. to make secure or pin down

_____ 4. a bit or a part

_____ 5. hair on the upper lip that is styled

B. Circle the word that does not belong.

1.	pasture	field	grassland	lake
2.	root	stem	branch	crop
3.	praise	tease	compliment	honor
4.	cheerful	happy	serious	sunny
5.	whisper	squawk	scream	screech

C. Complete the sentence with the best answer.

_____ 1. A serious person would giggle at a _____.

      a) collection of cars

      b) group of clowns

      c) bag of marbles

_____ 2. A farmer might find _____ in the *Planter's Annual Catalog*.

      a) prices for streetlights

      b) a list of seasonal crops

      c) a list of prehistoric animals

_____ 3. A rug maker who uses braided materials might use _____ for making his rugs.

      a) thick threads

      b) brown mustaches

      c) smooth leaves

_____ 4. A football player would practice _____.

      a) using a beater to whip pudding

      b) guarding a player

      c) tying knots

_____ 5. _____ is a sport you would practice in an open field.

      a) Water skiing

      b) Bowling

      c) Golf

  Vocabulary Power, Level 1, by Latrice M. Seals, Sharolyn D. Pollard-Durodola, Barbara R. Foorman, and Ashley M. Bradley

Review Unit 1

REVIEW DAY 1	REVIEW DAY 2	REVIEW DAY 3	REVIEW DAY 4	REVIEW DAY 5
Introduce Unit Review "I Spy" Game Assign At-Home 1	Semantic Feature Analysis Assign At-Home 2	Multiple Meanings: *Thick, Twist, Branch,* and *Field* Find It, Say It! Game Assign At-Home 3	Clueless Game Assign At-Home 4	Assessment

Words and Definitions

The following are target words for this week. If the word has multiple meanings, we provide only the definition listed in the text. ***Please review the definitions prior to instruction.***

1. **ignore**—to pay no attention to someone or something
2. **optician**—a person who makes or sells eyeglasses and other products for the eye
3. **powerful**—strong, influential
4. **piece**—a bit or part
5. **twist**—to curve or bend
6. **practice**—do again and again as a habit
7. **thick**—closely packed, crowded, dense
8. **guard**—to protect, keep safe, shield
9. **crater**—large hole in the moon's or Earth's surface; hole created by an explosion
10. **leave**—to discontinue association with; stop bothering someone or something
11. **counter**—a level surface over which business is conducted or food is prepared
12. **method**—a way or process of doing something
13. **prehistoric**—period of time before written history and during the early development of man
14. **mastodon**—an extinct animal known for its large teeth; ancestor of the elephant
15. **decide**—to make a decision, choice or judgment; to make up one's mind
16. **grunt**—a noise like the sound pigs make; groan
17. **unusually**—uncommon, rare; out of the ordinary
18. **strange**—different, unusual, not common
19. **field**—an open land area free of woods and buildings
20. **branch**—part of a tree
21. **squawk**—to make a loud, harsh sound or scream
22. **collection**—an accumulation or group of objects for enjoyment or display
23. **loosen**—to untie, to release and set free
24. **catalog**—book that contains a list of items
25. **even**—to make a surface flat and level

Review Day 1

Prepare for Lesson

 Materials: Student Workbooks, display copy of Unit 1 Word List (optional)

Introduce Unit Review

☆ Say: *Last week, we completed the last story in our unit. We have read four stories and learned many new words each week. This week, we will review some key words that we learned in Unit 1. At the end of the week, you will have an opportunity to demonstrate just how much you've learned.*

"I Spy" Game

25 min.

☆ Say: *How many of you have ever played "I Spy"? When we play "I Spy" we use clues to help us to identify words.*

☆ Say: *Turn to Unit 1: "I Spy" in your Student Workbook. Today, we will work as word detectives and use a list of clues to determine the review word. Let's read the clues and decide which word is being described. Write the word next to the appropriate clue. Remember, a good detective never gives up!*

☆ Read the sentences out loud, and call on students for answers. Say: *I am looking for a word that means . . . ,* then read the definition. Students should respond in the form, "I spy . . ." then say the vocabulary word.

Assign At-Home 1

Say: *Tonight you will . . .*

1. *Study the Unit 1 vocabulary words with definitions.*

2. *Make flashcards.*

Unit 1 Word List

ignore	optician	powerful
piece	twist	thick
guard	practice	crater
catalog	leave	counter
method	prehistoric	mastodon
decide	grunt	even
field	unusually	strange
branch	squawk	collection
loosen		

Prepare for Lesson

☆ Materials: Student Workbooks, display copy of Semantic Feature Analysis: Action Words

☆ Read Teacher Tip: Semantic Feature Analysis

Teacher Tip: Semantic Feature Analysis

Semantic Feature Analysis is an instructional method that helps students to see relationships between words that are close in meaning (e.g., *house, mansion, shack, shed, barn, tent, bungalow, shanty*; Nagy, 1988[1]).

The vertical columns at the top of the matrix are for the features or characteristics shared by some of the words.

The horizontal columns on the left of the matrix are for the words that are being compared.

Pluses (+) are used to indicate features that are shared for each word.

Minuses (–) are used to indicate features that are not present in a word. These pluses and minuses are arrived at through class discussion.

Zeros (0) are used if students cannot agree that a word has a certain feature.

Semantic Feature Analysis is done through class discussions. Many answers are open ended.

Semantic Feature Analysis

☆ Say: *The objective of today's activity is to compare different words and to decide how words are similar and different. The purpose of this activity is to help you to see how words are related to each other.*

☆ Say: *Some of the words that we've learned describe what people do. Let's make a comparison of how these actions are similar and different.*

☆ Say: *Turn to the Unit 1 Word List in your Student Workbook. Let's reread the list of words in the Review Unit and look for words that describe what people or things can do. These are action words, or verbs.*

☆ Say: *Let's think of some features of action words. For example, actions may be directed towards other people, objects, or places. Actions can describe sounds. Actions can be physical or they can exist in our minds and be mental. Some actions are positive, and some are negative. Some actions require little effort, and some actions require physical strength.*

☆ Say: *Turn to Semantic Feature Analysis: Action Words in your Student Workbook. The action words for Unit 1 are listed in the left column of the matrix.* Read the list of action words.

☆ Say: *The top row of the matrix lists features of actions words.* Read the list of features.

---

[1]Nagy, W.E. (1988). *Teaching vocabulary to improve reading comprehension.* Newark, DE: International Reading Association

☆ Say: *Let's think about each action and see what features it has or doesn't have. We will fill in the matrix with a plus or minus to indicate the presence or absence of each feature. If we can't agree, we will place a zero in the matrix.*

☆ After the matrix is complete, say: *Let's look at the matrix to see which features are shared by each type of action.* Discuss similar and different features.

☆ Help students discover that no two categories of actions have exactly the same pattern of pluses (similarities) and minuses (differences): none are identical. Even the categories that are most alike will reveal their differences if enough features are added.

Assign At-Home 2

Say: *Tonight you will study the vocabulary words on your flashcards.*

Semantic Feature Analysis: Action Words

	Directed toward objects	Directed toward people	Directed toward places	Sounds	Physical	Mental	Positive	Negative	Much effort	Little effort	
Ignore											
Twist											
Practice											
Guard											
Leave											
Decide											
Grunt											
Loosen											
Even											

Review Day 3

Prepare for Lesson

☆ Materials: Student Workbooks

 Multiple Meanings: *Thick, Twist, Branch,* **and** *Field*

☆ Say: *Today we are going to study some of the words from the past 4 weeks that have more than one meaning. In the first part of the activity, we will quickly review the different meanings for each word.*

☆ Say: *Who remembers one of the meanings for the word <u>thick</u>?* Continue until the students have identified as many definitions as they can for *thick.* Do the same for *twist, branch,* and *field.*

☆ Say: *Open your Student Workbook to Multiple Meanings: <u>Thick</u>, <u>Twist</u>, <u>Branch</u>, and <u>Field</u>. Let's see how many meanings we know for these words.*

☆ The Bonus Box contains two words that are homophones (*hole* and *whole*) and one word that sounds similar but has a different sound at the end (*hold*). Because many speakers tend to leave the endings off words, please direct students' attention to the final sound in *hold.*

 Find It, Say It! Game

☆ Say: *Next, we will play Find It, Say It! Turn to Unit 1: Find It, Say It!*

☆ Say: *When we play Find It, Say It! I first read the sentence with the underlined word and say, "Find it." You then go to the box of the underlined word and find the definition that best fits the way the word is used in each sentence. Without talking, write the letter for that definition in the space at the beginning of the sentence. When I say, "Say it," everyone will say the answer out loud together. Let's do the example together.*

☆ Say: *In the movie, Consuela and Carlos decided that they would tie the <u>knot</u> because they knew that they would love each other forever.*

☆ Say: *Find it!* Allow students approximately 7 seconds.

☆ Say: *Say It!* Students say *B* together.

Assign At-Home 3

Say: *Tonight you will study the vocabulary words on your flashcards.*

Prepare for Lesson

☆ Materials: Clue Cards, photocopies of Score Keeper Card

Clueless Game

25 min.

☆ Write the words "Class Score Keeper" and the numbers 1–10 on the board. Have a magnet or other device ready to point to one of the numbers.

☆ Say: *Today, we will play a game called Clueless. The objective of this game is to focus on single word clues that can help you to remember the words that you have learned. You may not use your Student Workbook to help you.*

☆ Divide students into teams. Students can play by rows if desired.

☆ Say: *We will appoint one score keeper for each team. Each team will have a Score Keeper Card to keep track of the team's points. The Score Keeper Card has boxes for four games. We will use the part for Review Unit 1.* Assign a person from each team to be the score keeper or allow teams to choose their own score keepers.

☆ Say: *I will place a marker on number 10 on the Class Score Keeper. Then, I will flash a Clue Card with a one-word clue. I will start with Team A. If Team A correctly identifies the word, they get the points indicated on the Class Score Keeper. If the marker is on 10, they get 10 points, and the team's score keeper records the value on the Score Keeper Card.*

☆ Say: *If the word is not guessed from the Clue Card, the marker on the Class Score Keeper is moved to 9, and it becomes the other team's turn. If they guess the word, they receive the points indicated by the Class Score Keeper.*

☆ Say: *Remember, if the word is not guessed from the first clue, the marker on the Class Score Keeper is moved to 9, and it becomes the other team's turn. If the next team cannot guess the word, the marker is moved to 8, and so forth. Each time the word is not guessed, the marker is moved one number lower.*

☆ Say: *Each time we read a new clue, the marker is placed back on 10, and the other team tries to identify the word from the next clue card.*

☆ Say: *We will continue to play until we have identified all of the clue words. The team with the highest total score is the winner.*

☆ Distribute Score Keeper Cards to each team. After playing the game, collect the Score Keeper Cards so that they can be used with the next review unit.

Assign At-Home 4

Say: *Tonight you will study for Friday's test.*

Clue Cards

level	list	untie	group	scream
tree	land	rare	different	pigs
decision	teeth	history	process	surface
discontinue	holes	protect	crowded	habit
bend	part	overlook	eyes	mighty

Score Keeper Card

☆ You are the Score Keeper for your team. Write the name of your team in the blank. Each time your team earns points for identifying a word, write the number of points on one of the lines. At the end of the game, add the points together to get the total. The team with the most points wins the game.

TEAM NAME: _____

Review Unit 1

1.	9.
2.	10.
3.	11.
4.	12.
5.	13.
6.	14.
7.	15.
8.	

Review Unit 2

1.	9.
2.	10.
3.	11.
4.	12.
5.	13.
6.	14.
7.	15.
8.	

Review Unit 3

1.	9.
2.	10.
3.	11.
4.	12.
5.	13.
6.	14.
7.	15.
8.	

Review Unit 4

1.	9.
2.	10.
3.	11.
4.	12.
5.	13.
6.	14.
7.	15.
8.	

Vocabulary Power, Level 1, by Latrice M. Seals, Sharolyn D. Pollard-Durodola, Barbara R. Foorman, and Ashley M. Bradley

Review Day 5

Prepare for Lesson

☆ Materials: photocopies of Assessment 5

 ## Assessment

☆ Distribute Assessment 5 to each student.

☆ Read the directions out loud.

☆ Read each vocabulary word out loud along with the answer choices. Allow students a few seconds to choose and write the letter for a definition.

☆ Collect assessments.

Name: _____ Date: _____

Assessment 5
Unit 1

Choose the letter that represents the best definition for each word.

___ 1. catalog
   a. an encyclopedia about cats
   b. written or printed material with a selection of objects
   c. a group of objects for display

___ 2. ignore
   a. to close one's eyes to others
   b. to see and notice others
   c. to speak to others

___ 3. even
   a. to make crooked or bent
   b. to make checkered, black and white
   c. to make smooth or level

___ 4. optician
   a. a person who wears eyeglasses
   b. a person who destroys eyeglasses
   c. a person who makes eyeglasses

___ 5. loosen
   a. to make taut and tight
   b. to free from pressure
   c. to free from homework

___ 6. piece
   a. whole
   b. divided into parts
   c. complete

___ 7. collection
   a. a group of things to be eaten or cooked
   b. a group of works or things kept together for show
   c. a group of shows or programs

___ 8. twist
   a. to smooth, flatten, straighten
   b. to unfold, unravel, unsnarl
   c. to wind, turn, weave

___ 9. branch
   a. a woody stem or limb
   b. a broken limb or leg
   c. a broken arm or finger

___ 10. practice
   a. to perform in a movie many times
   b. to repeat a drill many times
   c. to sleep for many hours

___ 11. squawk
   a. to whisper quietly
   b. to run swiftly
   c. to make a loud protest

___ 12. prehistoric
   a. a period of time before there were written accounts
   b. a period of time after there were written records
   c. a period of time in which there was no history

___ 13. guard
   a. to dress in a uniform on a daily basis
   b. to expose or lead into risky situations
   c. to shield from danger by careful watching

_____ 14. strange

    a. strained, stressed, nervous
    b. odd, peculiar, uncommon
    c. same, similar, identical

_____ 15. thick

    a. packed, crammed, overcrowded
    b. thin, slim, narrow
    c. empty, blank, unfilled

_____ 16. unusual

    a. ordinary, common, everyday
    b. bizarre, different, curious
    c. under, underneath, below

_____ 17. crater

    a. large cracks caused by heat or a big ice pick
    b. a pit or hole in the ground caused by the impact of an explosion
    c. a large cave for sheltering animals from the heat

_____ 18. decide

    a. to settle on a choice or selection
    b. to become confused about choices
    c. to become confused about life

_____ 19. leave

    a. to stop bothering something or someone
    b. to stop looking for an answer
    c. to grow on a tree or plant

_____ 20. mastodon

    a. an extinct animal found only at the zoo
    b. an extinct animal with large teeth
    c. a living animal with large teeth or tusks

_____ 21. counter

    a. an even surface on which money is counted
    b. a bed used for examining sick patients
    c. an even surface used for chopping wood

_____ 22. method

    a. a disorderly and unplanned way of doing something
    b. an orderly and planned way for doing something
    c. an ordinary and plain way for doing something

_____ 23. grunt

    a. to make a deep sound
    b. to make a loud whistle
    c. to make a soft murmur

_____ 24. field

    a. a small, narrow tunnel
    b. an expansive, wide area
    c. a sealed, closed box

_____ 25. powerful

    a. full of tricks
    b. full of strength and might
    c. full of weakness

Bonus: Earn extra points!

_____ 26. Which of the following is not a definition for *field*?

    a) division of a large organization
    b) a stream that flows into another
    c) a place for battles

_____ 27. Which of the following is not a definition for *twist*?

    a) to curve or bend
    b) to become mentally warped
    c) to award or honor with a medal

_____ 28. Which of the following is not a definition for *thick*?

    a) a division of a family extending from one's ancestors
    b) not very smart
    c) foggy or unclear

The Hundred Penny Box, Part I

by Sharon Bell Mathis

DAY 1 Preview of Lesson	DAY 2 Introduction	DAY 3 Using Words in Context	DAY 4 Expanding Meaning	DAY 5 Keys to Understanding
Read New Words	Vocabulary Review	Vocabulary Review	Vocabulary Review	Review At-Home 4
Say and Write New Words	Review At-Home 1	Review At-Home 2	Review At-Home 3	Bingo Game
Read Definitions	Predict the Storyline	Using Context Clues	Deep Processing	AAVE Idioms and Figurative Speech
Assign At-Home 1	Story Reading (pages 19–32)	Word Wizard	Assign At-Home 4	The Beauty of Conversational Speech
	Identifying Vocabulary in Text	Assign At-Home 3		Assessment
	Paraphrasing Vocabulary in Text			
	Assign At-Home 2			

Words and Definitions

The following are target words for this week. If the word has multiple meanings, we provide only the definition listed in the text. ***Please review the definitions prior to instruction.***

1. **impatient**—restless, anxious, short of temper when irritated
2. **furnace**—an enclosed structure in which heat is produced
3. **basement**—the part of a building that is below ground level
4. **britches**—pants, trousers
5. **bare-waisted**—exposed, naked to the waist
6. **desperate**—being beyond hope; feeling despair
7. **Reconstruction**—the act of rebuilding the South again after the Civil War
8. **pneumonia**—an inflammatory disease of the lungs
9. **depression**—a period of widespread unemployment; a state of feeling sad
10. **decent**—in good taste, modestly dressed, adequate
11. **quilt**—a bed coverlet made of two layers of cloth filled with padding (e.g., down, batting)
12. **Congress**—the legislative or law-making body of a country
13. **downstream**—in the direction of the mouth of a stream
14. **plank**—a heavy thick board
15. **fancy**—not plain or common; ornamental

Prepare for Lesson

 Materials: Student Workbooks, *The Hundred Penny Box* by Sharon Bell Mathis, display copy of Week 6 Word List

 Read Teacher Tip: Reading New Words (Week 1, page 8)

5 min.

Read New Words

 Say: *Today, we will begin a new book. Let's read the title of the story for this book together:* The Hundred Penny Box. *Remember, on Day 1, we always learn to read new words that you will study at home. The words we learn will help you to read this story better and will help you to express your thoughts on paper and when talking to others. Let's see if there are any words that you already know.*

 Display the Week 6 Word List. Cover the bottom box, leaving the word columns at the top of the page exposed. Say: *Which words do you already know?*

 Uncover the bottom box. Say: *Let's read these words. Sound out each syllable as I point to it. Be sure to say each sound clearly. Sound it out.*

 Students sound out each syllable. Say the word. Students repeat the word. Say: *Yes, the word is . . . .*

10 min.

Say and Write New Words

 Cover the bottom box, and use the word columns at the top of the page.

 Say: *Let's read the words together.* Point to each word and read one time.

 Say: *Take out your pencil and Student Workbook. Find the page that says Week 6: Say and Write New Words. Let's get ready to say and write each word.*

 Point to each word. Say: *What word?* Students say the word. *Write [the word].*

 Students write the word next to one that appears on Week 6: Say and Write New Words. Continue until all words are written.

5 min.

Read Definitions

 Say: *I will read the definitions so that we will understand what each word means. Some words have more than one meaning; however, these are the definitions that are used in the story.*

 Read the definitions out loud as students read silently. Choose a student to read each sentence.

Definitions

1. **impatient** (restless, anxious, short of temper when irritated)
   The little boy was <u>impatient</u> as he waited for his father to come home so that they could play.

2. **furnace** (an enclosed structure in which heat is produced)
   The children shivered during the night because the <u>furnace</u> was not working.

Week 6 Word List

impatien**t**	desper**a**te	qui**l**t
furn**ace**	Reconstruc**tion**	Congress
basemen**t**	pneumo**nia**	downstream
britch**es**	depress**ion**	plan**k**
bare-waist**ed**	decen**t**	fan**cy**

1. pa tien**t**
   im pa tient **ly**
2. fur na**ce**
3. base
   base men**t**
4. brit ch**es**
5. bare
   bare waist **ed**
6. des per a**te**
7. con struc**t**
   re con struc**t**
   Re con struct **ion**

8. pneu mo **nia**
9. press
   de press **ion**
10. de cen**t**
11. qui**l**t
12. Con gress
13. down stream
14. plan**k**
15. fan **cy**

3. **basement** (the part of a building that is below ground level)
    The <u>basement</u> was always cold and damp because it did not receive any sunlight.

4. **britches** (pants, trousers)
    The boy's denim <u>britches</u> tore when he slid under the wire fence.

5. **bare-waisted** (exposed, naked to the waist)
    During the summer months, the boys leave their shirts behind and play <u>bare-waisted</u>ly in the hot sun.

6. **desperate** (being beyond hope; feeling despair)
    We were <u>desperate</u> to find the $20 because we didn't have money for the bus.

7. **Reconstruction** (the act of rebuilding the South again after the Civil War)
    Our ancestors who lived during the era or time of <u>Reconstruction</u> left their hometowns to start a new life in the North.

8. **pneumonia** (an inflammatory disease of the lungs)
    Uncle Dave kept coughing because he was suffering from <u>pneumonia</u>.

9. **depression** (a period of widespread unemployment; a state of feeling sad)
    It was difficult to find a job during the Great <u>Depression</u>.

10. **decent** (in good taste, modestly dressed, adequate)
    The mattress was not <u>decent</u> enough for our new guests.

11. **quilt** (a bed coverlet made of two layers of cloth filled with padding like down or batting)
    Grandma sewed pieces of fabric into a decorative <u>quilt</u> for my bed.

12. **Congress** (the legislative or law-making body of a country)
    In this election, we voted for new members to serve in <u>Congress</u>.

13. **downstream** (moving in the direction of the mouth of a stream)
    My sisters and I watched sadly as our plastic boat floated <u>downstream</u> away from our campgrounds.

14. **plank** (a heavy thick board)
    The carpenter nailed the <u>plank</u>s together to make a doghouse for our pet.

15. **fancy** (not plain or common; ornamental)
    For the dinner party, we bought a <u>fancy</u>, lace tablecloth to display Mom's china.

Assign At-Home 1

Say: *Tonight you will . . .*

1. *Study the vocabulary words with definitions.*

2. *Complete the Riddle Page.*

3. *Do the Matching Activity.*

4. *Make flashcards.*

Day 2: Introduction

Prepare for Lesson

 Materials: Student Workbooks, *The Hundred Penny Box* by Sharon Bell Mathis

 Vocabulary Review (3 min.)

 Rapid review of vocabulary words (Students use the Week 6 Word List in their Student Workbooks.)

Review At-Home 1 (7 min.)

☆ Review the correct answers to At-Home 1.

☆ Review student work to confirm or clarify responses.

Predict the Storyline (8 min.)

☆ Students look at the cover of *The Hundred Penny Box* by Sharon Bell Mathis.

☆ Say: *Today, we will begin reading a new book, The Hundred Penny Box. In fact, we will read two chapters from this book for the next 2 weeks. In this story, one of the characters collects something special. Let's talk about collecting special objects.*

☆ Say: *Open your Student Workbook to Semantic Web: Collections. What are some objects that people collect? Why do people collect objects? Where do people store their special collections?*

☆ Say: *Now look at the picture on the front cover of The Hundred Penny Box. What special object do you think one of the characters collects? Why do you think the character collects pennies? Where might this special collection be kept? Yes, it looks like the pennies are kept in a special box. How many of you have a special collection?*

☆ Say: *Think of a question that you think the story will answer. Write the question at the bottom of Semantic Web: Collections.*

Story Reading 1: Identifying Vocabulary in Text (8–10 min.)

 Say: *As I read the story out loud, you will follow along silently. When you see a word from our vocabulary list, give a thumbs up.*

☆ Read pages 19–32.

☆ Discuss what students predicted would happen in the story.

Story Reading 2: Paraphrasing Vocabulary in Text

☆ Say: *As I read specific paragraphs of the story out loud again, let's paraphrase what the author has said by using our own words. Let's focus on the second paragraph on page 20. Follow along as I read out loud.* Read the paragraph (" 'Just in case,' Michael said impatiently . . .").

☆ Say: *What's another way of saying, "Michael said impatiently"? How does a person look when he or she is impatient? We could say, "Michael said while wiggling" or, "Michael said restlessly."*

☆ Help students to paraphrase the remaining sentences in the paragraph as appropriate.

Assign At-Home 2

Say: *Tonight you will . . .*

1. *Study your flashcards.*

2. *Complete Word Substitutions.*

3. *Complete Same and Different.*

Day 3: Using Words in Context

Prepare for Lesson

☆ Materials: Student Workbooks

☆ Read Teacher Tip: Word Wizard (Week 1, page 14)

Vocabulary Review

3 min.

☆ Rapid review of vocabulary words (Students use the Week 6 Word List in their Student Workbooks.)

Review At-Home 2

7 min.

☆ Review the correct answers to At-Home 2.

☆ Review student work to confirm or clarify responses.

Using Context Clues

15 min.

☆ Say: *Open your Student Workbook to Week 6: Using Context Clues. Today, we will use context clues to help us choose the word that fits in the blank by using the clues from other words and information in the sentence or sentences. I will read the sentences out loud. Raise your hand when you know which word best completes the sentence. Write the word in the blank. Sometimes the word might require an ending such as -ed, -s, or -ing. Each word will be used only one time.*

☆ Choose individual students to give answers. Have students point out context clues that helped them to choose the correct answer.

☆ Say: *Cross out words in the box as we use them. Write your answers in the blank, and write the context clues you used in the space below.*

Word Wizard

5 min.

☆ Say: *As Word Wizards this week, you must always be on the lookout for opportunities to use and demonstrate your word knowledge. Use your Word Wizard Journals to keep track of each time you hear one of this week's vocabulary words used in a sentence at home, school, or even on television. If you don't hear the words in a sentence, be creative and write original sentences using your new vocabulary knowledge. Next week, each group will read two of their sentences to the class!*

☆ Say: *Get in your Word Wizard Groups from Week 4, and share your best sentences.*

☆ Say: *Which group would like to read two of their sentences using the words from Week 4's lesson?* Tally the number of sentences per group, and record the amounts on the Word Wizard Chart.

Assign At-Home 3

Say: *Tonight you will . . .*

1. *Study your flashcards.*

2. *Complete the Word Wizard Journal.*

3. *Complete the Context Clues Activity.*

Day 4: Expanding Meaning

Prepare for Lesson

☆ Materials: Student Workbooks

☆ Read Teacher Tip: Deep Processing (Week 2, page 28)

3 min.

Vocabulary Review

☆ Rapid review of vocabulary words (Students use the Week 6 Word List in their Student Workbooks.)

7 min.

Review At-Home 3

☆ Review the correct answers to At-Home 3.

☆ Review student work to confirm or clarify responses.

20 min.

Deep Processing

☆ Say: *Does anyone remember what <u>deep processing</u> is? It is thinking about how words relate to each other.*

☆ Say: *We have learned the definitions of this week's vocabulary words, but definitions do not really teach us everything we need to know to really understand the meaning of a word. Remember, it is important to be able to use these words to describe your own experiences in life and to describe conditions in the world in general.*

☆ Say: *Open your Student Workbook to Deep Processing: <u>The Hundred Penny Box</u>, Part I. We will read each question together and decide what is a reasonable answer and why. Remember, the answers are not in the book we read but come from your own thinking. Think about the questions and about what would be a reasonable response. Remember, you must be able to explain why you chose your answer.*

Assign At-Home 4

Say: *Tonight you will . . .*

1. *Study your flashcards.*

2. *Complete the Crossword Puzzle.*

Day 5: Keys to Understanding

Prepare for Lesson

☆ Materials: Student Workbooks

☆ Read Teacher Tip: African American Vernacular English

Teacher Tip: African American Vernacular English

The author of this story uses idiomatic spellings and phrases. An *idiom* is a phrase or expression whose meaning cannot be understood from the ordinary meanings of the words. For example, *"Big deal"* is an idiom because *big* and *deal* have different meanings in this sentence than one would normally associate with either word. "Look like John just spit you out" is an idiomatic expression because "spit" has a meaning in this sentence that differs from a dictionary definition. African American Vernacular English (AAVE), which is used by characters in this book, frequently relies on idiomatic phrases and spellings. An example of an idiomatic spelling is when the final consonant is deleted, as in goin', comin', and talkin'.

The idioms used in this story appear in the Word Enrichment Vocabulary List. These idioms will be discussed with students during the Idioms and Figurative Speech activity.

---

7 min.

Review At-Home 4

 Review the correct answers to At-Home 4.

 Review student work to confirm or clarify responses.

8 min.

Bingo Game

☆ Say: *Choose nine words from the Week 6 Word List, and write them on the Bingo Card in your Student Workbook. When I read the definition, raise your hand to identify the word. If you have the word on your card, mark it with an X. The first person who has 3 Xs in a row (across, down, diagonally) wins the game.*

☆ Read the definitions. As students identify definitions, write the words on the board until someone wins the game.

> ### Word Enrichment Vocabulary List
>
> **Idiomatic expressions**
>
> 1. "Look like John just *spit you out."*
> 2. "And John . . .liked it most because he *was city."*
> 3. "It didn't *make them no never mind."*
> 4. ". . . *that boat old."*
>
> **Deletion of the final -s**
>
> 1. "What your *mamma* name?"

AAVE Idioms and Figurative Speech

12 min.

☆ Say: *Sometimes authors write the way we speak. That means that the author's written language will contain elements that we only hear when people are talking. For example, when talking, we might leave the endings off some words, such as* comin' *for* coming *and* talkin' *for* talking, *or we may change the sounds in a word when speaking. For example, we may say* dis *instead of* this.

☆ Say: *Open your Student Workbook to Week 6: Idioms and Figurative Speech. Let's read these expressions and think of a different way to express the same thoughts.* Ask students to read the idiomatic expressions aloud. Discuss.

☆ Say: *Now that we have discussed how the characters talked in the story, let's match these phrases with the appropriate meanings.*

☆ Say: *Read the sentences in Writing Practice, and rewrite them using the language you would use at school.* Give students a few minutes to rewrite the sentences. Then, discuss their answers.

☆ Say: *Which of the phrases on your page would you hear when talking? Which would you write in a paragraph at school?*

☆ Say: *Is either style of speakng better than the other? No! Remember, you may speak and write differently depending on where you are and your purpose in communicating.*

The Beauty of Conversational Speech

5 min.

☆ Discuss the poem *Lullaby* by Paul Laurence Dunbar that is written in AAVE. Read it out loud as students read silently. Discuss the value and beauty of using conversational speech patterns in narrative writings. See if students can paraphrase some of the lines in different ways. Discuss the beauty of AAVE in this poem.

Assessment

10 min.

☆ Distribute Assessment 6 to each student.

☆ For the Bonus Question 1, say: *Look like they mom just spit them out.*

☆ For Bonus Question 2, say: *My teacher so city she scared of anything green.*

Name: _____ Date: _____

Assessment 6
The Hundred Penny Box, Part I

A. Match the word with the appropriate definition.

a)	furnace	d)	desperate	g)	Depression	j)	impatient	m)	downstream
b)	basement	e)	pneumonia	h)	decent	k)	quilt	n)	plank
c)	britches	f)	bare-waisted	i)	Reconstruction	l)	Congress	o)	fancy

_____ 1. not wearing a shirt

_____ 2. adequate

_____ 3. anxious, restless

_____ 4. rebuilding the South after the Civil War

_____ 5. disease of the lungs

B. Circle the word or phrase that does not belong.

1.	kiln	oven	heater	refrigerator
2.	open-air market	dungeon	basement	crypt
3.	calm	hopeful	tranquil	desperate
4.	take apart	destroy	reconstruct	break
5.	skirt	pants	trousers	bloomers

C. Complete the sentence with the best answer.

_____ 1. During the Depression, Grandpa was desperate because he _____ money in the bank to pay the bills.

    a) had enough

    b) invested

    c) didn't have enough

_____ 2. The bare-waisted child was impatient because _____.

    a) his sweater was not warm enough

    b) his shirt still was not dry

    c) his t-shirt was a great fit

_____ 3. Because the apartment's furnace was decent, the children _____.

    a) decided to play outside

    b) cried because they were cold

    c) said they were very warm

_____ 4. The desperate worker suffered from pneumonia because he worked _____.

    a) in the rain

    b) in an office with a furnace

    c) in a computer lab

_____ 5. The Mayor decided to reconstruct the basement of the museum because _____.

    a) it didn't need any repairs

    b) the city suffered from an earthquake

    c) the marble floor was magnificent

Bonus

☆ Listen as I read two statements spoken in a conversation. Pick the letter of the sentence that expresses the same idea.

_____ 1. a) Matt and Rick are twins.

    b) Matt and Rick look like their mom.

_____ 2. a) My teacher likes to live in the city.

    b) My teacher was born in the city.

The Hundred Penny Box, Part II

by Sharon Bell Mathis

DAY 1 Preview of Lesson	DAY 2 Introduction	DAY 3 Using Words in Context	DAY 4 Expanding Meaning	DAY 5 Keys to Understanding
Read New Words	Vocabulary Review	Vocabulary Review	Vocabulary Review	Review At-Home 4
Say and Write New Words	Review At-Home 1	Review At-Home 2	Review At-Home 3	Bingo Game
Read Definitions	Predict the Storyline	Using Context Clues	Synonyms and Antonyms	AAVE Idioms and Figurative Speech
Assign At-Home 1	Story Reading (pages 33–47)	Word Wizard	Assign At-Home 4	The Beauty of Conversational Speech
	Identifying Vocabulary in Text	Assign At-Home 3		Assessment
	Paraphrasing Vocabulary in Text			
	Assign At-Home 2			

Words and Definitions

The following are target words for this week. If the word has multiple meanings, we provide only the definition listed in the text. *Please review the definitions prior to instruction.*

1. **stiff**—rigid, tense, not natural or easy to bend

2. **plain**—common, not fancy

3. **mahogany**—an American evergreen tree with reddish wood that is used in furniture

4. **protect**—to shield from injury or to guard

5. **perspiration**—sweat

6. **frail**—morally or physically weak

7. **stubborn**—firm, determined, not easily controlled

8. **freight**—heavy cargo, the carrying of goods by a train or other means of transportation

9. **creek**—a stream of water that is smaller than a river and larger than a brook

10. **irritable**—feeling angry or exasperated

11. **woodshop**—a class offered in school that teaches one how to make objects, furniture, and so forth from wood

12. **murmur**—to make a low continuous sound

13. **disappear**—to pass out of sight; to cease to be

14. **stuffing**—material used to fill an object

15. **dresser**—a chest of drawers with a mirror; bedroom furniture

Day 1: Preview of Lesson

Prepare for Lesson

☆ Materials: Student Workbooks, *The Hundred Penny Box* by Sharon Bell Mathis, display copy of Week 7 Word List

☆ Read Teacher Tip: Reading New Words (Week 1, page 8)

 5 min.

Read New Words

☆ Say: *Today, we will continue with The Hundred Penny Box. This week, we will complete the story. Remember, on Day 1, we always learn to read new words that you will study at home. The words we learn will help you to read this story better and will help you to express your thoughts on paper and when talking to others. Let's see if there are any words that you already know.*

☆ Display the Week 7 Word List. Cover the bottom box, leaving the word columns at the top of page exposed. Say: *Which words do you already know?*

☆ Uncover the bottom box. Say: *Let's read these words. Sound out each syllable as I point to it. Be sure to say each sound clearly. Sound it out.*

☆ Students sound out each syllable. Say the word. Students repeat the word. Say: *Yes, the word is . . . .*

 10 min.

Say and Write New Words

☆ Cover the bottom box, and use the word columns at the top of the page.

☆ Say: *Let's read the words together.* Point to each word, and read one time.

☆ Say: *Take out your pencil and Student Workbook. Find the page that says Week 7: Say and Write New Words. Let's get ready to say and write each word.*

☆ Point to each word. Say: *What word?* Students say the word. *Write [the word].*

☆ Students write the word on the appropriate line. Continue until all words are written.

 5 min.

Read Definitions

☆ Say: *I will read the definitions so that we will understand what each word means. Some words have more than one meaning; however, these are the definitions that are used in the story.*

☆ Read the definitions out loud as students read silently. Choose a student to read each sentence.

Definitions

1. **stiff** (rigid, tense, not natural or easy to bend)
   The patient walked in a <u>stiff</u> manner with his crutches towards the elevator door.

2. **plain** (common, not fancy)
   Although we named our dog Spot, a very <u>plain</u> name, he was an extraordinary and courageous pet.

Week 7 Word List

sti**ff**	frai**l**	woodsho**p**
pla**in**	stubbor**n**	murm**ur**
mahoga**ny**	freigh**t**	disappear
protec**t**	cree**k**	stuff**ing**
perspira**tion**	irritable	dress**er**

1. sti**ff**
   sti**ff ly**
2. pla**in**
3. ma hog a **ny**
4. pro tec**t**
5. per spir a **tion**
6. frai**l**
7. stub bor**n**
8. freigh**t**
9. cree**k**

10. ir ri tate
    ir ri ta ble
11. woo**d** sho**p**
12. mur m**ur**
13. ap pear
    dis ap pear
14. stu**ff**
    stuff **ing**
15. dress
    dress **er**

Vocabulary Power, Level 1, by Latrice M. Seals, Sharolyn D. Pollard-Durodola, Barbara R. Foorman, and Ashley M. Bradley

3. **mahogany** (an American evergreen tree with reddish wood that is used in furniture)
    My mother's bed is made of beautiful <u>mahogany</u> wood.

4. **protect** (to shield from injury or to guard)
    The kangaroo <u>protect</u>ed its baby as it slept soundly in her pouch.

5. **perspiration** (sweat)
    After playing basketball, the girls were sticky with <u>perspiration</u>.

6. **frail** (morally or physically weak)
    Candace wrapped her puppy in a blanket because it was sick and <u>frail</u>.

7. **stubborn** (firm, determined, not easily controlled)
    Braying and making loud noises, the <u>stubborn</u> mules refused to pull the heavy loads.

8. **freight** (heavy cargo, the carrying of goods by a train or other means of transportation)
    The men unloaded the <u>freight</u> from the train.

9. **creek** (a stream of water that is smaller than a river and larger than a brook)
    When I was a little girl, my grandma and I fished by the side of Martin <u>Creek</u>.

10. **irritable** (feeling angry or exasperated)
    Jasper felt itchy and <u>irritable</u> as he scratched the rash caused by poison ivy.

11. **woodshop** (a class offered in school that teaches one how to make objects, furniture, and so forth from wood)
    In high school, my brother made a bookcase in his <u>woodshop</u> class.

12. **murmur** (to make a low continuous sound)
    Looking to see if the teacher was watching, the two girls <u>murmur</u>ed something funny in the boy's ear.

13. **disappear** (to pass out of sight; to cease to be)
    Houdini, the famous magician, made himself <u>disappear</u> into thin air.

14. **stuffing** (material used to fill an object)
    My cat, Cuddles, pulled the cotton <u>stuffing</u> out of my favorite teddy bear.

15. **dresser** (a chest of drawers with a mirror; bedroom furniture)
    When I was a little girl, I would play with the perfume bottles on my mother's <u>dresser</u>.

Assign At-Home 1

Say: *Tonight you will . . .*

1. *Study the vocabulary words with definitions.*

2. *Complete the Riddle Page.*

3. *Do the Matching Activity.*

4. *Make flashcards.*

Day 2: Introduction

Prepare for Lesson

☆ Materials: Student Workbooks, *The Hundred Penny Box* by Sharon Bell Mathis

Vocabulary Review

☆ Rapid review of vocabulary words (Students use the Week 7 Word List in their Student Workbooks.)

Review At-Home 1

☆ Review the correct answers to At-Home 1.

☆ Review student work to confirm or clarify responses.

Predict the Storyline

☆ Students look at the illustrations on pages 43 and 46 of *The Hundred Penny Box* by Sharon Bell Mathis.

☆ Say: *Today we are going to continue reading <u>The Hundred Penny Box</u>. Last week, we introduced the story by focusing on a special collection of pennies that was collected by Aunt Dew. This week, we will introduce the story by looking at the theme of old age.*

☆ Say: *Open your Student Workbook to Semantic Web: Growing Old. Which characters in the story are growing old? What are some characteristics of old age? Which of these characteristics are physical? Which are emotional?*

☆ Say: *Where do people live when they grow old? Why? Do you know anyone who is growing old?*

☆ Say: *Think of a question that you think the story will answer. Write the question at the bottom of Semantic Web: Growing Old.*

Story Reading 1: Identifying Vocabulary in Text

☆ Say: *As I read the story out loud, you will follow along silently. When you see a word from our vocabulary list, give a thumbs up.*

☆ Read pages 33–47.

☆ Discuss what students predicted would happen in the story.

Story Reading 2: Paraphrasing Vocabulary in Text

☆ Say: *As I read specific paragraphs of the story out loud again, let's paraphrase what the author has said by using our own words. Let's focus on the first paragraph on page 40. Follow along as I read out loud.* Read the paragraph ("'Ain't nobody mean to Dewbet Thomas . . .").

☆ Say: *What's another way of saying, "Ain't nobody mean to Dewbet Thomas?" We could say, "No one is ever mean to me." In this paragraph, Aunt Dew uses the word <u>ain't</u>, which is a conjunction for am not. Let's figure out some other ways to communicate the same ideas without using <u>ain't</u>.*

☆ Help students to paraphrase the remaining sentences in the paragraph as appropriate.

Assign At-Home 2

Say: *Tonight you will . . .*

1. *Study your flashcards.*

2. *Complete Word Substitutions.*

3. *Complete Same and Different.*

Day 3: Using Words in Context

Prepare for Lesson

☆ Materials: Student Workbooks

☆ Read Teacher Tip: Word Wizard (Week 1, page 14)

Vocabulary Review

☆ Rapid review of vocabulary words (Students use the Week 7 Word List in their Student Workbooks.)

Review At-Home 2

☆ Review the correct answers to At-Home 2.

☆ Review student work to confirm or clarify responses.

Using Context Clues

☆ Say: *Open your Student Workbook to Week 7: Using Context Clues. Today, we will use context clues to help us choose the word that fits in the blank by using the clues from other words and information in the sentence or sentences. I will read the sentences out loud. Raise your hand when you know which word best completes the sentence. Write the word in the blank. Sometimes the word might require an ending such as -ed, -s, or -ing. Each word will be used only one time.*

☆ Choose individual students to give answers. Have students point out context clues that helped them to choose the correct answer.

☆ Say: *Cross out words in the box as we use them. Write your answers in the blank, and write the context clues you used in the space below.*

Word Wizard

☆ Say: *As Word Wizards this week, you must always be on the lookout for opportunities to use and demonstrate your word knowledge. Use your Word Wizard Journals to keep track of each time you hear one of this week's vocabulary words used in a sentence at home, school, or even on television. If you don't hear the words in a sentence, be creative and write original sentences using your new vocabulary knowledge. Next week, each group will read two of their sentences to the class!*

☆ Say: *Get in your Word Wizard Groups from Week 6, and share your best sentences.*

☆ Say: *Which group would like to read two of their sentences using the words from last week's lesson?* Tally the number of sentences per group, and record the amounts on the Word Wizard Chart.

Assign At-Home 3

Say: *Tonight you will . . .*

1. *Study your flashcards.*

2. *Complete the Word Wizard Journal.*

3. *Complete the Context Clues Activity.*

Day 4: Expanding Meaning

Prepare for Lesson

☆ Materials: Student Workbooks

Vocabulary Review

☆ Rapid review of vocabulary words (Students use the Week 7 Word List in their Student Workbooks.)

Review At-Home 3

☆ Review the correct answers to At-Home 3.

☆ Review student work to confirm or clarify responses.

Synonyms and Antonyms

☆ Say: *You have learned many new words this week. You might have noticed when using context clues yesterday that some words have the same meaning and some words are opposite in meaning. What do we call words that have the same meaning?* The answer is synonyms. *What do we call words that are opposite in meaning?* The answer is antonyms.

☆ Say: *In Week 3, we learned several synonyms for* special. *Can anyone tell us a synonym for* special? Answers include extraordinary and unique. *Can anyone give us an antonym for* special? Answers include common and ordinary.

☆ Say: *Today, we will learn to express ideas with words that are the same or opposite in meaning. We will concentrate on six words from our vocabulary list.*

☆ Say: *Open your Student Workbook to Week 7: Synonyms and Antonyms. This worksheet has sentences that you took home at the beginning of the week. Let's look at how we can rewrite some of these sentences to express ideas that are the opposite or same in meaning.*

☆ Say: *I will read the original sentence with the underlined word and the definition. Then, we will read the synonym or antonym sentences together. Remember, not every word has a synonym or antonym.* Read and discuss examples.

☆ Say: *Let's read a story about a boy named Sam. In the story, we will use synonyms and antonyms that we have learned today. First, I will read the story out loud. Then, I will read the story again. When you figure out what goes in the blank, raise your hand during the second reading of the story.*

Assign At-Home 4

Say: *Tonight you will . . .*

1. *Study your flashcards.*

2. *Complete the Crossword Puzzle.*

Day 5: Keys to Understanding

Prepare for Lesson

☆ Materials: Student Workbooks, photocopies of Assessment 7

☆ Read Teacher Tip: African American Vernacular English (Week 6, page 81)

☆ The idioms used in the story appear in the Word Enrichment Vocabulary List. These idioms will be discussed with students during the Idioms and Figurative Speech activity.

Word Enrichment Vocabulary List

Idiomatic expressions

1. "I *been* sleep all day."

2. "What your name is?"

3. "Your daddy *like to got bit* by a cotton mouth."

4. "I *make out like* I don't see her all the time."

Review At-Home 4

7 min.

☆ Review the correct answers to At-Home 4.

☆ Review student work to confirm or clarify responses.

Bingo Game

8 min.

☆ Say: *Choose nine words from the Week 7 Word List, and write them on the Bingo Card in your Student Workbook. When I read the definition, raise your hand to identify the word. If you have the word on your card, mark it with an X. The first person who has 3 Xs in a row (across, down, diagonally) wins the game.*

☆ Read the definitions. As students identify definitions, write the words on the board until someone wins the game.

AAVE Idioms and Figurative Speech

12 min.

☆ Say: *Last week, we looked at dialogue spoken by characters in* The Hundred Penny Box. *Remember, sometimes authors write the way we speak. That means that the author's written language will contain elements that we only hear when people are talking. Today, we will read more expressions from the story and decide how the same idea might be expressed in a different manner.*

☆ Say: *Open your Student Workbook to Week 7: Idioms and Figurative Speech. Let's read these expressions and think of a different way to express the same thoughts.* Ask students to read the idiomatic expressions aloud. Discuss.

☆ Say: *Now that we have discussed how the characters talked in the story, let's match these phrases with the appropriate meanings.*

☆ Say: *Read the sentences in Writing Practice, and rewrite them using the language you would use at school.* Give students a few minutes to rewrite the sentences. Then, discuss their answers.

☆ Say: *Which of the phrases on your page would you hear when talking? Which would you write in a paragraph at school?*

☆ Say: *Is either style of speaking better than the other? No! Remember, you may speak and write differently depending on where you are and your purpose in communicating.*

The Beauty of Conversational Speech

☆ If time permits, you may discuss the poem *Signs of the Times* by Paul Laurence Dunbar that is written in AAVE. Discuss the value and beauty of using conversational speech patterns in narrative writings.

☆ Read the poem out loud with expression, and ask students to rephrase some of the lines in their own words.

☆ Read the poem a second time, and say: *What signs indicate the approaching holiday? What holiday is approaching?* The answer is Thanksgiving.

☆ After the discussion of the signs of the approaching holiday, translate the ending stanza. Say: *At the end of the poem, the author says, "Look here, Turkey, and stop that gobbling. You haven't learned the sense of fear. You are foolish—your neck is in danger. Do you know that Thanksgiving is here?"*

Assessment

☆ Distribute Assessment 7 to each student.

Name: _____ Date: _____

Assessment 7
The Hundred Penny Box, Part II

A. Match the word with the appropriate definition.

a)	stiff	d)	perspiration	g)	stubborn	j)	irritable	m)	disappear
b)	plain	e)	protect	h)	freight	k)	woodshop	n)	stuffing
c)	mahogany	f)	frail	i)	creek	l)	murmur	o)	dresser

_____ 1. a class that teaches you how to make crafts from wood

_____ 2. feeble and weak

_____ 3. a small stream of water

_____ 4. sweat

_____ 5. heavy cargo

B. Circle the word that does not belong.

1.	flexible	bendable	pliable	stiff
2.	bed	dresser	bathtub	bureau
3.	stubborn	mulish	cooperative	obstinate
4.	appear	emerge	disappear	show
5.	shelter	safeguard	damage	protect

C. Complete the sentence with the best answer.

_____ 1. The little old ladies were murmuring over the jewelry counter about _____.

   a) the expensive prices

   b) the beautiful weather

   c) the cherry blossoms

_____ 2. _____ could be used as stuffing to help a frail straw hat maintain its shape.

   a) Crumpled newspaper

   b) Iron fillings

   c) Cotton candy

_____ 3. A frail child might become irritable while _____.

   a) playing with a favorite toy

   b) listening to the quiet murmuring of a creek

   c) reaching for a glass of water on a high shelf

_____ 4. Mrs. Jackson wiped the heavy perspiration from her face because she was _____.

   a) looking at herself in the mahogany mirror

   b) lifting freight in a woodshop

   c) sipping lemonade

_____ 5. Mr. Pollock decided to take extra measures to protect his stubborn nephew from _____.

   a) being kind to a frail child

   b) jumping into a creek

   c) taking a nap

 Vocabulary Power, Level 1, by Latrice M. Seals, Sharolyn D. Pollard-Durodola, Barbara R. Foorman, and Ashley M. Bradley

Donavan's Word Jar, Part I
by Monalisa DeGross

DAY 1 Preview of Lesson	DAY 2 Introduction	DAY 3 Using Words in Context	DAY 4 Expanding Meaning	DAY 5 Keys to Understanding
Read New Words Say and Write New Words Read Definitions Assign At-Home 1	Vocabulary Review Review At-Home 1 Predict the Storyline Story Reading (pages 3–14) Identifying Vocabulary in Text Paraphrasing Vocabulary in Text Assign At-Home 2	Vocabulary Review Review At-Home 2 Using Context Clues Word Wizard Assign At-Home 3	Vocabulary Review Review At-Home 3 Deep Processing Assign At-Home 4	Review At-Home 4 Bingo Game Word Roots: Terre Assessment

Words and Definitions

The following are target words for this week. If the word has multiple meanings, we provide only the definition listed in the text. **Please review the definitions prior to instruction.**

1. **collect**—to gather things together

2. **discovery**—a finding out about something

3. **nutrition**—the process of eating food that is healthy for your body

4. **boutique**—a small shop that sells clothes or other specialty items

5. **hieroglyphics**—writing made up of pictures and symbols used by Egyptians

6. **property**—anything that is owned

7. **profound**—deeply felt or thought

8. **solidarity**—agreement between people to work together for a common goal

9. **warrior**—a soldier or someone who fights in battles

10. **squabble**—to quarrel or argue about something that is unimportant

11. **extraterrestrial**—coming from outer space

12. **orchestral**—related to a large group of musicians who play instruments together

13. **billboard**—a large outdoor sign for advertising products

14. **private**—belonging to one person, group, and so forth and no one else

15. **cuddle**—to hold someone lovingly in ones arms

Day 1: Preview of Lesson

Prepare for Lesson

 Materials: Student Workbooks, *Donavan's Word Jar* by Monalisa DeGross, display copy of Week 8 Word List

☆ Read Teacher Tip: Reading New Words (Week 1, page 8)

5 min.

Read New Words

☆ Say: *Today, we will begin a new book, Donavan's Word Jar. We will read two chapters in this book this week: "Donavan" and "Donavan's Discovery." Remember, on Day 1 we learn to read new words that you will study at home. The words we learn will help you to read this story better and will help you to express your thoughts on paper and when talking to others. Let's see if there are any words that you already know.*

☆ Display the Week 8 Word List. Cover the bottom box, leaving the word columns at the top of page exposed. Say: *Which words do you already know?*

☆ Uncover the bottom box. Say: *Let's read these words. Sound out each syllable as I point to it. Be sure to say each sound clearly. Sound it out.*

☆ Students sound out each syllable. Say the word. Students repeat the word. Say: *Yes, the word is . . . .*

10 min.

Say and Write New Words

 Cover the bottom box, and use the word columns at the top of the page.

☆ Say: *Let's read the words together.* Point to each word, and read one time.

☆ Say: *Take out your pencil and Student Workbook. Find the page that says Week 8: Say and Write New Words. Let's get ready to say and write each word.*

☆ Point to each word. Say: *What word?* Students say the word. *Write [the word].*

☆ Students write the word on the appropriate line. Continue until all words are written.

5 min.

Read Definitions

 Say: *I will read the definitions so that we will understand what each word means. Some words have more than one meaning; however, these are the definitions that are used in the story.*

☆ Read the definitions out loud as students read silently. Choose a student to read each sentence.

Definitions

1. **collect** (to gather things together)
   Donavan decided to <u>collect</u> special words and place them in a word jar.

2. **discovery** (a finding out about something)
   The <u>discovery</u> of electricity modernized our existence so that all were able to enjoy the comfort of well-lit rooms.

Vocabulary Power, Level 1

Week 8 Word List

collec**t**	proper**ty**	extraterrestrial
discover**y**	profoun**d**	orchestral
nutri**tion**	solidari**ty**	billboar**d**
boutique	warri**or**	priva**te**
hieroglyphics	squabble	cud**dle**

1. col lec**t**
2. dis cov **er**
   dis cov er **y**
3. nu tri tious
   nu tri **tion**
4. bou tique
5. hi er o glyph ics
6. prop er
   prop er **ty**
7. pro foun**d**
8. sol id
   sol i dar i **ty**

9. war
   war ri **or**
10. squab ble
11. ex tra
    ex tra ter res tri al
12. or ches tra
    or ches tral
13. bill
    bill boar**d**
14. pri va**te**
15. cud **dle**

3. **nutrition** (the process of eating food that is healthy for your body)
   Good <u>nutrition</u> consists of eating a balance of fruits, vegetables, meats, breads, and dairy products.

4. **boutique** (a small shop that sells clothes or other specialty items)
   On 5th Avenue in New York City, there are many fashionable <u>boutique</u>s with the latest designs from Paris and London.

5. **hieroglyphics** (writing made up of pictures and symbols used by Egyptians)
   At the museum, the tour guide explained that only a few people within Egyptian society used <u>hieroglyphics</u> because they were so difficult to learn.

6. **property** (anything that is owned)
   Grandpa decided to place a fence around his <u>property</u> so that the cattle would not roam and get lost.

7. **profound** (deeply felt or thought)
   When Mother Teresa died, many felt <u>profound</u> sorrow that she would no longer be around to encourage and help the poor.

8. **solidarity** (agreement between people to work together for a common goal)
   The <u>solidarity</u> among the railroad workers helped to form a union, or organization that would influence labor laws.

9. **warrior** (a soldier or someone who fights in battles)
   Many years ago in West Africa, <u>warrior</u>s wore scars on their faces as identification of belonging to a specific tribe.

10. **squabble** (to quarrel or argue about something that is unimportant)
    Mom says that brothers and sisters should not <u>squabble</u> because one day they will need each other's help and friendship in order to survive in the world.

11. **extraterrestrial** (coming from outer space)
    The movie *E.T.* was about an <u>extraterrestrial</u> being who visited planet Earth.

12. **orchestral** (related to a large group of musicians who play instruments together)
    The <u>orchestral</u> sounds from the stage floated down the hall and into the classrooms.

    Note: This word comes from *orchestra* which means a large group of musicians who play together.

13. **billboard** (a large outdoor sign for advertising products)
    The advertisement on the <u>billboard</u> says that drinking milk is cool!

14. **private** (belonging to one person, group, and so forth and no one else)
    When I grow up, I can't wait to have my own <u>private</u> room because I am tired of sharing a room with my twin brothers.

15. **cuddle** (to hold someone lovingly in ones arms)
    Whenever I am afraid at night, my mom <u>cuddle</u>s me in her arms, and I feel safe.

Day 1: Preview of Lesson

Assign At-Home 1

Say: *Tonight you will . . .*

1.   *Study the vocabulary words with definitions.*

2.   *Complete the Riddle Page.*

3.   *Do the Matching Activity.*

4.   *Make flashcards.*

Day 2: Introduction

Prepare for Lesson

☆ Materials: Student Workbooks, *Donavan's Word Jar* by Monalisa DeGross

Vocabulary Review

(3 min.)

☆ Rapid review of vocabulary words (Students use the Week 8 Word List in their Student Workbooks.)

Review At Home 1

(7 min.)

☆ Review the correct answers to At-Home 1.

☆ Review student work to confirm or clarify responses.

Predict the Storyline

(8 min.)

☆ Students look at the cover of *Donavan's Word Jar* by Monalisa DeGross.

☆ Say: *Today we will begin reading a new book,* Donavan's Word Jar. *In fact, we will read two chapters from this book this week. The first chapter that we will read is "Donavan." The second brief chapter is "Donavan's Discovery." How many of you remember the character, Julian, from* The Stories Julian Tells? *Well, Donavan, is an inquisitive little boy just like Julian, and he encounters a problem that he has to solve.*

☆ Say: *Let's look at the illustration on the cover of the book. What do you think this book will be about?* Briefly discuss. *Yes, these stories probably have something to do with interesting words that Donavan may collect in a jar. Why do you think Donavan collects words? What kind of words could he collect?*

☆ Say: *Look at the words in red: Abracadabra! Words are magic! Open your Student Workbook to Semantic Web: Words, Words, Words. How can words be magic? Where can we find interesting words? It appears that Donavan enjoys collecting words. What kinds of words could he collect? What different kinds of words are there? Why do you think Donavan believes that words can be powerful? Have we read about another person who also believed that words are powerful? Richard Wright said that words could change your life.*

☆ Say: *Every week, you collect words just like Donavan. You can become Word Wizards and look and listen for words in many places. We keep our words in our Word Wizard Journals. Where do you predict Donavan will keep his words? Haven't we read about another character who also was a collector? In* The Hundred Penny Box, *the grandmother collects pennies and keeps them in a box.*

☆ Say: *Think of a question that you think the story will answer. Write the question at the bottom of Semantic Web: Words, Words, Words.*

Day 2: Introduction

 Story Reading 1: Identifying Vocabulary in Text

☆ Say: *As I read the story out loud, you will follow along silently. When you see a word from our vocabulary list, give a thumbs up.*

☆ Read pages 3–14.

☆ Discuss what students predicted would happen in the story.

 Story Reading 2: Paraphrasing Vocabulary in Text

☆ Say: *As I read specific paragraphs of the story out loud again, let's paraphrase what the author has said by using our own words. Let's focus on page 12, starting with the top of the page through the big paragraph in the middle of the page. Follow along as I read out loud.* Read the paragraphs (starting with "'Why?'" and ending with ". . . take some of his words.").

☆ Say: *What's another way of saying, "This is my collection, and it is private property. I don't want you messing with it"? What is <u>private property</u>? We might paraphrase the sentence as, "This is my word collection, and it belongs to me."*

☆ Help students to paraphrase the remaining sentences in the paragraphs as appropriate.

Assign At-Home 2

Say: *Tonight you will . . .*

1. *Study your flashcards.*

2. *Complete Word Substitutions.*

3. *Complete Same and Different.*

Day 3: Using Words in Context

Prepare for Lesson

☆ Materials: Student Workbooks

☆ Read Teacher Tip: Word Wizard (Week 1, page 14)

3 min.

Vocabulary Review

☆ Rapid review of vocabulary words (Students use the Week 8 Word List in their Student Workbooks.)

7 min.

Review At-Home 2

☆ Review the correct answers to At-Home 2.

☆ Review student work to confirm or clarify responses.

15 min.

Using Context Clues

☆ Say: *Open your Student Workbook to Week 8: Using Context Clues. Today, we will use context clues to help us choose the word that fits in the blank by using the clues from other words and information in the sentence or sentences. I will read the sentences out loud. Raise your hand when you know which word best completes the sentence. Write the word in the blank. Sometimes the word might require an ending such as -ed, -s, or -ing. Each word will be used only one time.*

☆ Choose individual students to give answers. Have students point out context clues that helped them to choose the correct answer.

☆ Say: *Cross out words in the box as we use them. Write your answers in the blank, and write the context clues you used in the space below.*

5 min.

Word Wizard

☆ Say: *As Word Wizards this week, you must always be on the lookout for opportunities to use and demonstrate your word knowledge. Use your Word Wizard Journals to keep track of each time you hear one of this week's vocabulary words used in a sentence at home, school, or even on television. If you don't hear the words in a sentence, be creative and write original sentences using your new vocabulary knowledge. Next week, each group will read two of their sentences to the class!*

☆ Say: *Get in your Word Wizard Groups from last week, and share your best sentences.*

☆ Say: *Which group would like to read two of their sentences using the words from last week's lesson?* Tally the number of sentences per group, and record the amounts on the Word Wizard Chart.

Assign At-Home 3

Say: *Tonight you will . . .*

1. *Study your flashcards.*

2. *Complete the Word Wizard Journal.*

3. *Complete the Context Clues Activity.*

Day 4: Expanding Meaning

Prepare for Lesson

☆ Materials: Student Workbooks

☆ Read Teacher Tip: Deep Processing (Week 2, page 28)

3 min.

Vocabulary Review

☆ Rapid review of vocabulary words (Students use the Week 8 Word List in their Student Workbooks.)

7 min.

Review At-Home 3

☆ Review the correct answers to At-Home 3.

☆ Review student work to confirm or clarify responses.

20 min.

Deep Processing

☆ Say: *Does anyone remember what <u>deep processing</u> is? It is thinking about how words relate to each other.*

☆ Say: *We have learned the definitions for this week's vocabulary words, but definitions do not really teach everything we need to know to really understand the meaning of a word. Remember, it is important to be able to use these words to describe your own experiences in life and to describe conditions in the world in general.*

☆ Say: *Open your Student Workbook to Deep Processing: <u>Donovan's Word Jar</u>, Part I. We will read each question together and decide what is a reasonable answer and why. Remember, the answers are not in the book we read but come from your own thinking. Think about the questions and what would be a reasonable response. Remember, you must be able to explain why you chose your answer.*

Assign At-Home 4

Say: *Tonight you will . . .*

1. *Study your flashcards.*

2. *Complete the Crossword Puzzle.*

Day 5: Keys to Understanding

Prepare for Lesson

☆ Materials: Student Workbooks

☆ Read Teacher Tip: Word Roots

Teacher Tip: Word Roots

It is important that students understand that some words, historically, derive from other words. These word *roots* constitute a unit of meaning to which other word parts can be added.

This activity is designed to help students figure out meaningful units in words and to use these roots to understand the meaning of unfamiliar words.

Explicit instruction is important so that students do not misidentify smaller words in bigger words (e.g., using the word *let* to define the word *letter*).

Throughout the day, it is important to have students point out meaningful word parts. Nagy (1998)[1] suggested the following teacher-guided think-aloud activity.

Say: *Here's a word we haven't seen before. First, I'll see whether I recognize any familiar word parts—prefix, root, or suffix—or maybe a compound word. Okay, I see that I can divide this word into a root I know and a suffix. So the meaning of this word must have something to do with.... Now I'll see if the meaning makes any sense in this sentence . . .*

Review At-Home 4

☆ Review the correct answers to At-Home 4.

☆ Review student work to confirm or clarify responses.

Bingo Game

☆ Say: *Choose nine words from the Week 8 Word List, and write them on the Bingo Card in your Student Workbook. When I read a definition, raise your hand to identify the word. If you have the word on your card, mark it with an X. The first person who has 3 Xs in a row (across, down, diagonally) wins the game.*

☆ Read the definitions. As students identify definitions, write the words on the board until someone wins the game.

---

[1]Nagy, W.E. (1988). *Teaching vocabulary to improve reading comprehension.* Newark, DE: International Reading Association.

Word Roots: *Terre*

8–10 min.

☆ Say: *Open your Student Workbook to Word Roots: Terre. Remember, just as we belong to a family with a history, words also belong to families with a history. When we look at some word histories, it becomes evident that some words come from other languages like Latin or Greek. Yes, we use words everyday in English that have word parts that come from other languages. These small word units are called roots. A root is a small part of a word that can help you to figure out what the whole word means. Roots are the base part or original part of a word.*

☆ Say: *Today, we will look at the word root terre. Terre is a Latin word root, and it means land, ground, or of the earth. When we define words using the definition of the word root, it does not always exactly match the actual definition. However, the root can help us understand the meaning of an unfamiliar word.*

☆ Say: *Let's look at Word Roots: Terre. We are going to define words containing the word root terre. Repeat these words after me: terrestrial, extraterrestrial, territory, terrarium, and terracotta. Who thinks they know the definition of terrestrial? Extraterrestrial? Territory? Terrarium? Terracotta? Using the word root, terre, let's read each sentence and write what you think the word means.*

☆ Once all five words have been defined, quickly review the actual word meanings, and ask students if the definitions that they wrote matched the dictionary definitions.

☆ Say: *Let's see how close we are to the actual meaning of the words.*

Dictionary Definitions

1. **terrestrial**—relating to the earth or the people who live on the earth
2. **extraterrestrial**—beings who come from outside of the Earth's atmosphere
3. **territory**—land belonging to a government
4. **terrarium**—enclosure with land used for raising small plants/animals
5. **terracotta**—clay that is the color of the earth

Assessment

10 min.

☆ Distribute Assessment 8 to each student.

Name: _____ Date: _____

Assessment 8
Donavan's Word Jar, Part I

A. Match the word with the appropriate definition.

a)	collect	d)	boutique	g)	profound	j)	squabble	m)	private
b)	discovery	e)	hieroglyphics	h)	solidarity	k)	extraterrestrial	n)	cuddle
c)	nutrition	f)	property	i)	warrior	l)	billboard	o)	orchestral

_____ 1.   from outer space

_____ 2.   a large sign used for advertising

_____ 3.   writing made up of pictures and symbols

_____ 4.   related to a group of musicians who play together

_____ 5.   the process of eating wholesome food

B. Circle the word or phrase that does not belong.

1.	confidential	private	communal	not public
2.	superficial	profound	thoughtful	intense
3.	cuddle	reject	hug	hold
4.	agree	squabble	bicker	argue
5.	extraterrestrial	universe	Earth	Mars

C. Complete the sentence with the best answer.

_____ 1. Our teacher told us that _____ was a profound discovery.

    a) electricity

    b) chalk

    c) gum

_____ 2. A warrior might own _____ as personal property.

    a) a washing machine

    b) spears and knives

    c) a swimming pool

_____ 3. A billboard on good nutrition might display a _____.

    a) chocolate bar

    b) six-layer cake with icing

    c) glass of milk

_____ 4. Solidarity among boutique owners might result in _____.

    a) the same store hours throughout the week

    b) a standard or common salary for workers

    c) all of the above

_____ 5. Orchestral sounds may be profound if _____.

    a) they inspire the listeners to dream about a better future

    b) the music is not harmonious because the musicians are unprepared

    c) it is impossible to hear the music because of structure of the concert hall

Donavan's Word Jar, Part II

by Monalisa DeGross

DAY 1 Preview of Lesson	DAY 2 Introduction	DAY 3 Using Words in Context	DAY 4 Expanding Meaning	DAY 5 Keys to Understanding
Read New Words Say and Write New Words Read Definitions Assign At-Home 1	Vocabulary Review Review At-Home 1 Predict the Storyline Story Reading (pages 15–30) Identifying Vocabulary in Text Paraphrasing Vocabulary in Text Assign At-Home 2	Vocabulary Review Review At-Home 2 Using Context Clues Word Wizard Assign At-Home 3	Vocabulary Review Review At-Home 3 Multiple Meanings: *Suggestion, Solution, Firm,* and *Gather* Assign At-Home 4	Review At-Home 4 Bingo Game Word Roots: *Rupt* Let's Go to the Writing Board (optional) Assessment

Words and Definitions

The following are target words for this week. If the word has multiple meanings, we provide only the definition listed in the text. ***Please review the definitions prior to instruction.***

1. **dilemma**—a difficult choice

2. **solution**—the answer to a problem

3. **definitive**—something that is final

4. **suggestion**—something that is mentioned or brought to mind

5. **file**—a folder, box, or cabinet used for keeping papers in order

6. **decision**—making up one's mind about something; the choice that is selected

7. **advice**—an opinion given on how to best do something

8. **patterned**—the arrangement of parts into a design

9. **concentrate**—to think with effort, to focus one's mind

10. **canvas**—a strong cotton cloth usually used for tents, oil painting, or sails

11. **interruption**—the act of breaking in on someone's conversation or actions

12. **firm**—steady, stable, not shaky

13. **gather**—to bring together in one group

14. **steady**—not changing; firm, not shaky

15. **partner**—a person who takes part in something with another

Day 1: Preview of Lesson

Prepare for Lesson

☆ Materials: Student Workbooks, *Donavan's Word Jar* by Monalisa DeGross, display copy of Week 9 Word List

☆ Read Teacher Tip: Reading New Words (Week 1, page 8)

Read New Words

☆ Say: *Today, we will continue with two new chapters in* Donavan's Word Jar: *"Donavan's Dilemma" and "Donavan's Decision." Remember, on Day 1 we learn to read new words that you will study at home. The words we learn will help you to read this story better and will help you to express your thoughts on paper and when talking to others. Let's see if there are any words that you already know.*

☆ Display the Week 9 Word List. Cover the bottom box, leaving the word columns at the top of page exposed. Say: *Which words do you already know?*

☆ Uncover the bottom box. Say: *Let's read these words. Sound out each syllable as I point to it. Be sure to say each sound clearly. Sound it out.*

☆ Students sound out each syllable. Say the word. Students repeat the word. Say: *Yes, the word is . . . .*

Say and Write New Words

☆ Cover the bottom box, and use the word columns at the top of the page.

☆ Say: *Let's read the words together.* Point to each word, and read one time.

☆ Say: *Take out your pencil and Student Workbook. Find the page that says Week 9: Say and Write New Words. Let's get ready to say and write each word.*

☆ Point to each word. Say: *What word?* Students say the word. *Write [the word].*

☆ Students write the word on the appropriate line. Continue until all words are written.

Read Definitions

☆ Say: *I will read the definitions so that we will understand what each word means. Some words have more than one meaning; however, these are the definitions that are used in the story.*

☆ Read the definitions out loud as students read silently. Choose a student to read each sentence.

Definitions

1. **dilemma** (a difficult choice)
   The hospital staff were faced with an endless <u>dilemma</u>. They could use the endowment to buy new equipment and increase their technology, but the patients who were poor would no longer be able to afford to be treated there.

Week 9 Word List

dilem**ma**	deci**sion**	interrup**tion**
solu**tion**	advi**ce**	fir**m**
defini**tive**	pat**terned**	gath**er**
sugges**tion**	concen**trate**	stead**y**
fi**le**	can**vas**	part**ner**

1. di lem **ma**
2. sol ute
   so lu **tion**
3. de fine
   de fin i **tive**
4. sug gest
   sug ges **tion**
5. fi**le**
6. de cide
   de ci **sion**
7. ad vi**ce**
8. pat tern
   pat **terned**
9. con cen **trate**
10. can
    can **vas**
11. in ter rupt
    in ter rup **tion**
12. fir**m**
13. gath **er**
14. stead
    stead **y**
15. part
    part **ner**

2. **solution** (the answer to a problem)
   The <u>solution</u> to the hospital's problem was to provide financial assistance to poor patients.

3. **definitive** (something that is final)
   Mother's <u>definitive</u> answer was that we could not attend the party.

4. **suggestion** (something that is mentioned or brought to mind)
   Our teacher made the <u>suggestion</u> that we choose an experiment for the science fair that we would be able to talk about in front of an audience.

5. **file** (a folder, box, or cabinet used for keeping papers in order)
   Grandma keeps a recipe <u>file</u> with recipes that have been passed down from our ancestors.

6. **decision** (making up one's mind about something; the choice that is selected)
   The <u>decision</u> was made that we would fly into Miami and then drive to Cape Canaveral to witness the launching of the new rocket.

7. **advice** (an opinion given on how to best do something)
   I think the best <u>advice</u> is to save as much money as possible before deciding which gift to purchase for Father's Day.

8. **patterned** (the arrangement of parts into a design)
   We chose a pink wallpaper <u>patterned</u> with ballerinas to decorate our baby sister's new room.

9. **concentrate** (to think with effort, to focus one's mind)
   It was impossible to <u>concentrate</u> during the test because of the noisy drilling coming from the construction site across the street.

10. **canvas** (a strong cotton cloth usually used for tents, oil painting, or sails)
    Before painting, my uncle and I stretch the <u>canvas</u> over a wooden support and nail it into place.

11. **interruption** (the act of breaking in on someone's conversation or actions)
    There were so many <u>interruption</u>s during the day that I was not able to complete the last chapter of the novel.

12. **firm** (steady, stable, not shaky)
    We placed our confidence and trust in the architect's ability to transform our home into a castle and sealed our agreement with a <u>firm</u> handshake.

13. **gather** (to bring together in one group)
    When the teacher heard the siren, she quickly <u>gather</u>ed the small children and prepared for the tornado.

14. **steady** (not changing; firm, not shaky)
    Grandpa warned us that if we sat in the chair we would fall because it was old and not <u>steady</u>.

15. **partner** (a person who takes part in something with another)
    The policeman expected his <u>partner</u> to guard the front door while he looked around for clues in the windowsill.

Day 1: Preview of Lesson

Assign At-Home 1

Say: *Tonight you will . . .*

1. *Study the vocabulary words with definitions.*
2. *Complete the Riddle Page.*
3. *Do the Matching Activity.*
4. *Make flashcards.*

Day 2: Introduction

Prepare for Lesson

 Materials: Student Workbooks, *Donavan's Word Jar* by Monalisa DeGross

3 min.

Vocabulary Review

 Rapid review of vocabulary words (Students use the Week 9 Word List in their Student Workbooks.)

7 min.

Review At-Home 1

 Review the correct answers to At-Home 1.

 Review student work to confirm or clarify responses.

8 min.

Predict the Storyline

 Students look at the illustrations on pages 22 and 25 of *Donavan's Word Jar* by Monalisa DeGross.

 Say: *Today we will begin reading two new chapters of Donavan's Word Jar. The first chapter we will read is "Donavan's Dilemma," and the second chapter is 'Donavan's Decision." When we look at the illustration on page 22, we see Donavan and his father working as partners. It looks as if they are painting, and in order to paint you must have steady hands. What do you think they are trying to build?*

 Say: *If you remember, the word <u>dilemma</u> means a difficult choice. What dilemma do you think Donavan will face in this chapter? Look at the illustration on page 25. What is going on in the picture? What clues are present that suggest the decision that Donavan will make to solve his dilemma? How many of you have ever had to make a difficult choice? What kinds of dilemmas do people face in life?*

 Say: *Open your Student Workbook to Semantic Web: Difficult Choices. What vocabulary words do we associate with difficult choices? Let's think of some people who make difficult choices. They might be forced to make these decisions because of their job. How do you feel when faced with a difficult decision? Now, let's think of some places where difficult decisions are made.*

 Say: *Think of a question that you think the story will answer. Write the question at the bottom of Semantic Web: Difficult Choices.*

8–10 min.

Story Reading 1: Identifying Vocabulary in Text

 Say: *As I read the story out loud, you will follow along silently. When you see a word from our vocabulary list, give a thumbs up.*

 Read pages 15–30.

 Discuss what students predicted would happen in the story.

Story Reading 2: Paraphrasing Vocabulary in Text

☆ Say: *As I read specific paragraphs of the story out loud again, let's paraphrase what the author has said by using our own words. Let's focus on the fourth paragraph on page 28. Follow along as I read out loud.* Read the paragraph. ("He is, but your father . . .").

☆ Say: *What's another way of saying, "He needs peace and quiet so that he can concentrate . . .?" We might say, "Dad would like you to be quiet so that he can finish his work."*

☆ Help students to paraphrase the remaining sentences in the paragraph as appropriate.

Assign At-Home 2

Say: *Tonight you will . . .*

1. *Study your flashcards.*

2. *Complete Word Substitutions.*

3. *Complete Same and Different.*

Day 3: Using Words in Context

Prepare for Lesson

☆ Materials: Student Workbooks

☆ Read Teacher Tip: Word Wizard (Week 1, page 14)

3 min.

Vocabulary Review

☆ Rapid review of vocabulary words (Students use the Week 9 Word List in their Student Workbooks.)

7 min.

Review At-Home 2

☆ Review the correct answers to At-Home 2.

☆ Review student work to confirm or clarify responses.

15 min.

Using Context Clues

☆ Say: *Open your Student Workbook to Week 9: Using Context Clues. Today, we will use context clues to help us choose the word that fits in the blank by using the clues from other words and information in the sentence or sentences. I will read the sentences out loud. Raise your hand when you know which word best completes the sentence. Write the word in the blank. Sometimes the word might require an ending such as -ed, -s, or -ing. Each word will be used only one time.*

☆ Choose individual students to give answers. Have students point out context clues that helped them to choose the correct answer.

☆ Say: *Cross out words in the box as we use them. Write your answers in the blank, and write the context clues you used in the space below.*

5 min.

Word Wizard

☆ Say: *As Word Wizards this week, you must always be on the lookout for opportunities to use and demonstrate your word knowledge. Use your Word Wizard Journals to keep track of each time you hear one of this week's vocabulary words used in a sentence at home, school, or even on television. If you don't hear the words in a sentence, be creative and write original sentences using your new vocabulary knowledge. Next week, each group will read two of their sentences to the class!*

☆ Say: *Get in your Word Wizard Groups from last week, and share your best sentences.*

☆ Say: *Which group would like to read two of their sentences using the words from last week's lesson?* Tally the number of sentences per group, and record the amounts on the Word Wizard Chart.

Assign At-Home 3

Say: *Tonight you will . . .*

1. *Study your flashcards.*

2. *Complete the Word Wizard Journal.*

3. *Complete the Context Clues Activity.*

Day 4: Expanding Meaning

Prepare for Lesson

 Materials: Student Workbooks

Vocabulary Review
3 min.

 Rapid review of vocabulary words (Students use the Week 9 Word List in their Student Workbooks.)

Review At-Home 3
7 min.

 Review the correct answers to At-Home 3.

 Review student work to confirm or clarify responses.

Multiple Meanings: *Suggestion, Solution, Firm,* and *Gather*
20 min.

★ Say: *Sometimes words have several meanings. For example, in Week 1 we studied different definitions for master and approach. The word master may mean a man who rules over animals or people or it could refer to an expert at some type of work. If you remember, the word approach can mean to draw closer to someone, but it can also mean to go to someone with a plan or request.*

★ Say: *Some of the words in this week's story also have multiple meanings. Let's look at solution, suggestion, firm, and gather. Open your Student Workbook to Multiple Meanings: Suggestion, Solution, Firm, and Gather. Let's read the definitions for these words.*

★ Say: *Let's read sentences using these words and look for context clues that can help us to choose the correct definition.*

★ Read the first sentence out loud. Say: *Which definition of solution are we using in the sentence?* The answer is b, a mixture of two or more sentences.

★ Say: *What context clues helped us to understand the meaning of the word?* Answers include mixed and completely dissolve.

★ Say: *I will read each sentence out loud, and you will choose the letter of the definition that describes how the word is used in the sentence.*

Assign At-Home 4

Say: *Tonight you will . . .*

1. *Study your flashcards.*

2. *Complete the Word Search.*

3. *Complete the Crossword Puzzle.*

Day 5: Keys to Understanding

Prepare for Lesson

⭐ Materials: Student Workbooks

⭐ Read Teacher Tip: Root Words (Week 8, page 106)

Review At-Home 4
(7 min.)

⭐ Review the correct answers to At-Home 4.

⭐ Review student work to confirm or clarify responses.

Bingo Game
(8 min.)

⭐ Say: *Choose nine words from the Week 9 Word List, and write them on the Bingo Card in your Student Workbook. When I read a definition, raise your hand to identify the word. If you have the word on your card, mark it with an* X. *The first person who has 3* Xs *in a row (across, down, diagonally) wins the game.*

⭐ Read the definitions. As students identify definitions, write the words on the board until someone wins the game.

Word Roots: *Rupt*
(8–10 min.)

⭐ Say: *Open your Student Workbook to Word Roots:* Rupt. *Do you remember what a word root is?* Call on a student. *That's right. Roots are small word units in words that come from other languages like Latin or Greek. They help us figure out the meaning of a word.*

⭐ Say: *Today, we will look at the word root* rupt. Rupt *is a Greek word root, and it means to break or burst. When we define words using the definition of the word root, it does not always exactly match the actual definition. However, the root can help us understand the meaning of an unfamiliar word.*

⭐ Say: *Let's look at Word Root:* Rupt. *We are going to define words containing the word* rupt. *Repeat these words after me:* interrupt, disrupt, rupture, corrupt, *and* erupt. *Who can tell us the meaning of* interrupt? Disrupt? Rupture? Corrupt? Erupt? *Using the word root,* rupt, *let's read each sentence and write what you think the word means.*

⭐ Once all five words have been defined, quickly review the actual word meanings, and ask students if the definitions that they wrote matched the dictionary definitions.

⭐ Say: *Let's see how close we are to the actual meaning of the words.*

Dictionary Definitions

1. **interrupt**—a break in one's conversation or actions

2. **disrupt**—to break up or disturb something that is taking place

3. **rupture**—to break open or burst

4. **corrupt**—to break one's moral code (a sense of what is right or wrong) so that one becomes bad or dishonest

5. **erupt**—when a volcano breaks open abruptly and hot lava and rocks are spewed forth

Let's Go to the Writing Board (optional)

15–20 min.

☆ The following steps can be used for scaffolding the writing process. Students are expected to dictate seven sentences for you to write on the board. As you write the sentences, emphasize correct grammatical structures while focusing on appropriate content. Students should also write what is dictated and check and edit their work by comparing what they have written to what you have written on the board.

☆ Step 1—Brainstorm the kinds of decisions that children make, and select one topic as a class (e.g., telling the truth, confronting a bully) to write about. Discuss the topic.

☆ Step 2—Have students write the title of the paragraph on the page.

☆ Step 3—Remind students to begin each sentence with a capital letter and to end sentences with appropriate punctuation marks.

☆ Step 4—Write the first sentence on the board. You may use one of the following sentence stems or create your own:

   a.   One day I had to make a big decision.

   b.   One day I was faced with a challenging dilemma.

☆ Step 5—Solicit sentences from students by asking guiding questions such as the following examples:

   a.   Describe the two options the student is facing.

   b.   Tell why the decision is important.

   c.   Describe how one feels in selecting option A of the decision.

   d.   Describe how one feels in selecting choice B of the decision.

   e.   What suggestions do other people give to help the student make the decision?

   f.   What decision is finally made and why.

☆ Step 6—Solicit student participation by asking

   a.   All boys to contribute the next sentence as a group.

   b.   All girls to contribute a sentence as a group.

   c.   Each cooperative group or row of students to supply a sentence.

☆ This is an activity that builds both oral and written vocabulary skills!

Assessment

10 min.

☆ Distribute Assessment 9 to each student.

Name: _____ Date: _____

Assessment 9
Donavan's Word Jar, Part II

A. Match the word with the appropriate definition.

a)	dilemma	d)	suggestion	g)	advice	j)	canvas	m)	gather
b)	solution	e)	file	h)	patterned	k)	interruption	n)	steady
c)	definitive	f)	decision	i)	concentrate	l)	firm	o)	partner

_____ 1. a person who assists or helps another

_____ 2. a system for organizing information

_____ 3. a strong cotton cloth used for painting

_____ 4. to collect

_____ 5. a break in service or conversation

B. Circle the word that does not belong.

1.	suggestion	advice	decision	opinion
2.	steady	secure	flimsy	firm
3.	solution	dilemma	problem	trouble
4.	conclusive	beginning	definitive	final
5.	concentrate	think	drift	focus

C. Write the letter of the item in the blank that completes the sentences.

_____ 1. When facing a dilemma, an important decision may be made after gathering advice from _____.

     a)   a parent

     b)   a stranger

     c)   your baby sister

_____ 2. When visiting an optometrist, she might ask you to concentrate on different visual patterns in order to gather information about your _____.

     a)   hearing

     b)   eyesight

     c)   sense of smell

_____ 3. The president of the United States might issue a firm, definitive response to _____.

     a)   an invitation to a display of oil paintings on canvases

     b)   a threat of war from a neighboring country

     c)   a steady pattern of rain and sleet that has lasted over a week

_____ 4. An interruption such as _____ would require an immediate solution.

     a)   an intermission during the circus

     b)   a pause during storytelling

     c)   a disconnection of one's telephone service

_____ 5. A farmer might give advice about _____.

     a)   gathering vegetables from the vine when they are not firm

     b)   working with a partner so that one can concentrate and move quickly

     c)   constructing a mahogany table in a woodshop class

 Vocabulary Power, Level 1, by Latrice M. Seals, Sharolyn D. Pollard-Durodola, Barbara R. Foorman, and Ashley M. Bradley

Review Unit 2

REVIEW DAY 1	REVIEW DAY 2	REVIEW DAY 3	REVIEW DAY 4	REVIEW DAY 5
Introduce Unit Review "I Spy" Game Assign At-Home 1	Semantic Feature Analysis Assign At-Home 2	Multiple Meanings Find It, Say It! Game Assign At-Home 3	Clueless Game Assign At-Home 4	Assessment

Words and Definitions

The following are target words for this week. If the word has multiple meanings, we provide only the definition listed in the text. *Please review the definitions prior to instruction.*

1. **firm**—steady, stable, not shaky
2. **Reconstruction**—the act of rebuilding the South after the Civil War
3. **solution**—the answer to a problem
4. **concentrate**—to think with effort, to focus one's mind
5. **suggestion**—something that was mentioned or brought to mind
6. **irritable**—feeling angry or exasperated
7. **disappear**—to pass out of sight; to cease to be
8. **impatient**—restless, anxious, short of temper when irritated
9. **profound**—deeply felt or thought
10. **depression**—a period of widespread unemployment; a state of feeling sad
11. **discovery**—a finding out about something
12. **warrior**—a soldier or someone who fights in battles
13. **furnace**—an enclosed structure in which heat is produced
14. **private**—belonging to one person, group, and so forth and no one else
15. **solidarity**—agreement between people to work together for a common goal
16. **mahogany**—an American evergreen tree with reddish wood that is used in furniture
17. **creek**—a stream of water that is smaller than a river and larger than a brook
18. **extraterrestrial**—coming from outer space
19. **canvas**—a strong cotton cloth usually used for tents, oil painting, or sails
20. **file**—a folder, box, or cabinet used for keeping papers in order
21. **freight**—cargo, the carrying of goods by a train or other means of transportation
22. **frail**—morally or physically weak
23. **basement**—the part of a building that is below ground level
24. **partner**—a person who takes part in something with another
25. **nutrition**—the process of eating food that is healthy for your body

Review Day 1

Prepare for Lesson

 Materials: Student Workbooks, display copy of Unit 2 Word List (optional)

Introduce Unit Review

☆ Say: *Last week, we completed the last story in our unit. We have read four stories and learned many new words each week. This week we will review some key words that we learned in Unit 2. At the end of the week, you will have an opportunity to demonstrate just how much you've learned.*

"I Spy" Game

25 min.

☆ Say: *How many of you remember playing "I Spy"? When we play "I Spy" we use clues to help us to identify words.*

☆ Say: *Turn to Unit 2: "I Spy" in your Student Workbook. Today, we will work as word detectives and use a list of clues to determine the review word. Let's read the clues and decide which word is being described. Write the word next to the appropriate clue. Remember, a good detective never gives up!*

☆ Read the sentences out loud, and call on students for answers. Say: *I am looking for a word that means . . . ,* then read the definition. Students should respond in the form, "I spy . . ." then say the vocabulary word.

Assign At-Home 1

Say: *Tonight you will . . .*

1. *Study the Unit 2 vocabulary words with definitions.*

2. *Make flashcards.*

Unit 2 Word List

firm	Reconstruction	solution
concentrate	suggestion	irritable
disappear	impatient	profound
depression	discovery	warrior
furnace	private	solidarity
mahogany	creek	extraterrestrial
canvas	file	freight
frail	basement	partner
nutrition		

Review Day 2

Prepare for Lesson

☆ Materials: Student Workbooks, display copy of Semantic Feature Analysis: Heating Systems

☆ Read Teacher Tip: Semantic Feature Analysis (Week 5, page 62)

25 min.

Semantic Feature Analysis

☆ Say: *The objective of today's activity is to compare different words and to decide how words are similar and different. The purpose of this activity is to help you to see how words are related to each other.*

☆ Say: *In the Review Unit 1, we categorized words that describe what people do. We looked for action words and then described features of those words in a special matrix. This week, we will focus on heating systems. Who remembers one of our vocabulary words that describes a large system for producing heat?* The answer is furnace. *We saw the word <u>furnace</u> used in <u>A Hundred Penny Box</u> when Michael tells Aunt Dew that he is afraid that his mother will put Aunt Dew's belongings in the furnace in the basement.*

☆ Say: *Not everyone uses a furnace. In fact, there are many techniques and systems used for producing heat. Can you think of other kinds of heating systems? For example, in older brownstones in New York City, the owners rely on a huge boiler in the basement to heat the building. How is your room, apartment, or house heated?*

☆ Say: *Open your Student Workbook to Semantic Feature Analysis: Heating Systems. Let's look at the heating systems listed in the left column of the matrix. Does the list contain the types of systems that we have just discussed in class?* Read through the list with students. Add any heating systems that were discussed in class but that are not on the list.

☆ Say: *Let's look at some features of heating systems. Look at the top row of the matrix. Can you think of any other features that should be listed here?* Any additional features may be added. You might want to add "uses electricity" and "uses gas."

☆ Say: *Let's discuss the features of different heating systems. We will fill in the matrix with a plus or minus to indicate the presence or absence of each feature. If we can't agree, we will place a zero in the matrix.*

☆ After the matrix is complete, say: *Let's look at the matrix to see which features are shared by the different heating systems.* Discuss similar and different features.

☆ Help students discover that no two heating systems have exactly the same pattern of pluses (similarities) and minuses (differences): none are identical. Even the categories that are most alike will reveal their differences if enough features are added.

Assign At-Home 2

Say: *Tonight you will study the vocabulary words on your flashcards.*

Semantic Feature Analysis: Heating Systems

	Heats the building	Makes faucet water hot	Cooks food	Bakes pottery	Uses water	Uses coal	Heats a room	Uses oil		
Radiator										
Heater										
Oven										
Boiler										
Furnace										
Central Heat										
Kiln										

Prepare for Lesson

 Materials: Student Workbooks

15 min.
Multiple Meanings

 Say: *Today we are going to study some of the words from the past 4 weeks that have more than one meaning. In the first part of the activity, we will quickly review the different meanings for each word.*

⭐ Say: *Who remembers one of the meanings for the word <u>firm</u>?* Continue until the students have identified as many definitions as they can for *firm*. Do the same for *solution, file, depression,* and *reconstruction.*

⭐ Say: *Open your Student Workbook to Unit 2: Multiple Meanings. Let's see how many meanings we know for these words.*

15 min.
Find It, Say It! Game

⭐ Say: *Next, we will play Find It, Say It! Turn to Unit 2: Find It, Say It!*

⭐ Say: *Remember, when we play Find It, Say It! I first read the sentence with the underlined word and say, "Find It!" You then go to the box of the underlined word and find the definition that best fits the way the word is used in each sentence. Without talking, you write the letter for that definition in the space at the beginning of the sentence. When I say, "Say It," everyone will say the answer out loud together.*

⭐ After asking students to find the answer, allow them approximately 7 seconds before asking them to say it.

Assign At-Home 3

Say: *Tonight you will study the vocabulary words on your flashcards.*

Review Day 4

Prepare for Lesson

☆ Materials: Clue Cards, photocopies of Score Keeper Card (from Week 5)

25 min.

Clueless Game

☆ Write the words "Class Score Keeper" and the numbers 1–10 on the board, Have a magnet or other device ready to point to one of the numbers.

☆ Say: *Today, we will play Clueless. As you may recall from last unit review, the objective of this game is to focus on single word clues that can help you to remember the words that you have learned. Remember, you may not use your Student Workbook to help you.*

☆ Say: *Do you remember your groups from last time?* If necessary, create new groups.

☆ Say: *We will appoint a new score keeper for each team. We will use the part of the Score Keeper Card for Review Unit 2.* Assign a person from each group to be the score keeper or allow teams to choose their own score keepers.

☆ Say: *Let's review the rules. I will place a marker on 10 on the Class Score Keeper. Then, I will flash a Clue Card with a one-word clue. I will start with Team A. If Team A correctly identifies the word, they get the points indicated on the Class Score Keeper. If the marker is on 10, they get 10 points, and the team's score keeper records the value on the Score Keeper Card.*

☆ Say: *If the word is not guessed from the Clue Card, the marker on the Class Score Keeper is moved to 9, and it becomes the other team's turn. If they guess the word, they receive the points indicated by the Class Score Keeper.*

☆ Say: *Remember, if the word is not guessed from the first clue, the marker on the Class Score Keeper is moved to 9, and it becomes the other team's turn. If the next team cannot guess the word, the marker is moved to 8, and so forth. Each time the word is not guessed the marker is moved one number lower.*

☆ Say: *Each time we read a new clue, the marker is placed back on 10, and the other team tries to identify the word from the next clue card.*

☆ Say: *We continue to play until we have identified all the clue words. The team with the highest total score is the winner.*

☆ Distribute the Score Keeper Cards for each team. After playing the game, collect the Score Keeper Cards so that they can be used with the next review unit.

Assign At-Home 4

Say: *Tonight you will study for Friday's test.*

individual	anxious	health	wood	answer
heat	rebuild	cargo	paintings	papers
finding	agreement	focus	co-worker	deep
underground	vanish	stream	idea	soldier
feeble	angry	sadness	space	secure

 Vocabulary Power, Level 1, by Latrice M. Seals, Sharolyn D. Pollard-Durodola, Barbara R. Foorman, and Ashley M. Bradley

Review Day 5

Prepare for Lesson

☆ Materials: photocopies of Assessment 10

Assessment

☆ Distribute Assessment 10 to each student.

☆ Read the directions out loud.

☆ Read each vocabulary word out loud along with the answer choices. Allow students a few seconds to choose and write the letter for a definition.

☆ Collect assessments.

Name: _____ Date: _____

Assessment 10
Unit 2

Choose the letter that represents the best definition for each word.

___ 1. nutrition
   a. spoiled food
   b. fatty food
   c. healthy food

___ 2. creek
   a. a wide ocean
   b. a small stream
   c. a long river

___ 3. solution
   a. an explanation
   b. a problem
   c. a puzzle

___ 4. extraterrestrial
   a. one planet
   b. from outer space
   c. from Earth

___ 5. impatient
   a. anxious, not being able to wait
   b. calm, being able to wait
   c. tranquil, full of peace

___ 6. furnace
   a. air conditioning
   b. a heating system
   c. a ceiling fan

___ 7. partner
   a. a co-worker
   b. a borrower
   c. a miser

___ 8. basement
   a. a room under the ground
   b. a room above the ground
   c. a room with a metal base

___ 9. firm
   a. poor
   b. frail
   c. stable

___ 10. canvas
   a. strong cloth
   b. wet cloth
   c. ancient cloth

___ 11. solidarity
   a. disagreement
   b. unity
   c. conversation

___ 12. warrior
   a. soldier
   b. secretary
   c. civilian

___ 13. reconstruction
   a. to destroy
   b. to build again
   c. to draw again

___ 14. mahogany
   a. a white wood
   b. a red wood
   c. a soft wood

_____ 15. concentrate

    a. to focus on

    b. to write about

    c. to speak to

_____ 16. private

    a. one group

    b. everyone

    c. no one

_____ 17. file

    a. a cabinet with food

    b. a cabinet with dishes

    c. a cabinet with papers

_____ 18. frail

    a. tired

    b. robust

    c. cheerful

_____ 19. profound

    a. to feel deeply

    b. to forget quickly

    c. to find slowly

_____ 20. disappear

    a. to become visible

    b. to become desperate

    c. to leave one's sight

_____ 21. suggestion

    a. a plan

    b. a book

    c. a composition

_____ 22. freight

    a. letters

    b. a shipment

    c. tickets

_____ 23. discovery

    a. something unearthed

    b. something hidden

    c. something destroyed

_____ 24. depression

    a. feeling happy

    b. feeling unhappy

    c. feeling the same

_____ 25. irritable

    a. feeling angry

    b. feeling joyful

    c. feeling hopeful

Donavan's Word Jar, Part III

by Monalisa DeGross

DAY 1 Preview of Lesson	DAY 2 Introduction	DAY 3 Using Words in Context	DAY 4 Expanding Meaning	DAY 5 Keys to Understanding
Read New Words Say and Write New Words Read Definitions Assign At-Home 1	Vocabulary Review Review At-Home 1 Predict the Storyline Story Reading (pages 55–71) Identifying Vocabulary in Text Paraphrasing Vocabulary in Text Assign At-Home 2	Vocabulary Review Review At-Home 2 Using Context Clues Word Wizard Assign At-Home 3	Vocabulary Review Review At-Home 3 Multiple Meanings: *Relief, Security,* and *Exchange* Assign At-Home 4	Review At-Home 4 Bingo Game Deep Processing Let's Pick a Word (optional) Assessment

Words and Definitions

The following are target words for this week. If the word has multiple meanings, we provide only the definition listed in the text. ***Please review the definitions prior to instruction.***

1. **diplomacy**—conducting peaceful negotiations among different people or countries

2. **lounge**—a comfortable room for relaxing

3. **perseverance**—the ability to keep going and not give up when faced with difficulties

4. **timid**—shy and easily frightened

5. **boisterous**—to behave in a loud and noisy way

6. **leisure**—free time

7. **serendipity**—discovering something pleasant without looking for it to occur

8. **compromise**—an agreement reached between people with opposing views in which they accept something that is not exactly what they wanted

9. **security**—freedom from danger and anxiety or worry

10. **exchange**—to give one thing in return for another

11. **stern**—harsh or strict

12. **hassock**—a cushion or low stool that serves as a leg rest or place to sit

13. **gruff**—rough or stern manner

14. **relief**—feeling of freedom from worry and pain

15. **delight**—great pleasure

Day 1: Preview of Lesson

Prepare for Lesson

☆ Materials: Student Workbooks, *Donavan's Word Jar* by Monalisa DeGross, display copy of Week 11 Word List

☆ Read Teacher Tip: Reading New Words (Week 1, page 8)

Read New Words

☆ Say: *Today, we will continue with two new stories in* <u>Donavan's Word Jar</u>*: "Donavan's Diplomacy" and "Donavan's Delight." Remember, on Day 1 we learn to read new words that you will study at home. The words we learn will help you to read this story better and will help you to express your thoughts on paper and when talking to others. Let's see if there are any words that you already know.*

☆ Display the Week 11 Word List. Cover the bottom box, leaving the word columns at the top of page exposed. Say: *Which of the words do you already know?*

☆ Uncover the bottom box. Say: *Let's read these words. Sound out each syllable as I point to it. Be sure to say each sound clearly. Sound it out.*

☆ Students sound out each syllable. Say the word. Students repeat the word. Say: *Yes, the word is . . . .*

Say and Write New Words

☆ Cover the bottom box, and use the word columns at the top of the page.

☆ Say: *Let's read the words together.* Point to each word, and read one time.

☆ Say: *Take out your pencil and Student Workbook. Find the page that says Week 11: Say and Write New Words. Let's get ready to say and write each word.*

☆ Point to each word. Say: *What word?* Students say the word. *Write [the word].*

☆ Students write the word on the appropriate line. Continue until all words are written.

Read Definitions

☆ Say: *I will read the definitions so that we will understand what each word means. Some words have more than one meaning; however, these are the definitions that are used in the story.*

☆ Read the definitions out loud as students read silently. Choose a student to read each sentence.

Week 11 Word List

diploma**cy**	leisure	ster**n**
loun**ge**	serendipi**ty**	hasso**ck**
perseverance	compromise	gru**ff**
tim**id**	securi**ty**	relie**f**
boister**ous**	exchan**ge**	deligh**t**

1. dipl o ma**t**
   dip lo ma**cy**
2. loun**ge**
3. per sev ere
   per sev er ance
4. tim **id**
5. boi ster **ous**
6. lei sure
7. ser en di pi **ty**
8. com pro mise
9. sec ure
   se cu ri **ty**
10. change
    ex chan**ge**
11. ster**n**
12. has so**ck**
13. gru**ff**
14. re lie**f**
15. de ligh**t**

Vocabulary Power, Level 1, by Latrice M. Seals, Sharolyn D. Pollard-Durodola, Barbara R. Foorman, and Ashley M. Bradley

Definitions

1. **diplomacy** (conducting peaceful negotiations among different people or countries)
   As an ambassador to France, Benjamin Franklin was known for his tactful <u>diplomacy</u> with the French government.

2. **lounge** (a comfortable room for relaxing)
   We decided to move our guests to the <u>lounge</u> for lemonade and other refreshments.

3. **perseverance** (the ability to keep going and not give up when faced with difficulties)
   In her <u>perseverance</u>, Harriet Tubman was successful in raising funds to assist former slaves with food, education, and needed shelter.

4. **timid** (shy and easily frightened)
   At the circus, the <u>timid</u> child was easily frightened by the ferocious tigers that stood on their hind legs, roaring at the ringmaster.

5. **boisterous** (to behave in a loud and noisy way)
   The end-of-year school dance was so <u>boisterous</u> that Mr. Card, the principal, turned the music off and threatened to discontinue everything.

6. **leisure** (free time)
   During our <u>leisure</u> time on weekends, the Girls' Book Club decided to read *Dear Mr. President: Abraham Lincoln Letters From a Slave Girl.*

7. **serendipity** (discovering something pleasant without looking for it to occur)
   It was only by <u>serendipity</u> that we discovered that the coveted quilt that was exhibited at the museum turned out to be the very one that our great, great grandmother had stitched when she was first married.

8. **compromise** (an agreement reached between people with opposing views in which they accept something that is not exactly what they wanted)
   My brother and I made a <u>compromise</u> with our younger sister that we would take her to the movies if she would stop sharing our personal secrets with her best friends.

9. **security** (freedom from danger and anxiety or worry)
   The alarm on the <u>security</u> system sounded loud and clear at 2:00 in the morning because we forgot to turn it off before entering into the dark, quiet house.

10. **exchange** (to give one thing in return for another)
    At the end of the voyage, the students <u>exchange</u>d telephone numbers and e-mails so that they could remain friends forever.

11. **stern** (harsh or strict)
    Our piano instructor is so <u>stern</u> that he gives us a theory test every month in addition to requiring that we practice 2 hours every night.

12. **hassock** (a cushion or low stool that serves as a leg rest or place to sit)
    In the lounge, Uncle Jack rested his tired, aching feet on the brown, leather <u>hassock</u> while we ran to the kitchen to get a cool drink of water to quench his thirst.

13. **gruff** (rough or stern manner)
    The army sergeant's voice was <u>gruff</u> and unrelenting as he scolded the men for their boisterous behavior in the barracks.

14. **relief** (feeling of freedom from worry and pain)

We experienced great <u>relief</u> when we learned that the war had ended and that civilian life would become more peaceful.

15. **delight** (great pleasure)

Janet and Haile took great <u>delight</u> in sampling the assortment of chocolate at the candy store.

Assign At-Home 1

Say: *Tonight you will . . .*

1. *Study the vocabulary words with definitions.*

2. *Complete the Riddle Page.*

3. *Do the Matching Activity.*

4. *Make flashcards.*

Day 2: Introduction

Prepare for Lesson

☆ Materials: Student Workbooks, *Donavan's Word Jar* by Monalisa DeGross

Vocabulary Review

3 min.

☆ Rapid review of vocabulary words (Students use the Week 11 Word List in their Student Workbooks.)

Review At-Home 1

7 min.

☆ Review the correct answers to At-Home 1.

☆ Review student work to confirm or clarify responses.

Predict the Storyline

8 min.

☆ Students look at the illustrations on pages 59 and 64 of *Donavan's Word Jar* by Monalisa DeGross.

☆ Say: *Today we will begin reading two new chapters of <u>Donavan's Word Jar</u>. The first chapter we will read is "Donavan's Diplomacy," and the second chapter is "Donavan's Delight." Let's compare the illustrations on pages 59 and 64.* Point out the fact that Donovan's friends and relatives appear to be arguing in the first illustration but no longer seem to be upset in the second illustration.

☆ Say: *In Week 1, Richard Wright taught us the meaning of the word <u>powerful</u>. Who remembers what this word means? What do you think was so powerful that a change was brought about in the attitude of Donavan's friends and relatives who had been arguing? The key lies in the words <u>diplomacy</u> and <u>compromise</u>. What is diplomacy? How can people who disagree eventually reach a compromise?*

☆ Say: *Open your Student Workbook to Semantic Web: Effective Diplomacy. Look at the picture. Are these two people in agreement or disagreement. Let's discuss the following three steps to effective and powerful diplomacy. How do you think Donavan might use his word jar to bring about diplomacy and compromise between his neighbors?*

☆ Say: *Think of a question that you think the story will answer. Write the question at the bottom of Semantic Web: Effective Diplomacy.*

Story Reading 1: Identifying Vocabulary in Text

8–10 min.

☆ Say: *As I read the story out loud, you will follow along silently. When you see a word from our vocabulary list, give a thumbs up.*

☆ Read pages 55–71.

☆ Discuss what students predicted would happen in the story.

Day 2: Introduction

Story Reading 2: Paraphrasing Vocabulary in Text

☆ Say: *As I read specific paragraphs of the story out loud again, let's paraphrase what the author has said by using our own words. Let's focus on the first four paragraphs on page 57. Follow along as I read out loud.* Read the paragraphs (starting with " 'Miz Marylou, . . ." and ending with ". . . almost as loudly.").

☆ Say: *What's another way of saying "Miz Marylou?" We would use the word* Miss *or* Ms. *for* Miz. *What's another way of saying "I say that people who live here should set the time?"*

☆ Help students to paraphrase the remaining sentences in the passage as appropriate.

Assign At-Home 2

Say: *Tonight you will . . .*

1. *Study your flashcards.*

2. *Complete Word Substitutions.*

3. *Complete Same and Different.*

Day 3: Using Words in Context

Prepare for Lesson

☆ Materials: Student Workbooks

☆ Read Teacher Tip: Word Wizard (Week 1, page 14)

Vocabulary Review

☆ Rapid review of vocabulary words (Students use the Week 11 Word List in their Student Workbooks.)

Review At-Home 2

☆ Review the correct answers to At-Home 2.

☆ Review student work to confirm or clarify responses.

Using Context Clues

☆ Say: *Open your Student Workbook to Week 11: Using Context Clues. Today, we will use context clues to help us choose the word that fits in the blank by using the clues from other words and information in the sentence or sentences. I will read the sentences out loud. Raise your hand when you know which word best completes the sentence. Write the word in the blank. Sometimes the word might require an ending such as -ed, -s, or -ing. Each word will be used only one time.*

☆ Choose individual students to give answers. Have students point out context clues that helped them to choose the correct answer.

☆ Say: *Cross out words in the box as we use them. Write your answers in the blank, and write the context clues you used in the space below.*

Word Wizard

☆ Say: *As Word Wizards this week, you must always be on the lookout for opportunities to use and demonstrate your word knowledge. Use your Word Wizard Journals to keep track of each time you hear one of this week's vocabulary words used in a sentence at home, school, or even on television. If you don't hear the words in a sentence, be creative and write original sentences using your new vocabulary knowledge. Next week, each group will read two of their sentences to the class!*

☆ Say: *Get in your Word Wizard Groups from last week, and share your best sentences.*

☆ Say: *Which group would like to read two of their sentences using the words from Week 9's lesson?* Tally the number of sentences per group, and record the amounts on the Word Wizard Chart.

Assign At-Home 3

Say: *Tonight you will . . .*

1. *Study your flashcards.*

2. *Complete the Word Wizard Journal.*

3. *Complete the Context Clues Activity.*

Day 4: Expanding Meaning

Prepare for Lesson

☆ Materials: Student Workbooks

Vocabulary Review

☆ Rapid review of vocabulary words (Students use the Week 11 Word List in their Student Workbooks.)

Review At-Home 3

☆ Review the correct answers to At-Home 3.

☆ Review student work to confirm or clarify responses.

Multiple Meanings: *Relief, Security,* and *Exchange*

☆ Say: *Sometimes words have several meanings. For example, in Week 9, we studied different definitions for the words <u>solution</u>, <u>suggestion</u>, <u>firm</u>, and <u>gather</u>. For example, the word <u>gather</u> may mean to pick a crop or it could refer to bringing something together in a group. If you remember, the word <u>solution</u> can mean the answer to a problem, but it can also mean a mixture of two or more substances in science.*

☆ Say: *Some of the words in this week's story also have multiple meanings. Let's look at <u>relief</u>, <u>security</u>, and <u>exchange</u>. Open your Student Workbook to Multiple Meanings: <u>Relief</u>, <u>Security</u>, and <u>Exchange</u>. Let's read the definitions for these words.*

☆ Say: *Let's read sentences using these words and look for context clues that can help us to choose the correct definition.*

☆ Read the first sentence out loud. Say: *Which definition of <u>relief</u> are we using in this sentence?* The correct answer is a, a feeling of freedom from worry and pain.

☆ Say: *What context clues helped us to understand the meaning of the word?* Answers include cream and from itching.

☆ Say: *I will read each sentence out loud, and you will choose the letter of the definition that describes how the word is used in the sentence.*

Assign At-Home 4

Say: *Tonight you will . . .*

1. *Study your flashcards.*

2. *Complete the Crossword Puzzle.*

Day 5: Keys to Understanding

Prepare for Lesson

 Materials: Student Workbooks, photocopies of Assessment 11

 Read Teacher Tip: Deep Processing (Week 2, page 28)

7 min.

Review At-Home 4

☆ Review the correct answers to At-Home 4.

☆ Review student work to confirm or clarify responses.

8 min.

Bingo Game

☆ Say: *Choose nine words from the Week 11 Word List, and write them on the Bingo Card in your Student Workbook. When I read a definition, raise your hand to identify the word. If you have the word on your card, mark it with an <u>X</u>. The first person who has 3 <u>X</u>s in a row (across, down, diagonally) wins the game.*

☆ Read the definitions. As students identify definitions, write the words on the board until someone wins the game.

9–10 min.

Deep Processing

☆ Say: *Does anyone remember what <u>deep processing</u> is? It is thinking about how words relate to each other.*

☆ Say: *We have learned the definitions for this week's vocabulary words, but definitions do not really teach everything you need to know to really understand the meaning of a word. Remember, it is important to be able to use these words to describe your own experiences in life and to describe conditions in the world in general.*

☆ Say: *Open your Student Workbook to Deep Processing: <u>Donovan's Word Jar</u>, Part III. We will read each question together and decide what is a reasonable answer and why. Remember, the answers are not in the novel we read but come from your own thinking. Think about the questions and what would be a reasonable response. Remember, you must be able to explain why you chose your answer.*

25 min.

Let's Pick a Word (optional)

☆ The following steps can be used for scaffolding the writing process. Students are expected to write seven sentences about a word and how it inspires them to be a better person.

☆ **Step 1**—Review the word selected by each neighbor in *Donovan's Word Jar* and how each word inspired the neighbor to be a better person. For example, Miss Millie chose the word *boisterous*. This inspired her to speak up with confidence. To assist the review process, you may write each character's name on the board and let the students tell you which word was selected and how the word changed the character's life.

    a. Mr. Crawford (mailman): *perseverance*

    b. Miss Millie: *boisterous*

    c.   Mr. Foote: *timid*

    d.   Mr. Kincaid: *leisure*

    e.   Mr. Mike: *chortle* (to sing, chant, or laugh happily)

    f.   Donavan: *serendipity*

☆ **Step 2**—Explain that words are powerful and can make people feel better or worse. Ask students to think of a word that they have heard that made them feel self-confident or discouraged. For example, when hearing the word *industrious,* maybe someone was inspired to work really hard for a goal. On the other hand, when hearing the word *slothful,* one might feel that maybe he or she did not have the capacity to work harder or more diligently.

☆ **Step 3**—Make slips of paper with the following words and definitions on them. Place the slips of paper in a jar. Make sure that there are enough words for all students. Allow students to choose a word from a jar and to write seven sentences about how the word makes them feel. What does the word inspire them to do?

    a.   *connoisseur*—someone who knows much about a topic and appreciates the good things in life (Example: A connoisseur of good books, art, or music)

    b.   *broad-minded*—being open to new ideas and view points

    c.   *ambivalent*—to have two different opinions about something at the same time

    d.   *irresponsible*—to be reckless and refusing to take the blame for one's actions; someone who is not sensible and cannot be trusted

    e.   *futuristic*—of or relating to the future; modern

    f.   *tough-minded*—realistic in one's outlook; sensible and practical

    g.   *tenacity*—having the quality of courage (Example: Crispus Attucks was known for his tenacity during the Revolutionary War.)

    h.   *rigid*—someone who is unyielding or is not willing to change his or her opinion

    i.   *procrastinate*—to put off doing something because you do not want to do it

    j.   *enlighten*—to teach or help others to understand

☆ **Step 4**—Write the word *callous* on the board with the definition "hardened and feeling no sympathy for others." Say the following seven sentences as an example of what students could write about their words.

    a.   This is a word that I would not want to describe myself.

    b.   A callous person is one who does not feel the pain of others.

    c.   To live successfully in this world, it is important that we develop empathy and that we care about others.

    d.   A person who is callous is one who might see someone in need and choose not to do anything.

    e.   A person who is callous is insensitive and cruel.

    f.   I would like to be the opposite of callous—warmhearted.

    g.   Hearing the word callous makes me want to extend myself to others and to be careful that I am not self-centered.

☆ **Step 5**—Allow students to write seven sentences about the word chosen. Monitor to make sure each student understands the word description.

☆ **Step 6**—Students can read their paragraphs out loud on this day or on another.

☆ This is an activity that builds both oral and written vocabulary skills!

Assessment

☆ Distribute Assessment 11 to each student.

Name: _____ Date: _____

Assessment 11
Donavan's Word Jar, Part III

A. Match the word with the appropriate definition.

a) diplomacy	d) timid	g) serendipity	j) security	m) hassock
b) lounge	e) boisterous	h) delight	k) exchange	n) gruff
c) perseverance	f) leisure	i) compromise	l) stern	o) relief

_____ 1. a room for relaxation

_____ 2. a cushion or low stool

_____ 3. freedom from pain

_____ 4. a stern manner

_____ 5. great joy or happiness

B. Circle the word that does not belong.

1.	exchange	substitute	loose	trade
2.	willpower	perseverance	feeble	persistence
3.	tactlessness	diplomacy	skill	carefulness
4.	gruff	curt	pleasant	harsh
5.	calm	serene	boisterous	relaxed

C. Write the letter of the item in the blank that completes the sentences.

_____ 1. In order to get two parties to reach a compromise, a good arbitrator would
_____.

    a)   speak with diplomacy

    b)   encourage an exchange of ideas

    c)   all of the above

_____ 2. _____ might make a lounge a delightful place.

    a)   Boisterous voices

    b)   Broken hassocks

    c)   Leisure activities

_____ 3. A good president would provide _____.

    a)   national security

    b)   leisure time

    c)   illegal financial exchanges

_____ 4. A timid employee who wants relief from working with a stern boss might
_____.

    a)   ignore his work to rest his feet on a hassock

    b)   exchange heated words with his supervisor

    c)   practice the skill of diplomacy

_____ 5. By serendipity, a child might find delight in discovering _____ in a
school lounge.

    a)   two quarters

    b)   a broken soda machine

    c)   a stern teacher

Vocabulary Power, Level 1, by Latrice M. Seals, Sharolyn D. Pollard-Durodola, Barbara R. Foorman, and Ashley M. Bradley

More Stories Huey Tells
The Treasure
by Ann Cameron

DAY 1 Preview of Lesson	DAY 2 Introduction	DAY 3 Using Words in Context	DAY 4 Expanding Meaning	DAY 5 Keys to Understanding
Read New Words Say and Write New Words Read Definitions Assign At-Home 1	Vocabulary Review Review At-Home 1 Predict the Storyline Story Reading (pages 86–118) Identifying Vocabulary in Text Paraphrasing Vocabulary in Text Assign At-Home 2	Vocabulary Review Review At-Home 2 Using Context Clues Word Wizard Assign At-Home 3	Vocabulary Review Review At-Home 3 Synonyms and Antonyms Assign At-Home 4	Review At-Home 4 Bingo Game Deep Processing Be a Miner (optional) Assessment

Words and Definitions

The following are target words for this week. If the word has multiple meanings, we provide only the definition listed in the text. *Please review the definitions prior to instruction.*

1. **desert**—very dry land

2. **prospector**—a person who explores an area for minerals

3. **stake**—a pointed stick

4. **valuable**—worth a good price or a lot of money

5. **complain**—to express unhappiness or pain

6. **rot**—to break up into parts by a chemical process; to go to ruin

7. **miner**—one who digs in the earth for minerals and/or valuable materials

8. **figure**—to conclude or decide

9. **reinforcement**—something that strengthens by giving additional support

10. **clammy**—being damp, soft, sticky, and usually cool

11. **treasure**—wealth, riches, or something of great value

12. **engineer**—a designer or builder

13. **mica**—a mineral through which light can shine, which is crystal-like and can be separated into very thin leaves

14. **preserve**—to keep or save from decomposition or rotting

15. **yardstick**—a measuring stick that is 3 feet (36 inches) long

Day 1: Preview of Lesson

Prepare for Lesson

☆ Materials: Student Workbooks, *More Stories Huey Tells* by Ann Cameron, display copy of Week 12 Word List

☆ Read Teacher Tip: Reading New Words (Week 1, page 8)

Read New Words

5 min.

☆ Say: *Today, we will begin a new story, "The Treasure." Remember, on Day 1 we learn to read new words that you will study at home. The words we learn will help you to read this story better and will help you to express your thoughts on paper and when talking to others. Let's see if there are any words that you already know.*

☆ Display the Week 12 Word List. Cover the bottom box, leaving the word columns at the top of page exposed. Say: *Which of the words do you already know?*

☆ Uncover the bottom box. Say: *Let's read these words. Sound out each syllable as I point to it. Be sure to say each sound clearly. Sound it out.*

☆ Students sound out each syllable. Say the word. Students repeat the word. Say: *Yes, the word is . . . .*

Say and Write New Words

10 min.

☆ Cover bottom box and use the word columns at the top of the page.

☆ Say: *Let's read the words together.* Point to each word, and read one time.

☆ Say: *Take out your pencil and Student Workbook. Find the page that says Week 12: Say and Write New Words. Let's get ready to say and write each word.*

☆ Point to each word. Say: *What word?* Students say the word. *Write [the word].*

☆ Students write the word on the appropriate line. Continue until all words are written.

Read Definitions

5 min.

☆ Say: *I will read the definitions so that we will understand what each word means. Some words have more than one meaning; however, these are the definitions that are used in the story.*

☆ Read the definitions out loud as students read silently. Choose a student to read each sentence.

Week 12 Word List

deser**t**	ro**t**	treasu**re**
prospec**tor**	min**er**	engineer
sta**ke**	figu**re**	mica
valuable	reinforcemen**t**	preser**ve**
complai**n**	clammy	yardsti**ck**

1. des er**t**
2. pros pec**t**
   pros pec **tor**
3. sta**ke**
4. val ue
   val u a ble
5. com plai**n**
6. ro**t**
7. mine
   min **er**

8. fig u**re**
9. re in force
   re in force men**t**
10. clam my
11. trea su**re**
12. en gi neer
13. mi ca
14. pre ser**ve**
15. yard sti**ck**

153

Definitions

1. **desert** (very dry land)
    When traveling in the Sahara <u>Desert</u>, one has to carry quite a bit of water because the air and land are very dry in that environment.

2. **prospector** (a person who explores an area for minerals)
    Thirty thousand <u>prospector</u>s traveled to Canada's Yukon Territory in the 1898 Gold Rush, but only a few actually found gold.

3. **stake** (a pointed stick)
    Sam hammered a <u>stake</u> into the ground to mark the spot where he wanted to plant the oak tree.

4. **valuable** (worth a good price or a lot of money)
    Jimmy is saving his baseball cards in hopes that one day they will be <u>valuable</u> and he can sell them to a collector for a good price.

5. **complain** (to express unhappiness or pain)
    Roderick <u>complain</u>s constantly about his headache.

6. **rot** (to break up into parts by a chemical process; to go to ruin)
    If an apple falls from a tree and no one picks it up for days, it will soon <u>rot</u> and no longer be good for eating.

7. **miner** (one who digs in the earth for minerals and/or valuable materials)
    Howard's uncle worked as a <u>miner</u> in Argentina, digging for silver that was later used to make jewelry.

8. **figure** (to conclude or decide)
    I've thought about this for a while, and I <u>figure</u> if we leave the house at 1:45, we will make it to the airport in time for our flight.

9. **reinforcement** (something that strengthens by giving additional support)
    The knee of Bobby's jeans was wearing thin, so his mother sewed a patch on as a <u>reinforcement</u> to keep the jeans from ripping.

10. **clammy** (being damp, soft, sticky, and usually cool)
    Jackie's hands are always wet and <u>clammy</u> when she is nervous before a test.

11. **treasure** (wealth, riches, or something of great value)
    It is rumored that pirates who robbed wealthy merchants out at sea would then bury their <u>treasure</u> on this very beach.

12. **engineer** (a designer or builder)
    The <u>engineer</u> of this building was very clever to figure out how to build such a wide-open lobby without columns or walls for support.

13. **mica** (a mineral through which light can shine, which is crystal-like and can be separated into very thin leaves)
    While hiking on Pike's Peak in Colorado, Erin saw many flaky pieces of <u>mica</u> laying along the trail, reflecting the sunlight.

14. **preserve** (to keep or save from decomposition or rotting)
     I bought a special photo album with acid-free pages so that I can <u>preserve</u> my pictures and memories for a very long time.

15. **yardstick** (a measuring stick that is 3 feet [36 inches] long)
     In math class, we used a <u>yardstick</u> to measure the length and width of the classroom.

Assign At-Home 1

Say: *Tonight you will . . .*

1. *Study the vocabulary words with definitions.*

2. *Complete the Riddle Page.*

3. *Do the Matching Activity.*

4. *Make flashcards.*

Prepare for Lesson

☆ Materials: Student Workbooks, *More Stories Huey Tells* by Ann Cameron

3 min.

Vocabulary Review

☆ Rapid review of vocabulary words (Students use the Week 12 Word List in their Student Workbooks.)

7 min.

Review At-Home 1

☆ Review the correct answers to At-Home 1.

☆ Review student work to confirm or clarify responses.

8 min.

Predict the Storyline

☆ Students look at the illustration on page 86 of *More Stories Huey Tells* by Ann Cameron.

☆ Say: *Today we will begin reading a new story from <u>More Stories Huey Tells</u>. This chapter is called "The Treasure." This is the last chapter in the book. In "The Treasure," Julian, Gloria, and Huey decide to become prospectors and search for gold. Why do you think the chapter is called, "The Treasure"? Let's talk about searching for treasures.*

☆ Say: *Open your Student Workbook to Semantic Web: Treasures. What kinds of treasure can you think of? Who searches for treasure? What equipment do they need? Where do they look for treasure?*

☆ Say: *Are treasures always objects? Can people be treasures? Name some of the people in your life who are like a valuable treasure.*

☆ Say: *Think of a question that you think the story will answer. Write the question at the bottom of Semantic Web: Treasures.*

8–10 min.

Story Reading 1: Identifying Vocabulary in Text

☆ Say: *As I read the story out loud, you will follow along silently. When you see a word from our vocabulary list, give a thumbs up.*

☆ Read pages 86–118.

☆ Discuss what students predicted would happen in the story.

6 min.

Story Reading 2: Paraphrasing Vocabulary in Text

☆ Say: *As I read specific paragraphs of the story out loud again, let's paraphrase what the author has said by using our own words. Let's focus on the middle paragraph on page 87. Follow along as I read out loud.* Read the paragraph ("I saw a place just like this . . .").

☆ Say: *What's another way of saying, "An old prospector made camp"? We might say, "A man who was looking for gold set up a tent."*

☆ Help students to paraphrase the remaining sentences in the paragraph as appropriate.

Day 2: Introduction

Assign At-Home 2

Say: *Tonight you will . . .*

1. *Study your flashcards.*

2. *Complete Word Substitutions.*

3. *Complete Same and Different.*

Day 3: Using Words in Context

Prepare for Lesson

☆ Materials: Student Workbooks

☆ Read Teacher Tip: Word Wizard (Week 1, page 14)

3 min.

Vocabulary Review

☆ Rapid review of vocabulary words. (Students use the Week 12 Word List in their Student Workbooks.)

7 min.

Review At-Home 2

☆ Review the correct answers to At-Home 2.

☆ Review student work to confirm or clarify responses.

15 min.

Using Context Clues

☆ Say: *Open your Student Workbook to Week 12: Using Context Clues. Today, we will use context clues to help us choose the word that fits in the blank by using the clues from other words and information in the sentence or sentences. I will read the sentences out loud. Raise your hand when you know which word best completes the sentence. Write the word in the blank. Sometimes the word might require an ending such as -ed, -s, or -ing. Each word will be used only one time.*

☆ Choose individual students to give answers. Have students point out context clues that helped them to choose the correct answer.

☆ Say: *Cross out words in the box as we use them. Write your answers in the blank, and write the context clues you used in the space below.*

5 min.

Word Wizard

☆ Say: *As Word Wizards this week, you must always be on the lookout for opportunities to use and demonstrate your word knowledge. Use your Word Wizard Journals to keep track of each time you hear one of this week's vocabulary words used in a sentence at home, school, or even on television. If you don't hear the words used in a sentence, be creative and write original sentences using your new vocabulary knowledge. Next week, each group will read two of their favorite sentences to the class!*

☆ Say: *Get in your Word Wizard Groups from last week, and share your best sentences.*

☆ Say: *Which group would like to read two of their sentences using the words from last week's lesson?* Tally the number of sentences per group, and record the amount on the Word Wizard Chart.

Assign At-Home 3

Say: *Tonight you will . . .*

1. *Study your flashcards.*

2. *Complete the Word Wizard Journal.*

3. *Complete the Context Clues Activity.*

Day 4: Expanding Meaning

Prepare for Lesson

 Materials: Student Workbooks

Vocabulary Review

3 min.

 Rapid review of vocabulary words (Students use the Week 12 Word List in their Student Workbooks.)

Review At-Home 3

7 min.

 Review the correct answers to At-Home 3.

☆ Review student work to confirm or clarify responses.

Synonyms and Antonyms

20 min.

☆ Say: *You have learned many new words this week. You might have noticed when using context clues yesterday that some words have the same meaning and some words are opposite in meaning. What do we call words that have the same meaning?* The answer is synonyms. *What do we call words that are opposite in meaning?* The answer is antonyms.

☆ Say: *In Week 7, we learned several synonyms for the word* <u>protect</u>. *Can anyone tell us a synonym for* <u>protect</u>? Answers include shelter and guard. *Can someone give us an antonym for* <u>protect</u>? Answers include injure and damage.

☆ Say: *Today, we will learn to express ideas with words that are the same or opposite in meaning. We will concentrate on four words from our vocabulary list.*

☆ Say: *Open your Student Workbook to Week 12: Synonyms and Antonyms. This worksheet has sentences that you took home at the beginning of the week. Let's look at how we can rewrite some of these sentences to express ideas that are opposite or same in meaning.*

☆ Say: *I will read the original sentence with the underlined word and the definition. Then, we will read the synonym or antonym sentences together. Remember, not every word has a synonym or antonym.* Read and discuss examples.

☆ Say: *Let's read a story about a boy named Sam. In the story, we will use synonyms and antonyms that we have learned today. First, I will read the story out loud. Then, I will read the story again. When you figure out what goes in the blank, raise your hand during the second reading of the story.*

Assign At-Home 4

Say: *Tonight you will . . .*

1. *Study your flashcards.*

2. *Complete the Crossword Puzzle.*

Day 5: Keys to Understanding

Prepare for Lesson

☆ Materials: Student Workbooks, photocopies of Assessment 12

☆ Read Teacher Tip: Deep Processing (Week 2, page 28)

7 min.

Review At-Home 4

☆ Review the correct answers to At-Home 4.

☆ Review student work to confirm or clarify responses.

8 min.

Bingo Game

☆ Say: *Choose nine words from the Week 12 Word List, and write them on the Bingo Card in your Student Workbook. When I read a definition, raise your hand to identify the word. If you have the word on your card, mark it with an X. The first person who has 3 Xs in a row (across, down, diagonally) wins the game.*

☆ Read the definitions. As students identify definitions, write the words on the board until someone wins the game.

12 min.

Deep Processing

☆ Say: *Does anyone remember what deep processing is? It is thinking about how words relate to each other.*

☆ Say: *We have learned the definitions for this week's vocabulary words, but definitions do not really teach everything you need to know to really understand the meaning of a word. Remember, it is important to be able to use these words to describe your own experiences in life and to describe conditions in the world in general.*

☆ Say: *Open your Student Workbook to Deep Processing: More Stories Huey Tells. We will read each question together and decide what is a reasonable answer and why. Remember, the answers are not in the novel we read but come from your own thinking. Think about the questions and about what would be a reasonable response. Remember, you must be able to explain why you chose your answer.*

20 min.

Be a Miner (optional)

☆ Students use a dictionary and/or encyclopedia to categorize gemstones by color.

10 min.

Assessment

☆ Distribute Assessment 12 to each student.

Name: _____ Date: _____

Assessment 12
More Stories Huey Tells
The Treasure

A. Match the word with the appropriate definition.

a) desert	d) prospector	g) stake	j) valuable	m) complain
b) rot	e) miner	h) figure	k) reinforcement	n) clammy
c) treasure	f) engineer	i) mica	l) preserve	o) yardstick

_____ 1. a mineral that is crystal-like

_____ 2. to decay, to ruin

_____ 3. riches, great wealth

_____ 4. a pointed stick that is driven into the ground as a support

_____ 5. to consider, to decide

B. Circle the word or phrase that does not belong.

1.	yardstick	measuring tape	inches	ruler
2.	praise	grumble	complain	fuss
3.	destroy	damage	rot	preserve
4.	clammy	dry	damp	sticky
5.	valuable	precious	important	worthless

Vocabulary Power, Level 1, by Latrice M. Seals, Sharolyn D. Pollard-Durodola, Barbara R. Foorman, and Ashley M. Bradley

C. Complete the sentence with the best answer.

_____ 1. The prospector used _____ in her search for gold.

    a) needle, thread, and a sewing machine

    b) maps, books, and computers

    c) a fork, knife, and spoon

_____ 2. A stake might be used with _____.

    a) signs and tents

    b) apples and oranges

    c) books and magazines

_____ 3. An engineer is valuable because he or she know how to _____.

    a) take care of animals

    b) sell materials to the right person

    c) use the right materials in the best way

_____ 4. Reinforcements might be needed for _____.

    a) batteries that work well in a watch

    b) the torn elbows of a jacket

    c) a new car

_____ 5. A miner might complain about working in _____.

    a) a hot desert

    b) someone's backyard

    c) a swimming pool

Vocabulary Power, Level 1, by Latrice M. Seals, Sharolyn D. Pollard-Durodola, Barbara R. Foorman, and Ashley M. Bradley

Five Notable Inventors
Jan Ernst Matzeliger
by Wade Hudson

DAY 1 Preview of Lesson	DAY 2 Introduction	DAY 3 Using Words in Context	DAY 4 Expanding Meaning	DAY 5 Keys to Understanding
Read New Words Say and Write New Words Read Definitions Assign At-Home 1	Vocabulary Review Review At-Home 1 Predict the Storyline Story Reading (pages 5–13) Identifying Vocabulary in Text Paraphrasing Vocabulary in Text Assign At-Home 2	Vocabulary Review Review At-Home 2 Using Context Clues Word Wizard Assign At-Home 3	Vocabulary Review Review At-Home 3 Word Roots: *Fac* Assign At-Home 4	Review At-Home 4 Bingo Game Deep Processing A Pair of (optional) Assessment

Words and Definitions

The following are target words for this week. If the word has multiple meanings, we provide only the definition listed in the text. ***Please review the definitions prior to instruction.***

1. **inventor**—a person who produces something for the first time
2. **pair**— two things designed for use together
3. **operator**—one who controls a machine
4. **hire**—to provide with a job that pays a salary; to employ
5. **shop**—a business for the making or repair of goods or machinery
6. **sole**—the bottom part of a shoe
7. **factory**—a building where products are manufactured or made
8. **finished**—complete
9. **patent**—a writing that guarantees an inventor the right to make, use, or sell an invention
10. **share**—an equal interest or right into which the capital stock (money) of a corporation is divided; a portion
11. **metal**—a material that is shiny and allows electricity and heat to flow through it (for example, iron, gold, and aluminum)
12. **industry**—a department of a craft or large manufacturing business
13. **union**—people joined together in support of better working conditions
14. **scrap**—manufactured materials or parts (such as metal) that have been rejected and thrown away
15. **model**—a small version of something to be made

Day 1: Preview of Lesson

Prepare for Lesson

☆ Materials: Student Workbooks, *Five Notable Inventors* by Wade Hudson, display copy of Week 13 Word List

☆ Read Teacher Tip: Reading New Words (Week 1, page 8)

Read New Words

5 min.

☆ Say: *Today, we will begin a new story, "Jan Ernst Matzeliger," from a new book called* Five Notable Inventors. *Remember, on Day 1 we learn to read new words that you will study at home. The words we learn will help you to read this story better and will help you to express your thoughts on paper and when talking to others. Let's see if there are any words that you already know.*

☆ Display the Week 13 Word List. Cover the bottom box, leaving the word columns at the top of page exposed. Say: *Which words do you already know?*

☆ Uncover the bottom box. Say: *Let's read these words. Sound out each syllable as I point to it. Be sure to say each sound clearly. Sound it out.*

☆ Students sound out each syllable. Say the word. Students repeat the word. Say: *Yes, the word is . . . .*

Say and Write New Words

10 min.

☆ Cover the bottom box and use the word columns at the top of the page.

☆ Say: *Let's read the words together.* Point to each word, and read one time.

☆ Say: *Take out your pencil and Student Workbook. Find the page that says Week 13: Say and Write New Words. Let's get ready to say and write each word.*

☆ Point to each word. Say: *What word?* Students say the word. *Write [the word].*

☆ Students write the word on the appropriate line. Continue until all words are written.

Read Definitions

5 min.

☆ Say: *I will read the definitions so that we will understand what each word means. Some words have more than one meaning; however, these are the definitions that are used in the story.*

☆ Read the definitions out loud as students read silently. Choose a student to read each sentence.

Definitions

1. **inventor** (a person who produces something for the first time)
   Thomas Edison was the <u>inventor</u> of the electric lightbulb.

2. **pair** (two things designed for use together)
   Julian received a new <u>pair</u> of shoes for his birthday.

Week 13 Word List

inventor	sole	metal
pair	factory	industry
operator	finished	union
hire	patent	scrap
shop	share	model

1. in ven tor
2. pair
3. op er ate
   op er a tor
4. hire
5. shop
6. sole
   soles
7. fac to ry

8. fin ish
   fin ished
9. pat ent
10. share
11. met al
12. in dus try
13. un ion
14. scrap
15. mod el

3. **operator** (one who controls a machine)
    At the carnival, the Ferris wheel <u>operator</u> waited until all of the chairs were filled before he started the ride.

4. **hire** (to provide with a job that pays a salary; to employ)
    The company is growing so much that the boss will <u>hire</u> two new employees next month.

5. **shop** (a business for the making or repair of goods or machinery)
    Mrs. Lincoln took her car to the mechanic's <u>shop</u> for repairs.

6. **sole** (the bottom part of a shoe)
    The <u>sole</u> of Jeff's left shoe is wearing thin because he always scuffs it along the ground when he walks.

7. **factory** (a building where products are manufactured or made)
    The BMW <u>factory</u> in Dingolfing, Germany, produces 280,000 cars annually.

8. **finished** (complete)
    Even though I knew the <u>finished</u> product would be a beautiful, hand-painted vase, it was hard to believe that a lump of clay could turn into anything attractive.

9. **patent** (a writing that guarantees an inventor the right to make, use, or sell an invention)
    If you ever come up with a good idea for a product, be sure to get a <u>patent</u> so that no one else can take credit for your idea.

10. **share** (an equal interest or right into which the capital stock [money] of a corporation is divided; a portion)
    Workers at Shop Now grocery stores each receive a <u>share</u> in the company so that they will feel ownership and responsibility for the place where they work.

11. **metal** (a material that is shiny and allows electricity and heat to flow through it [for example, iron, gold, and aluminum])
    The scientist heated the <u>metal</u> and hammered it until it was formed into a U-shaped horseshoe.

12. **industry** (a department of a craft or large manufacturing business)
    Many people think of Detroit as America's car <u>industry</u> capital because so many cars are manufactured and sold there.

13. **union** (people joined together in support of better working conditions)
    "Newsies," the boys who sold newspapers on street corners, finally started to make a decent amount of money after the newspaper <u>union</u> fought for higher wages.

14. **scrap** (manufactured materials or parts [such as metal] that have been rejected and thrown away)
    Barney collects <u>scrap</u> metal from the junkyard, then recycles it for money.

15. **model** (a small version of something to be made)
    Ricky just built an airplane <u>model</u> to add to the collection of miniature planes hanging from his ceiling.

Day 1: Preview of Lesson

Assign At-Home 1

Say: *Tonight you will . . .*

1.   *Study the vocabulary words with definitions.*

2.   *Complete the Riddle Page.*

3.   *Do the Matching Activity.*

4.   *Make flashcards.*

Day 2: Introduction

Prepare for Lesson

☆ Materials: Student Workbooks, *Five Notable Inventors* by Wade Hudson

3 min.

Vocabulary Review

☆ Rapid review of vocabulary words (Students use the Week 13 Word List in their Student Workbooks.)

7 min.

Review At-Home 1

☆ Review the correct answers to At-Home 1.

☆ Review student work to confirm or clarify responses.

8 min.

Predict the Storyline

☆ Students look at the illustration on page 4 of *Five Notable Inventors* by Wade Hudson.

☆ Say: *Today we will begin reading a new story from <u>Five Notable Inventors</u>. This chapter is called "Jan Ernst Matzeliger" and says "He made shoes to last." Why do you think it is called this? What does it mean to make shoes to last?*

☆ Say: *Open your Student Workbook to Semantic Web: Shoes. What kinds of shoes can you think of? Who makes shoes? What are the parts of a shoe? What equipment is needed for shoemaking?*

☆ Say: *Think of a question that you think the story will answer. Write the question at the bottom of Semantic Web: Shoes.*

10 min.

Story Reading 1: Identifying Vocabulary in Text

☆ Say: *As I read the story out loud, you will follow along silently. When you see a word from our vocabulary list, give a thumbs up.*

☆ Read pages 5–13.

☆ Discuss what students predicted would happen in the story.

6 min.

Story Reading 2: Paraphrasing Vocabulary in Text

☆ Say: *As I read specific paragraphs of the story out loud again, let's paraphrase what the author has said by using our own words. Let's focus on the second paragraph on page 6. Follow along as I read out loud.* Read the paragraph ("At the age of 19 . . .").

☆ Say: *What's another way of saying, "At the age of 19, Jan became a seaman?" We might say, "When he was 19, Jan sailed."*

☆ Help students to paraphrase the remaining sentences in the paragraph as appropriate.

Assign At-Home 2

Say: *Tonight you will . . .*

1. *Study your flashcards.*

2. *Complete Word Substitutions.*

3. *Complete Same and Different.*

Day 3: Using Words in Context

Prepare for Lesson

☆ Materials: Student Workbooks

☆ Read Teacher Tip: Word Wizard (Week 1, page 14)

3 min.

Vocabulary Review

☆ Rapid review of vocabulary words. (Students use the Week 13 Word List in their Student Workbooks.)

7 min.

Review At-Home 2

☆ Review the correct answers to At-Home 2.

☆ Review student work to confirm or clarify responses.

15 min.

Using Context Clues

☆ Say: *Open your Student Workbook to Week 13: Using Context Clues. Today, we will use context clues to help us choose the word that fits in the blank by using the clues from other words and information in the sentence or sentences. I will read the sentences out loud. Raise your hand when you know which word best completes the sentence. Write the word in the blank. Sometimes the word might require an ending such as -ed, -s, or -ing. Each word will be used only one time.*

☆ Choose individual students to give answers. Have students point out context clues that helped them to choose the correct answer.

☆ Say: *Cross out words in the box as we use them. Write your answers in the blank, and write the context clues you used in the space below.*

5 min.

Word Wizard

☆ Say: *As Word Wizards this week, you must always be on the lookout for opportunities to use and demonstrate your word knowledge. Use your Word Wizard Journals to keep track of each time you hear one of this week's vocabulary words used in a sentence at home, school, or even on television. If you don't hear the words used in a sentence, be creative and write original sentences using your new vocabulary knowledge. Next week, each group will read two of their favorite sentences to the class!*

☆ Say: *Get in your Word Wizard Groups from last week, and share your best sentences.*

☆ Say: *Which group would like to read two of their sentences using the words from last week's lesson?* Tally the number of sentences per group, and record the amount on the Word Wizard Chart.

Assign At-Home 3

Say: *Tonight you will . . .*

1. *Study your flashcards.*

2. *Complete the Word Wizard Journal.*

3. *Complete the Context Clues Activity.*

Day 4: Expanding Meaning

Prepare for Lesson

☆ Materials: Student Workbooks

☆ Read Teacher Tip: Word Roots (Week 8, page 106)

3 min. Vocabulary Review

☆ Rapid review of vocabulary words. (Students use the Week 13 Word List in their Student Workbooks.)

7 min. Review At-Home 3

☆ Review the correct answers to At-Home 3.

☆ Review student work to confirm or clarify responses.

20 min. Word Roots: *Fac*

☆ Say: *Open your Student Workbook to Word Roots: Fac. Do you remember what a word root is?* Call on a student. *That's right. Roots are small word units in words that come from other languages like Latin or Greek. They help us to figure out the meaning of a word.*

☆ Say: *Today, we will look at the word root fac. Fac is a Latin word root, and it means to do or to make. When we define words using the definition of the word root, it does not always exactly match the actual definition. However, the root can help us understand the meaning of an unfamiliar word.*

☆ Say: *Let's look at Word Root: Fac. We are going to define words containing the word fac. Repeat these words after me: factory, fact, satisfaction, manufacture, and benefactor. Who can tell us the meaning of factory? Fact? Satisfaction? Manufacture? Benefactor? Using the word root, fac, let's read each sentence and write what you think the word means.*

☆ Once all five words have been defined, quickly review the actual word meaning, and ask students if the definitions that they wrote matched the dictionary definitions.

☆ Say: *Let's see how close we are to the actual meaning of the words.*

Dictionary Definitions

1. **factory**—a building where products are made

2. **fact**—something that is done

3. **satisfaction**—to make one's needs or wants fulfilled

4. **manufacture**—the process of making something by hand or machine

5. **benefactor**—a person who makes a charitable gift or donation

Day 4: Expanding Meaning

Assign At-Home 4

Say: *Tonight you will . . .*

1. *Study your flashcards.*

2. *Complete the Crossword Puzzle.*

Day 5: Keys to Understanding

Prepare for Lesson

☆ Materials: Student Workbooks, photocopies of Assessment 13

☆ Read Teacher Tip: Deep Processing (Week 2, page 28)

7 min. | Review At Home 4

☆ Review the correct answers to At-Home 4.

☆ Review student work to confirm or clarify responses.

8 min. | Bingo Game

☆ Say: *Choose nine words from the Week 13 Word List, and write them on the Bingo Card in your Student Workbook. When I read a definition, raise your hand to identify the word. If you have the word on your card, mark it with an X. The first person who has 3 Xs in a row (across, down, diagonally) wins the game.*

☆ Read the definitions. As students identify definitions, write the words on the board until someone wins the game.

12 min. | Deep Processing

☆ Say: *Does anyone remember what <u>deep processing</u> is? It is thinking about how words relate to each other.*

☆ Say: *We have learned the definitions for this week's vocabulary words, but definitions do not really teach everything you need to know to really understand the meaning of a word. Remember, it is important to be able to use these words to describe your own experiences in life and to describe conditions in the world in general.*

☆ Say: *Open your Student Workbook to Deep Processing: <u>Five Notable Inventors</u>: Jan Ernst Matzeliger. We will read each question together and decide what is a reasonable answer and why. Remember, the answers are not in the novel we read but come from your own thinking. Think about the questions and about what would be a reasonable response. Remember, you must be able to explain why you chose your answer.*

25 min. | A Pair of (optional)

☆ The word *pair* is used to describe a group of two objects. In this activity, students read other words that describe a collection or group of objects.

10 min. | Assessment

☆ Distribute Assessment 13 to each student.

Name: _____ Date: _____

Assessment 13
Five Notable Inventors
Jan Ernst Matzeliger

A. Match the word with the appropriate definition.

a) inventor	d) hire	g) factory	j) share	m) union
b) pair	e) shop	h) finished	k) metal	n) scrap
c) operator	f) soles	i) patent	l) industry	o) model

_____ 1.   a branch of a large, manufacturing business

_____ 2.   a person whose job is to control a machine

_____ 3.   a person who creates something for the first time

_____ 4.   two things designed for use together

_____ 5.   a document that guarantees an inventor the right to make, use, or sell an invention

B. Circle the word that does not belong.

1.	pair	couple	twosome	one
2.	factory	shop	store	restaurant
3.	begin	finish	complete	cease
4.	fire	terminate	release	hire
5.	model	copy	imitation	original

C. Complete the sentence with the best answer.

_____ 1. When I stepped on the sticky gum on the floor, the soles of my shoes
_____.

    a) remained glued to the wooden surface

    b) slid across the room

    c) made a hole in the surface

_____ 2. My best friend and I had a lemonade stand during the summer. We hired
_____ to help finish our sales.

    a) telephone operators

    b) factory workers

    c) our relatives

_____ 3. I wanted to be an inventor so I used metal scraps to _____.

    a) build a fire

    b) design a new go cart

    c) repair my old bike

_____ 4. Most people trade shares of a company for _____.

    a) pizza

    b) books

    c) money

_____ 5. The union at the factory said that workers should _____.

    a) be covered by health insurance

    b) be fired without pay

    c) should work throughout the weekend

Five Notable Inventors
Madam C. J. Walker
by Wade Hudson

DAY 1 Preview of Lesson	DAY 2 Introduction	DAY 3 Using Words in Context	DAY 4 Expanding Meaning	DAY 5 Keys to Understanding
Read New Words	Vocabulary Review	Vocabulary Review	Vocabulary Review	Review At-Home 4
Say and Write New Words	Review At-Home 1	Review At-Home 2	Review At-Home 3	Bingo Game
Read Definitions	Predict the Storyline	Using Context Clues	Morphographic Elements: -ment	Word Roots: Duc
Assign At-Home 1	Story Reading (pages 31–39)	Word Wizard	Assign At-Home 4	A Cure for the Common Cold (optional)
	Identifying Vocabulary in Text	Assign At-Home 3		Assessment
	Paraphrasing Vocabulary in Text			
	Assign At-Home 2			

Words and Definitions

The following are target words for this week. If the word has multiple meanings, we provide only the definition listed in the text. ***Please review the definitions prior to instruction.***

1. **common**—happening frequently or often; familiar
2. **product**—something created or made
3. **harvest**—the season for gathering in a crop
4. **establish**—to bring into existence; to found; to start
5. **fever**—a rise of body temperature above normal or a disease with this symptom
6. **mixture**—a combination of several different kinds of ingredients
7. **attic**—a room or space right below the roof of a building
8. **demonstration**—a showing of the merits or good points of a product to a possible buyer
9. **laboratory**—a place equipped and furnished for conducting tests or experiments
10. **object**—goal or purpose of an effort or activity
11. **donate**—to make a gift, especially to a charity or an organization
12. **cure**—recovery or relief from a disease
13. **ingredients**—the individual parts in a mixture or a recipe
14. **training**—the process or method of teaching someone a new skill or new knowledge
15. **treatment**—the act of caring for a medical problem

Day 1: Preview of Lesson

Prepare for Lesson

☆ Materials: Student Workbooks, *Five Notable Inventors* by Wade Hudson, display copy of Week 14 Word List

☆ Read Teacher Tip: Reading New Words (Week 1, page 8)

 ## Read New Words

☆ Say: *Today, we will begin a new story, "Madam C. J. Walker." Remember, on Day 1 we learn to read new words that you will study at home. The words we learn will help you to read this story better and will help you to express your thoughts on paper and when talking to others. Let's see if there are any words that you already know.*

☆ Display the Week 14 Word List. Cover the bottom box, leaving the word columns at the top of the page exposed. Say: *Which words do you already know?*

☆ Uncover the bottom box. Say: *Let's read these words. Sound out each syllable as I point to it. Be sure to say each sound clearly. Sound it out.*

☆ Students sound out each syllable. Say the word. Students repeat the word. Say: *Yes, the word is . . . .*

 ## Say and Write New Words

☆ Cover the bottom box and use the word columns at the top of the page.

☆ Say: *Let's read the words together.* Point to each word and read one time.

☆ Say: *Take out your pencil and Student Workbook. Find the page that says Week 14: Say and Write New Words. Let's get ready to say and write each word.*

☆ Point to each word. Say: *What word?* Students say the word. *Write [the word].*

☆ Students write the word on the appropriate line. Continue until all words are written.

 ## Read Definitions

☆ Say: *I will read the definitions so that we will understand what each word means. Some words have more than one meaning; however, these are the definitions that are used in the story.*

☆ Read the definitions out loud as students read silently. Choose a student to read each sentence.

Week 14 Word List

commo**n**	mixtu**re**	dona**te**
produc**t**	atti**c**	cure
harves**t**	demonstra**tion**	ingredien**ts**
establi**sh**	laborato**ry**	trainin**g**
feve**r**	objec**t**	treatmen**t**

1. com mo**n**
2. prod uc**t**
3. har ves**t**
4. es tab li**sh**
5. fe ve**r**
6. mix tu**re**
7. at ti**c**
8. dem on stra**te**
   dem on stra **tion**
9. lab o ra to **ry**
10. ob jec**t**
11. do na**te**
12. cure
13. in gre di en**ts**
14. train
    train in**g**
15. treat men**t**

Vocabulary Power, Level 1, by Latrice M. Seals, Sharolyn D. Pollard-Durodola, Barbara R. Foorman, and Ashley M. Bradley

Definitions

1. **common** (happening frequently or often; familiar)
   Seattle is thought of as a wet city because rain is very <u>common</u>.

2. **product** (something created or made)
   The Frito-Lay company makes many different chip <u>product</u>s.

3. **harvest** (the season for gathering in a crop)
   When the <u>harvest</u> time for cotton arrives, workers spend their days picking the soft, woolly boll from the plant.

4. **establish** (to bring into existence; to found; to start)
   Ella wants to open or <u>establish</u> her own beauty parlor when she finishes cosmetology school.

5. **fever** (a rise of the body temperature above normal or a disease with this symptom)
   Hope's father realized she had a <u>fever</u> when he measured her temperature and it was 5 degrees above normal.

6. **mixture** (a combination of several different kinds of ingredients)
   Marge made a delicious smoothie drink, which was a <u>mixture</u> of apple juice, milk, bananas, and strawberries.

7. **attic** (a room or space right below the roof of a building)
   The <u>attic</u> of our house becomes hot in the summer because it is right under the roof and has no air conditioning.

8. **demonstration** (a showing of the merits or good points of a product to a potential buyer)
   The vacuum salesman gave Mr. and Mrs. Wright a <u>demonstration</u> of his superior product by cleaning up spilled grape juice and mud with the vacuum cleaner he was trying to sell to them.

9. **laboratory** (a place equipped and furnished for conducting tests or experiments)
   The scientist experimented with some new chemicals in his <u>laboratory</u>.

10. **object** (goal or purpose of an effort or activity)
    The <u>object</u> of this lesson is for you to learn 15 new words by the end of the week.

11. **donate** (to make a gift, especially to a charity or an organization)
    Mr. Garcia won the lottery and decided to <u>donate</u> half of his money to his church.

12. **cure** (recovery or relief from a disease)
    Owen took some aspirin as a <u>cure</u> for his pounding headache.

13. **ingredients** (the individual parts in a mixture or a recipe)
    Chocolate milk only has two <u>ingredients</u>: milk and chocolate syrup.

14. **training** (the process or method of teaching someone a new skill or new knowledge)
    Joseph went to a 9-week <u>training</u> program to learn how to be a flight attendant.

15. **treatment** (the act of caring for a medical problem)
    The recommended <u>treatment</u> for dandruff is to use a medicated anti-itch shampoo.

Day 1: Preview of Lesson

Assign At-Home 1

Say: *Tonight you will . . .*

1. *Study the vocabulary words with definitions.*

2. *Complete the Riddle Page.*

3. *Do the Matching Activity.*

4. *Make flashcards.*

Day 2: Introduction

Prepare for Lesson

☆ Materials: Student Workbooks, *Five Notable Inventors* by Wade Hudson

Vocabulary Review

☆ Rapid review of vocabulary words (Students use the Week 14 Word List in their Student Workbooks.)

Review At-Home 1

☆ Review the correct answers to At-Home 1.

☆ Review student work to confirm or clarify responses.

Predict the Storyline

☆ Students look at the illustration on page 30 of *Five Notable Inventors* by Wade Hudson.

☆ Say: *Today we will begin reading a new story from* Five Notable Inventors. *This chapter is called "Madam C. J. Walker" and says "A Millionaire Inventor." What is a millionaire?*

☆ Say: *Open your Student Workbook to Semantic Web: Millionaires. What famous millionaires can you name? How can someone become a millionaire? What do some rich people donate their money to? What are some words that describe millionaires?*

☆ Say: *Think of a question that you think the story will answer. Write the question at the bottom of Semantic Web: Millionaires.*

Story Reading 1: Identifying Vocabulary in Text

☆ Say: *As I read the story out loud, you will follow along silently. When you see a word from our vocabulary list, give a thumbs up.*

☆ Read pages 31–39.

☆ Discuss what students predicted would happen in the story.

Story Reading 2: Paraphrasing Vocabulary in Text

☆ Say: *As I read specific paragraphs of the story out loud again, let's paraphrase what the author has said by using our own words. Let's focus on the first paragraph on page 31. Follow along as I read out loud.* Read the paragraph ("A common problem helped . . .").

☆ Say: *What's another way of saying, "A common problem?" We might say, "One ordinary problem."*

☆ Help students to paraphrase the remaining sentences in the paragraph as appropriate.

Assign At-Home 2

Say: *Tonight you will . . .*

1. *Study your flashcards.*

2. *Complete Word Substitutions.*

3. *Complete Same and Different.*

Day 3: Using Words in Context

Prepare for Lesson

 Materials: Student Workbooks

 Read Teacher Tip: Word Wizard (Week 1, page 14)

3 min.
Vocabulary Review

 Rapid review of vocabulary words (Students use the Week 14 Word List in their Student Workbooks.)

7 min.
Review At-Home 2

 Review the correct answers to At-Home 2.

 Review student work to confirm or clarify responses.

15 min.
Using Context Clues

 Say: *Open your Student Workbook to Week 14: Using Context Clues. Today, we will use context clues to help us choose the word that fits in the blank by using the clues from other words and information in the sentence or sentences. I will read the sentences out loud. Raise your hand when you know which word best completes the sentence. Write the word in the blank. Sometimes the word might require an ending such as -ed, -s, or -ing. Each word will be used only one time.*

 Choose individual students to give answers. Have students point out context clues that helped them to choose the correct answer.

 Say: *Cross out words in the box as we use them. Write your answers in the blank, and write the context clues you used in the space below.*

5 min.
Word Wizard

 Say: *As Word Wizards this week, you must always be on the lookout for opportunities to use and demonstrate your word knowledge. Use your Word Wizard Journals to keep track of each time you hear one of this week's vocabulary words used in a sentence at home, school, or even on television. If you don't hear the words used in a sentence, be creative and write original sentences using your new vocabulary knowledge. Next week, each group will read two of their favorite sentences to the class!*

 Say: *Get in your Word Wizard Groups from last week, and share your best sentences.*

 Say: *Which group would like to read two of their sentences using the words from last week's lesson?* Tally the number of sentences per group, and record the amount on the Word Wizard Chart.

Assign At-Home 3

Say: *Tonight you will . . .*

1. *Study your flashcards.*

2. *Complete the Word Wizard Journal.*

3. *Complete the Context Clues Activity.*

Day 4: Expanding Meaning

Prepare for Lesson

☆ Materials: Student Workbooks

☆ Read Teacher Tip: Morphographic Elements (Week 1, page 17)

3 min. Vocabulary Review

☆ Rapid review of vocabulary words (Students use the Week 14 Word List in their Student Workbooks.)

7 min. Review At-Home 3

☆ Review the correct answers to At-Home 3.

☆ Review student work to confirm or clarify responses.

20 min. Morphographic Elements: *-ment*

☆ Say: *Today we will look at a suffix that is present in one of this week's vocabulary words. Find Morphographic Elements: -ment in your Student Workbook.*

☆ Say: *Let's look at the information in the top box. Suffixes are word parts that can be added to the end of a word. Can you think of any suffixes that you have studied?* Briefly discuss. *Today, we will look at words that use the suffix -ment.*

☆ Read the definition for *-ment*. Say: *Let's look in the box and read words that use this suffix. Read the word, definition, and the sentence that corresponds with the word using the suffix -ment.*

☆ Say: *Suffixes help us to see relationships between words when we read. Let's read and discuss the word cousins that appear in Part A.* Read the word cousins together.

☆ Say: *Let's look at Part B. Each underlined word is written with the suffix that we have studied today. We will read the word in a sentence and then use context clues and the meaning of the suffix to help us to select the best definition.*

Assign At-Home 4

Say: *Tonight you will . . .*

1. *Study your flashcards.*

2. *Complete the Crossword Puzzle.*

Day 5: Keys to Understanding

Prepare for Lesson

☆ Materials: Student Workbooks, photocopies of Assessment 14

☆ Read Teacher Tip: Word Roots (Week 8, page 106)

Review At-Home 4

☆ Review the correct answers to At-Home 4.

☆ Review student work to confirm or clarify responses.

Bingo Game

☆ Say: *Choose nine words from the Week 14 Word List, and write them on the Bingo Card in your Student Workbook. When I read a definition, raise your hand to identify the word. If you have the word on your card, mark it with an X. The first person who has 3 Xs in a row (across, down, diagonally) wins the game.*

☆ Read the definitions. As students identify definitions, write the words on the board until someone wins the game.

Word Roots: *Duc*

☆ Say: *Open your Student Workbook to Word Roots: Duc. Do you remember what a word root is?* Call on a student. *That's right. Roots are small word units in words that come from other languages like Latin or Greek. They help us to figure out the meaning of a word.*

☆ Say: *Today, we will look at the word root duc. Duc is a Latin root word that means to lead. When we define words using the definition of the word root, it does not always exactly match the actual definition. However, the root can help us understand the meaning of an unfamiliar word.*

☆ Say: *Let's look at Word Roots: Duc. We are going to define words containing the word duc. Repeat these words after me: product, conduct, educate, aqueduct, and introduce. Who can tell us the meaning of product? Conduct? Educate? Aqueduct? Introduce? Using the word root, duc, let's read each sentence and write what you think the word means.*

☆ Once all five words have been defined, quickly review the actual word meanings, and ask students if the definitions that they wrote matched the dictionary definitions.

☆ Say: *Let's see how close we are to the actual meaning of the words.*

Dictionary Definitions

1. **product**—something that is lead out of the work done by one's hands or by machinery

2. **conduct**—to lead or direct others in an activity

3. **educate**—to lead or direct the growth of one's mind through or by instruction

4. **aqueduct**—a man-made channel for leading or carrying a large quantity of flowing water

5. **introduce**—to lead to or make known by a formal act or announcement

A Cure for the Common Cold (optional)

☆ Students use vocabulary words from Weeks 1–14 to describe a cure for the common cold.

 Assessment

☆ Distribute Assessment 14 to each student.

Name: _____ Date: _____

Assessment 14
Five Notable Inventors
Madam C. J. Walker

A. Match the word with the appropriate definition.

a) common	d) establish	g) attic	j) object	m) ingredients
b) product	e) fever	h) demonstration	k) donate	n) training
c) harvest	f) mixture	i) laboratory	l) cure	o) treatment

_____ 1. a place for conducting tests and experiments

_____ 2. a combination of ingredients that are used together

_____ 3. a rise of body temperature

_____ 4. a room near the roof

_____ 5. familiar; to happen often

B. Circle the word that does not belong.

1.	healing	cure	treatment	disease
2.	confusion	purpose	object	intention
3.	pick	collect	plant	harvest
4.	demonstration	explosion	presentation	explanation
5.	donate	take	give	contribute

C. Complete the sentence with the best answer.

_____ 1. At the training, each salesperson made a demonstration to show _____.

    a) the new products that were available

    b) an expensive treatment that would not work

    c) boxes from an attic

_____ 2. The cook would not reveal the secret ingredients that made his salad dressing a success because he wanted to _____.

    a) establish a business for himself

    b) find a cure for fever

    c) buy shares in companies

_____ 3. The following items can be made in a laboratory: _____.

    a) optician, caveman, congressman

    b) comets, stars, and galaxies

    c) vaccines, medicines, and treatments

_____ 4. The doctor's main objective in life was to _____.

    a) set up a clinic in an attic

    b) create a mixture of lettuce and tomatoes

    c) develop a cure for yellow fever

_____ 5. Mr. De Soto established a hospital that would donate _____.

    a) bacteria, diseases, and contagious fevers

    b) common medicines, training, and treatments

    c) products from a harvest

Review Unit 3

REVIEW DAY 1	REVIEW DAY 2	REVIEW DAY 3	REVIEW DAY 4	REVIEW DAY 5
Introduce Unit Review "I Spy" Game Assign At-Home 1	Semantic Feature Analysis Assign At-Home 2	Multiple Meanings Find It, Say It! Game Assign At-Home 3	Clueless Game Assign At-Home 4	Assessment

Words and Definitions

The following are target words for this week. If the word has multiple meanings, we provide only the definition listed in the text. *Please review the definitions prior to instruction.*

1. **union**—people joined together in support of better working conditions
2. **scrap**—manufactured materials or parts (such as metal) that have been rejected and thrown away
3. **fever**—a rise of the body temperature above normal or a disease with this symptom
4. **common**—happening frequently or often; familiar
5. **harvest**—the season for gathering in a crop
6. **demonstration**—a showing of the merits or good points of a product to a possible buyer
7. **cure**—recovery or relief from a disease
8. **factory**—a building where products are manufactured or made
9. **shop**—a business for the making or repair of goods or machinery
10. **yardstick**—a measuring stick which is 3 feet (36 inches) long
11. **figure**—to conclude or decide
12. **preserve**—to keep or save from decomposition or rotting
13. **compromise**—an agreement reached between people with opposing views in which they accept something that is not exactly what they wanted
14. **perseverance**—the ability to keep going and not give up when faced with difficulties
15. **relief**—feeling of freedom from worry and pain
16. **reinforcement**—something that strengthens by giving additional support
17. **treasure**—wealth, riches, or something of great value
18. **complain**—to express unhappiness or pain
19. **patent**—a writing that guarantees an inventor the right to make, use, or sell an invention
20. **hire**—to provide with a job that pays a salary; to employ
21. **donate**—to make a gift, especially to a charity or organization
22. **mixture**—a combination of several different kinds of ingredients
23. **treatment**—the act of caring for a medical problem
24. **training**—the process or method of teaching someone a new skill or new knowledge
25. **clammy**—being damp, soft, sticky, and usually cool

Prepare for Lesson

☆ Materials: Student Workbooks, display copy of Unit 3 Word List (optional)

Introduce Unit Review

☆ Say: *Last week, we completed the last story in our unit. We have read four stories and learned many new words each week. This week, we will review some key words that we learned in Unit 3. At the end of the week, you will have an opportunity to demonstrate just how much you've learned.*

"I Spy" Game

25 min.

☆ Say: *How many of you remember playing "I Spy"? When we play "I Spy" we use clues to help us identify words.*

☆ Say: *Turn to Unit 3: "I Spy" in your Student Workbook. Today, we will work as word detectives and use a list of clues to determine the review word. Let's read the clues and decide which word is being described. Write the word next to the appropriate clue. Remember, a good detective never gives up!*

☆ Read the sentences out loud, and call on students for answers. Say: *I am looking for a word that means . . .* , then read the definition. Students should respond in the form, "I spy . . ." then say the vocabulary word.

Assign At-Home 1

Say: *Tonight you will . . .*

1. *Study the Unit 3 vocabulary words with definitions.*

2. *Make flashcards.*

Unit 3 Word List

union	scrap	fever
common	harvest	demonstration
cure	factory	shop
yardstick	figure	preserve
compromise	clammy	perseverance
relief	reinforcement	treasure
complain	patent	hire
donate	mixture	treatment
training		

Review Day 2

Prepare for Lesson

☆ Materials: Student Workbooks, display copy of Semantic Feature Analysis: Shops

☆ Read Teacher Tip: Semantic Feature Analysis (Week 5, page 62)

Semantic Feature Analysis

25 min.

☆ Say: *The objective of today's activity is to compare different words and to decide how words are similar and different. The purpose of this activity is to help you to see how words are related to each other.*

☆ Say: *In the Review Unit 2, we categorized words that describe different kinds of heating systems. We looked for action words and then described features of those words in a special matrix. This week, we will focus on types of stores. Who remembers one of our vocabulary words that describes a business where goods are made or repaired?* The answer is shop. *We saw the word <u>shop</u> used in <u>Five Notable Inventors</u> in the story about Jan Ernst Matzeliger, the shoemaker. In the story, Jan works in a shop for making and repairing shoes.*

☆ Say: *The word <u>shop</u> can also refer to a kind of store—a place where merchandise is purchased. In fact, there are many different kinds of stores or shops. Can you think of words that describe other kinds of shops?*

☆ Say: *Open your Student Workbook to Semantic Feature Analysis: Shops. Let's look at the shops listed in the left column of the matrix. Does the list contain the types of shops that we have just discussed in class?* Read through the list with students. Add any shops that were discussed in class but that are not on the list.

☆ Say: *Let's look at some features of these shops. Look at the top row of the matrix. Can you think of any other features that should be listed here?* Any additional features may be added.

☆ Say: *Let's discuss the features of different shops. We will fill in the matrix with a plus or minus to indicate the presence or absence of each feature. If we can't agree, we will place a zero in the matrix.*

☆ After the matrix is complete, say: *Let's look at the matrix and compare the different kinds of shops.* Discuss similar and different features.

☆ Help students discover that no two kinds of stores have exactly the same pattern of pluses (similiarities) and minuses (differences): none are identical. Even the categories that are most alike will reveal their differences if enough features are added.

Assign At-Home 2

Say: *Tonight you will study the vocabulary words on your flashcards.*

Semantic Feature Analysis: Shops

	Sells food	Sells clothing	Sells something besides food or clothes	Is privately owned	Inexpensive	Expensive	Chic atmosphere	Ordinary atmosphere	Inner-city	Rural	Single store	Multiple stores	Single employee	Multiple employees	Accepts cash	Accepts credit
Shop																
Chain																
Deli																
Department store																
Emporium																
Five-and-dime																
Market																
Outlet																
Stand																
Supermarket																
Store																

Review Day 3

Prepare for Lesson

 Materials: Student Workbooks

15 min.

Multiple Meanings

☆ Say: *Today we are going to study some of the words from the past 4 weeks that have more than one meaning. In the first part of the activity, we will quickly review the different meanings for each word.*

☆ Say: *Who remembers one of the meanings for the word <u>common</u>?* Continue until the students have identified as many definitions as they can for *common*. Do the same for *union, fever,* and *demonstration.*

☆ Say: *Open your Student Workbook to Week 15: Multiple Meanings. Let's see how many meanings we know for these words.*

15 min.

Find It, Say It! Game

☆ Say: *Next, we will play Find It, Say It! Turn to Week 15: Find It, Say It!*

 Say: *Remember, when we play Find It, Say It! I first read the sentence with the underlined word and say, "Find It!" You then go to the box of the underlined word and find the definition that best fits the way the word is used in each sentence. Without talking, you write the letter for that definition in the space at the beginning of the sentence. When I say, "Say It," everyone will say the answer out loud together.*

☆ After asking students to find the answer, allow them approximately 7 seconds before asking them to say it.

Assign At-Home 3

Say: *Tonight you will study the vocabulary words on your flashcards.*

Review Day 4

Prepare for Lesson

☆ Materials: Clue Cards, photocopies of Score Keeper Card

Clueless Game

☆ Write the words "Class Score Keeper" and the numbers 1–10 on the board.

☆ Say: *Today, we will play Clueless. As you may recall from the last unit review, the objective of this game is to focus on single word clues that can help you to remember the words that you have learned. Remember, you may not use your Student Workbook to help you.*

☆ Say: *Do you remember your groups from last time?* If necessary, create new groups.

☆ Say: *We will appoint a new score keeper for each team. We will use the part of the Score Keeper Card for Review Unit 3.* Assign a person from each group to be the score keeper or allow teams to choose their own score keepers.

☆ Say: *Let's review the rules. I will place a marker on 10 on the Class Score Keeper. Then, I will flash a Clue Card with a one-word clue. I will start with Team A. If Team A correctly identifies the word, they get the points indicated on the Class Score Keeper. If the marker is on 10, they get 10 points, and the team's score keeper records the value on the Score Keeper Card.*

☆ Say: *If the word is not guessed from the Clue Card, the marker on the Class Score Keeper is moved to 9, and it becomes the other team's turn. If they guess the word, they receive the points indicated by the Class Score Keeper.*

☆ Say: *Remember, if the word is not guessed from the first clue, the marker on the Class Score Keeper is moved to 9, and it becomes the other team's turn. If the next team cannot guess the word, the marker is moved to 8, and so forth. Each time the word is not guessed the marker is moved one number lower.*

☆ Say: *Each time we read a new clue, the marker is placed back on 10, and the other team tries to identify the word from the next clue card.*

☆ Say: *We continue to play until we have identified all the clue words. The team with the highest total score is the winner.*

☆ Distribute the Score Keeper Cards for each team. After playing the game, collect the Score Keeper Cards so that they can be used with the next review unit.

Assign At-Home 4

Say: *Tonight you will study for Friday's test.*

Clue Cards

employ	teaching	settlement	crop	support
valuable	sweaty	decide	care	often
organization	willpower	business	combination	freedom
pieces	healing	building	save	grumble
inventor	gift	measurement	temperature	showing

Review Day 5

Prepare for Lesson

☆ Materials: photocopies of Assessment 15

Assessment

☆ Distribute Assessment 15 to each student.

☆ Read the directions out loud.

☆ Read each vocabulary word out loud along with the answer choices. Allow students a few seconds to choose and write the letter for a definition.

☆ Collect assessments.

Name: _____   Date: _____

Assessment 15
Unit 3

Choose the letter that represents the best definition for each word.

___ 1. treatment
   a. a legal document that establishes peace
   b. therapy or care for a medical problem
   c. ingredient in a recipe or mixture

___ 2. complain
   a. to gripe or grumble
   b. to praise or compliment
   c. to investigate or research

___ 3. common
   a. unknown, unusual
   b. comparable, equal
   c. familiar, generally known

___ 4. training
   a. teaching, instruction, preparation
   b. cargo, shipment, boxes
   c. test, experiment, trial

___ 5. demonstration
   a. inventing a product
   b. packaging a product
   c. displaying a product

___ 6. perseverance
   a. weakness
   b. determination
   c. confusion

___ 7. patent
   a. a legal document that establishes ownership of an invention
   b. a legal document that establishes the birth of a child
   c. a legal document that establishes citizenship of a person

___ 8. factory
   a. a school for training
   b. a building for manufacturing
   c. a number for factoring

___ 9. relief
   a. to experience more pain
   b. to experience less pain
   c. to experience the same pain

___ 10. mixture
   a. a combination of ingredients
   b. a separation of ingredients
   c. a collection of ingredients

___ 11. yardstick
   a. a tool for cooking food
   b. a tool for gardening plants
   c. a tool for measuring objects

___ 12. harvest
   a. season for fertilizing crops
   b. season for gathering crops
   c. season for planting crops

_____ 13. clammy

    a. dry and scratchy

    b. sweaty and sticky

    c. thick and dense

_____ 14. treasure

    a. wealth of any kind

    b. poverty of any kind

    c. shortage of any kind

_____ 15. union

    a. one person within an organization

    b. organization of workers who have a common interest

    c. organization of people who are divided

_____ 16. fever

    a. a rise in body temperature

    b. oven temperature

    c. a heating system

_____ 17. hire

    a. to dismiss a person from a job

    b. to pay someone for doing a job

    c. to advertise a job

_____ 18. donate

    a. to pay a salary to an employee

    b. to make money as a salary

    c. to give something valuable to a charity

_____ 19. scrap

    a. materials that are listed in a patent

    b. materials that have been thrown away

    c. materials and supplies used for training

_____ 20. shop

    a. a laboratory used for testing

    b. a business for repairing products

    c. a machine used for recycling scraps

_____ 21. compromise

    a. an agreement between cooperating sides

    b. a standoff between football players

    c. an deadlock between enemy troops

_____ 22. cure

    a. fever from a disease

    b. recovery from a disease

    c. diagnosis of a disease

_____ 23. figure

    a. to write a poem

    b. to daydream

    c. to conclude or decide

_____ 24. reinforcement

    a. something that weakens the muscles

    b. something that gives additional support

    c. something that is recycled again

_____ 25. preserve

    a. to keep from rotting

    b. to decompose or decay

    c. to sell a crop

Justin and the Best Biscuits in the World, Part I
by Mildred Pitts Walter

DAY 1 Preview of Lesson	DAY 2 Introduction	DAY 3 Using Words in Context	DAY 4 Expanding Meaning	DAY 5 Keys to Understanding
Read New Words Say and Write New Words Read Definitions Assign At-Home 1	Vocabulary Review Review At-Home 1 Predict the Storyline Story Reading (pages 1–18) Identifying Vocabulary in Text Paraphrasing Vocabulary in Text Assign At-Home 2	Vocabulary Review Review At-Home 2 Using Context Clues Word Wizard Assign At-Home 3	Vocabulary Review Review At-Home 3 Bingo Game Morphographic Elements: -ness Assign At-Home 4	Review At-Home 4 Word Roots: Tort Assessment

Words and Definitions

The following are target words for this week. If the word has multiple meanings, we provide only the definition listed in the text. **Please review the definitions prior to instruction.**

1. **challenge**—to invite or dare to take part in a contest
2. **strain**—to stretch beyond a natural limit
3. **weakness**—object of special desire or fondness
4. **scatter**—to cause to separate widely or in different directions
5. **glance**—to look at quickly or hastily
6. **experiment**—a test; a trial
7. **reek**—to give a strong impression of something unpleasant
8. **exhausted**—a state in which all of one's mental or physical energy has been used up
9. **aggressive**—showing readiness to fight or attack
10. **mimic**—to make fun of by imitating
11. **retort**—to answer angrily or sharply
12. **rebound**—a bouncing back
13. **organize**—to put into order
14. **ground**—to prohibit from participating in an activity
15. **urge**—a sudden feeling or desire to do something

Day 1: Preview of Lesson

Prepare for Lesson

☆ Materials: Student Workbooks, *Justin and the Best Biscuits in the World* by Mildred Pitts Walter, display copy of Week 16 Word List

☆ Read Teacher Tip: Reading New Words (Week 1, page 8)

Read New Words

☆ Say: *Today, we will begin a new book, <u>Justin and the Best Biscuits in the World</u>. We will read the first two chapters, "Justin is Grounded" and "Women's Work." Remember, on Day 1 we learn to read new words that you will study at home. The words we learn will help you to read this story better and will help you to express your thoughts on paper and when talking to others. Let's see if there are any words that you already know.*

☆ Display the Week 16 Word List. Cover the bottom box, leaving the word columns at the top of the page exposed. Say: *Which words do you already know?*

☆ Uncover the bottom box. Say: *Let's read these words. Sound out each syllable as I point to it. Be sure to say each sound clearly. Sound it out.*

☆ Students sound out each syllable. Say the word. Students repeat the word. Say: *Yes, the word is . . . .*

Say and Write New Words

☆ Cover the bottom box and use the word columns at the top of the page.

☆ Say: *Let's read the words together.* Point to each word and read one time.

☆ Say: *Take out your pencil and Student Workbook. Find the page that says Week 16: Say and Write New Words. Let's get ready to say and write each word.*

☆ Point to each word. Say: *What word?* Students say the word. *Write [the word].*

☆ Students write the word on the appropriate line. Continue until all words are written.

Read Definitions

☆ Say: *I will read the definitions so that we will understand what each word means. Some words have more than one meaning; however, these are the definitions that are used in the story.*

☆ Read the definitions out loud as students read silently. Choose a student to read each sentence.

Definitions

1. **challenge** (to invite or dare to take part in a contest)
   George plans to <u>challenge</u> José to a game of chess after school.

2. **strain** (to stretch beyond a natural limit)
   The weightlifter grunted and <u>strain</u>ed as he lifted the 250-pound bar.

Week 16 Word List

challenge	experiment	retort
strain	reek	urge
weakness	exhausted	organize
scatter	aggressive	ground
glance	mimic	rebound

1. chal lenge
2. strain
3. weak
   weak ness
4. scat ter
5. glance
6. ex per i ment
7. reek
8. ex haust
   ex haust ed

9. ag gres sive
10. mim ic
11. re tort
12. urge
13. or ga nize
14. ground
15. bound
    re bound

3. **weakness** (object of special desire or fondness)
   Dogs are Susan's <u>weakness</u>; she loves every dog she has ever met.

4. **scatter** (to cause to separate widely or in different directions)
   If someone drops a handful of peanuts, they will <u>scatter</u> all over the floor.

5. **glance** (to look at quickly or hastily)
   When I am about to turn a corner on my bike, I <u>glance</u> over my shoulder to see if any cars are coming.

6. **experiment** (a test; a trial)
   Karen did an <u>experiment</u> with flour and water to see if she could make her own playdough.

7. **reek** (to give a strong impression of something unpleasant)
   Driving to school in her brand new BMW and carrying a very expensive purse, Susie <u>reeked</u> of wealth.

8. **exhausted** (a state in which all of one's mental or physical energy has been used up)
   I was <u>exhausted</u> after running 3 miles because I don't usually run that far.

9. **aggressive** (showing readiness to fight or attack)
   Our cat is very <u>aggressive</u> and swats at the dog's nose whenever he walks past her.

10. **mimic** (to make fun of by imitating)
    When we were younger, my brother would <u>mimic</u> me by repeating everything I said in a silly, high-pitched voice.

11. **retort** (to answer angrily or sharply)
    "I don't think that's fair," <u>retort</u>ed Julian when his dad took away his basketball as a punishment for not doing his homework.

12. **rebound** (a bouncing back)
    The basketball player caught the ball on the <u>rebound</u>.

13. **organize** (to put into order)
    Rachel plans to <u>organize</u> her closet by separating her winter and summer clothes, then arranging them according to color.

14. **ground** (to prohibit from participating in an activity)
    If Matt stays out too late, his parents will <u>ground</u> him from using the telephone for a month.

15. **urge** (a sudden feeling or desire to do something)
    After watching the commercial, my sister and I had the sudden <u>urge</u> to buy Double Dutch chocolate ice cream.

Assign At-Home 1

Say: *Tonight you will . . .*

1. *Study the vocabulary words with definitions.*

2. *Complete the Riddle Page.*

3. *Do the Matching Activity.*

4. *Make flashcards.*

Day 2: Introduction

Prepare for Lesson

☆ Materials: Student Workbooks, *Justin and the Best Biscuits in the World* by Mildred Pitts Walter

3 min.

Vocabulary Review

☆ Rapid review of vocabulary words (Students use the Week 16 Word List in their Student Workbooks.)

7 min.

Review At-Home 1

☆ Review the correct answers to At-Home 1.

☆ Review student work to confirm or clarify responses.

8 min.

Predict the Storyline

☆ Students look at the illustration on page 17 of *Justin and the Best Biscuits in the World* by Mildred Pitts Walter.

☆ Say: *Today we will begin reading a new book, Justin and the Best Biscuits in the World. The first two chapters are "Justin is Grounded" and "Women's Work." In these two chapters, Justin complains about work that he has to do at home. Everyone has to work. Even as students, you work at school. Let's talk about the different ways in which we work.*

☆ Say: *Open your Student Workbook to Semantic Web: Work. What types of work can you think of? Housework? Schoolwork? What activities fall under each of these categories? What are some places where people work?*

☆ Say: *Looking at the different kinds of work that people do, do you think that from this list of things there is work that only women should do? Is there any kind of work listed here that is only appropriate for men? Why do you feel that way?*

☆ Say: *In this story, the main character, Justin, dislikes doing housework. How many of you in class have to do housework? Can you think of reasons why Justin would dislike housework?*

☆ Say: *As you read you will discover that Justin dislikes housework because he considers it to be women's work. However, as we continue to read, Justin's grandfather causes him to question the concept of women's work versus men's work. The readings this week will definitely give us a lot to think about.*

☆ Say: *Think of a question that you think the story will answer. Write the question at the bottom of Semantic Web: Work.*

10 min.

Story Reading 1: Identifying Vocabulary in Text

☆ Say: *As I read the story out loud, you will follow along silently. When you see a word from our vocabulary list, give a thumbs up.*

☆ Read pages 1–18.

☆ Discuss what students predicted would happen in the story.

Story Reading 2: Paraphrasing Vocabulary in Text

☆ Say: *As I read specific paragraphs of the story out loud again, let's paraphrase what the author has said by using our own words. Let's focus on the paragraph that begins on the last line of page 1. Follow along as I read out loud.* Read the paragraph ("Justin wanted to play . . .").

☆ Say: *What's another way of saying "there was no one left to challenge him"? We might say, "Nobody was left to dare Justin to play."*

☆ Help students to paraphrase the remaining sentences in the paragraph as appropriate.

Assign At-Home 2

Say: *Tonight you will . . .*

1. *Study your flashcards.*

2. *Complete Word Substitutions.*

3. *Complete Same and Different.*

Day 3: Using Words in Context

Prepare for Lesson

 Materials: Student Workbooks

 Read Teacher Tip: Word Wizard (Week 1, page 14)

 Vocabulary Review
3 min.

 Rapid review of vocabulary words (Students use the Week 16 Word List in their Student Workbooks.)

 Review At-Home 2
7 min.

 Review the correct answers to At-Home 2.

 Review student work to confirm or clarify responses.

Using Context Clues
15 min.

 Say: *Open your Student Workbook to Week 16: Using Context Clues. Today, we will use context clues to help us choose the word that fits in the blank by using the clues from other words and information in the sentence or sentences. I will read the sentences out loud. Raise your hand when you know which word best completes the sentence. Write the word in the blank. Sometimes the word might require an ending such as -ed, -s, or -ing. Each word will be used only one time.*

 Choose individual students to give answers. Have students point out context clues that helped them to choose the correct answer.

 Say: *Cross out words in the box as we use them. Write your answers in the blank, and write the context clues you used in the space below.*

 Word Wizard
5 min.

 Say: *As Word Wizards this week, you must always be on the lookout for opportunities to use and demonstrate your word knowledge. Use your Word Wizard Journals to keep track of each time you hear one of this week's vocabulary words used in a sentence at home, school, or even on television. If you don't hear the words used in a sentence, be creative and write original sentences using your new vocabulary knowledge. Next week, each group will read two of their favorite sentences to the class!*

 Say: *Get in your Word Wizard Groups from Week 14, and share your best sentences.*

 Say: *Which group would like to read two of their sentences using the words from last week's lesson?* Tally the number of sentences per group, and record the amount on the Word Wizard Chart.

Assign At-Home 3

Say: *Tonight you will . . .*

1. *Study your flashcards.*

2. *Complete the Word Wizard Journal.*

3. *Complete the Context Clues Activity.*

Day 4: Expanding Meaning

Prepare for Lesson

☆ Materials: Student Workbooks

☆ Read Teacher Tip: Morphographic Elements (Week 1, page 17)

Vocabulary Review

☆ Rapid review of vocabulary words (Students use the Week 16 Word List in their Student Workbooks.)

Review At-Home 3

☆ Review the correct answers to At-Home 3.

☆ Review student work to confirm or clarify responses.

Morphographic Elements: *-ness*

☆ Say: *Today we will look at a suffix that is present in one of this week's vocabulary words. Find Morphographic Elements: -ness in your Student Workbook.*

☆ Say: *Let's look at the information in the top box. Suffixes are word parts that can be added to the end of a word. Can you think of any suffixes that you have studied?* Briefly discuss. *Today, we will look at words that use the suffix -ness.*

☆ Read the definition for -ness. Say: *Let's look in the box and read words that use this suffix.* Read the word, definition, and the sentence that corresponds with the word using the suffix *-ness.*

☆ Say: *Suffixes help us to see relationships between words when we read. Let's read and discuss the word cousins that appear in Part A.* Read the word cousins together.

☆ *Let's look at Part B. Each underlined word is written with the suffix that we have studied today. We will read the word in a sentence and then use context clues and the meaning of the suffix to help us to select the best definition.*

Assign At-Home 4

Say: *Tonight you will . . .*

1. *Study your flashcards.*

2. *Complete the Crossword Puzzle.*

Day 5: Keys to Understanding

Prepare for Lesson

 Materials: Student Workbooks, photocopies of Assessment 16

☆ Read Teacher Tip: Word Roots (Week 8, page 106)

7 min. Review At-Home 4

☆ Review the correct answers to At-Home 4.

☆ Review student work to confirm or clarify responses.

8 min. Bingo Game

☆ Say: *Choose nine words from the Week 16 Word List, and write them on the Bingo Card in your Student Workbook. When I read a definition, raise your hand to identify the word. If you have the word on your card, mark it with an <u>X</u>. The first person who has 3 <u>X</u>s in a row (across, down, diagonally) wins the game.*

☆ Read the definitions. As students identify definitions, write the words on the board until someone wins the game.

8–10 min. Word Roots: *Tort*

☆ Say: *Open your Student Workbook to Word Roots: <u>Tort</u>. Do you remember what a word root is?* Call on a student. *That's right. Roots are small word units in words that come from other languages like Latin or Greek. They help us figure out the meaning of a word.*

☆ Say: *Today, we will look at the word root <u>tort</u>. <u>Tort</u> is a Latin word that means to twist back or to hurl back. Each time you see a word with <u>tort</u>, you will know that it has something to do with twisting or hurling, throwing something back either physically or with words.*

☆ Say: *Let's look at Word Roots: <u>Tort</u>. We are going to try to define words containing the word <u>tort</u>. Repeat these words after me: <u>retort</u>, <u>distort</u>, <u>extort</u>, <u>torture</u>, and <u>contortion</u>. Who can tell us the meaning of <u>retort</u>? <u>Distort</u>? <u>Extort</u>? <u>Torture</u>? <u>Contortion</u>? Using the word root, <u>tort</u>, let's read each sentence and write what you think the word means.*

☆ Once all five words have been defined, quickly review the actual word meanings, and ask students if the definitions that they wrote matched the dictionary definitions.

☆ Say: *Let's see how close we are to the actual meaning of the words.*

Dictionary Definitions

1. **retort**—to answer or hurl angry words back at someone

2. **distort**—to change or twist the true meaning or shape of something

3. **extort**—to wring; to twist or force the truth out of someone by force or pressure

4. **torture**—to cause suffering by twisting or bending out of shape

5. **contortion**—to twist into a strained shape or facial expression

Assessment

☆ Distribute Assessment 16 to each student.

Name: _____   Date: _____

Assessment 16
Justin and the Best Biscuits in the World, Part I

A. Match the word with the appropriate definition.

a) challenge	d) scatter	g) reek	j) mimic	m) organize
b) strain	e) glance	h) exhausted	k) retort	n) ground
c) weakness	f) experiment	i) aggressive	l) urge	o) rebound

_____ 1.   to answer in an angry manner

_____ 2.   to look at quickly or briefly

_____ 3.   to dare or invite someone to take part in a contest

_____ 4.   a trial or test

_____ 5.   a strong or disagreeable smell or odor

B. Circle the word that does not belong.

1.	urge	wish	dislike	desire
2.	imitate	fake	copy	create
3.	organize	arrange	messy	sort
4.	violent	destructive	aggressive	friendly
5.	spread	separate	gather	scatter

C. Complete the sentence with the best answer.

_____ 1. My mother said that she would ground me if I _____.

    a)   finish my homework every night

    b)   eat my vegetables

    c)   don't do my chores after school

_____ 2. If I throw the rubber ball at the wall and it rebounds, I will _____.

    a)   catch it in my glove

    b)   buy a new ball

    c)   play ball with my sister

_____ 3. When my dad is exhausted, he likes to _____.

    a)   take a hot shower and sleep

    b)   lift 200 pounds at the gym

    c)   take a singing lesson

_____ 4. You might strain your back if you _____.

    a)   lift a book

    b)   lift a bookcase

    c)   lift a bookmark

_____ 5. If chocolate is your weakness, you would rather eat a giant _____.

    a)   Hershey's bar

    b)   bag of potato chips

    c)   apple

Justin and the Best Biscuits in the World, Part II
by Mildred Pitts Walter

DAY 1 Preview of Lesson	DAY 2 Introduction	DAY 3 Using Words in Context	DAY 4 Expanding Meaning	DAY 5 Keys to Understanding
Read New Words Say and Write New Words Read Definitions Assign At-Home 1	Vocabulary Review Review At-Home 1 Predict the Storyline Story Reading (pages 19–35) Identifying Vocabulary in Text Paraphrasing Vocabulary in Text Assign At-Home 2	Vocabulary Review Review At-Home 2 Using Context Clues Word Wizard Assign At-Home 3	Vocabulary Review Review At-Home 3 Deep Processing Assign At-Home 4	Review At-Home 4 Bingo Game Synonyms and Antonyms Assessment

Words and Definitions

The following are target words for this week. If the word has multiple meanings, we provide only the definition listed in the text. *Please review the definitions prior to instruction.*

1. **utensils**—useful tools

2. **dangling**—hanging loosely

3. **gaze**—to fix the eyes in a steady and intent look

4. **clutter**—to fill or cover with a disorderly scattering of things

5. **disposition**—one's attitude or mood

6. **inspection**—an official review or examination

7. **link**—to join together as in a chain

8. **trail**—a path marked to show a route through a wilderness region

9. **depend**—to rely on for support

10. **herd**—a number of animals of one kind kept or stored together

11. **speckled**—covered by small marks

12. **plains**—a broad area of level or rolling treeless country

13. **horizon**—the line where the earth or sea and the sky seem to meet

14. **relieve**—to release from a post or duty

15. **imagine**—to form a mental picture of something

Day 1: Preview of Lesson

Prepare for Lesson

☆ Materials: Student Workbooks, *Justin and the Best Biscuits in the World* by Mildred Pitts Walter, display copy of Week 17 Word List

☆ Read Teacher Tip: Reading New Words (Week 1, page 8)

Read New Words

☆ Say: *Today, we will begin a new section of* Justin and the Best Biscuits in the World, *two chapters called "Grandpa Arrives" and "A Visit to Q-T Ranch." Remember, on Day 1 we learn to read new words that you will study at home. The words we learn will help you to read this story better and will help you to express your thoughts on paper and when talking to others. Let's see if there are any words that you already know.*

☆ Display the Week 17 Word List. Cover the bottom box, leaving the word columns at the top of the page exposed. Say: *Which words do you already know?*

☆ Uncover the bottom box. Say: *Let's read these words. Sound out each syllable as I point to it. Be sure to say each sound clearly. Sound it out.*

☆ Students sound out each syllable. Say the word. Students repeat the word. Say: *Yes, the word is . . . .*

Say and Write New Words

☆ Cover the bottom box, and use the word columns at the top of the page.

☆ Say: *Let's read the words together.* Point to each word and read one time.

☆ Say: *Take out your pencil and Student Workbook. Find the page that says Week 17: Say and Write New Words. Let's get ready to say and write each word.*

☆ Point to each word. Say: *What word?* Students say the word. *Write [the word].*

☆ Students write the word on the appropriate line. Continue until all words are written.

Read Definitions

☆ Say: *I will read the definitions so that we will understand what each word means. Some words have more than one meaning; however, these are the definitions that are used in the story.*

☆ Read the definitions out loud as students read silently. Choose a student to read each sentence.

Definitions

1. **utensils** (useful tools)
   Jeff sets the table before dinner, setting a plate and <u>utensils</u> at each place.

2. **dangling** (hanging loosely)
   The fisherman sat on the end of the dock with his feet <u>dangling</u> off the pier.

Week 17 Word List

utensi**ls**	inspec**tion**	speckle**d**
dangl**ing**	lin**k**	plain**s**
ga**z**e	trai**l**	hori**z**o**n**
clutt**er**	depen**d**	relie**v**e
disposi**tion**	her**d**	imagi**n**e

1. u ten si**l**
   u ten si**ls**
2. dan **gle**
   dan gl**ing**
3. ga**z**e
4. clut t**er**
5. dis po si **tion**
6. in spect
   in spec **tion**
7. lin**k**
8. trai**l**
9. de pen**d**
10. her**d**
11. speck le
    speck le**d**
12. plain
    plain**s**
13. ho ri **z**o**n**
14. re lie**v**e
15. im ag i**n**e

Vocabulary Power, Level 1, by Latrice M. Seals, Sharolyn D. Pollard-Durodola, Barbara R. Foorman, and Ashley M. Bradley

213

3. **gaze** (to fix the eyes in a steady and intent look)
   When I lie in bed at night, I <u>gaze</u> at the glow-in-the-dark stars I have stuck to the ceiling and pretend I'm sleeping outdoors.

4. **clutter** (to fill or cover with a disorderly scattering of things)
   When Justin came home from school in the afternoons, he would <u>clutter</u> his bedroom by dropping books, shoes, and clothes all over the floor.

5. **disposition** (one's attitude or mood)
   Mrs. Campbell's new baby has a sweet and pleasant <u>disposition</u>.

6. **inspection** (an official review or examination)
   At boot camp, the military officers held an <u>inspection</u> at 6:00 every morning to see if the soldiers were dressed in uniform and had their beds properly made.

7. **link** (to join together as a chain)
   The driver used a chain to <u>link</u> the broken-down car to the tow truck.

8. **trail** (a path marked to show a route through a wilderness region)
   We hiked in the park on a <u>trail</u> marked with wooden signs on stakes.

9. **depend** (to rely on for support)
   After he broke his hip, Mr. Rosenthal had to <u>depend</u> on a cane for support.

10. **herd** (a number of animals of one kind kept or stored together)
    As we drove through New Mexico, we noticed a <u>herd</u> of almost 100 buffalo in the pasture alongside the highway.

11. **speckled** (covered by small marks)
    Palaver, Grandpa's dapple horse, was <u>speckled</u> gray and white.

12. **plains** (a broad area of level or rolling treeless country)
    The cowboys rode across the <u>plains</u> for many days on the cattle drive.

13. **horizon** (the line where the earth or sea and the sky seem to meet)
    Sunset officially begins when the bottom edge of the sun starts to drop below the <u>horizon</u>.

14. **relieve** (to release from a post or duty)
    Henry will <u>relieve</u> Susan of guard duty and take his own turn when her shift ends at midnight.

15. **imagine** (to form a mental picture of something)
    Many young girls like to <u>imagine</u> what their wedding day will one day be like.

Assign At-Home 1

Say: *Tonight you will . . .*

1. *Study the vocabulary words with definitions.*

2. *Complete the Riddle Page.*

3. *Do the Matching Activity.*

4. *Make flashcards.*

Day 2: Introduction

Prepare for Lesson

☆ Materials: Student Workbooks, *Justin and the Best Biscuits in the World* by Mildred Pitts Walter

Vocabulary Review

☆ Rapid review of vocabulary words (Students use the Week 17 Word List in their Student Workbooks.)

Review At-Home 1

☆ Review the correct answers to At-Home 1.

☆ Review student work to confirm or clarify responses.

Predict the Storyline

☆ Students look at the chapter titles on pages 19 and 28 of *Justin and the Best Biscuits in the World* by Mildred Pitts Walter.

☆ Say: *Today we will read the next two chapters of <u>Justin and the Best Biscuits in the World</u>, "Grandpa Arrives" and "A Visit to Q-T Ranch." In these two chapters, Justin is invited to go with Grandpa to his ranch, and he stays up late that night imagining his trip and thinking about the life of a cowboy.*

☆ Say: *Open your Student Workbook to Semantic Web: Life on a Ranch with Cowboys. Let's explore what you know about ranches and the life of cowboys. Who lives and works on a ranch, and what kinds of animals are kept on a ranch? What type of work is done on a ranch?*

☆ Say: *What do cowboys eat? What type of traveling did a cowboy have to do in the Old West? What do cowboys wear?*

☆ Say: *Think of a question that you think the story will answer. Write the question at the bottom of Semantic Web: Life on a Ranch with Cowboys.*

Story Reading 1: Identifying Vocabulary in Text

☆ Say: *As I read the story out loud, you will follow along silently. When you see a word from our vocabulary list, give a thumbs up.*

☆ Read pages 19–35.

☆ Discuss what students predicted would happen in the story.

Story Reading 2: Paraphrasing Vocabulary in Text

☆ Say: *As I read specific paragraphs of the story out loud again, let's paraphrase what the author has said by using our own words. Let's focus on the first paragraph on page 22. Follow along as I read out loud.* Read the paragraph ("Throwing himself across . . .").

☆ Say: *What's another way of saying, "Throwing himself across the bed, he lay with his feet dangling to the floor"? We might say, "Justin hurled himself onto his bed with his feet hanging off the side."*

☆ Help students to paraphrase the remaining sentences in the paragraph as appropriate.

Assign At-Home 2

Say: *Tonight you will . . .*

1. *Study your flashcards.*

2. *Complete Word Substitutions.*

3. *Complete Same and Different.*

Day 3: Using Words in Context

Prepare for Lesson

 Materials: Student Workbooks

 Read Teacher Tip: Word Wizard (Week 1, page 14)

3 min. Vocabulary Review

 Rapid review of vocabulary words (Students use the Week 17 Word List in their Student Workbooks.)

7 min. Review At-Home 2

 Review the correct answers to At-Home 2.

 Review student work to confirm or clarify responses.

15 min. Using Context Clues

 Say: *Open your Student Workbook to Week 17: Using Context Clues. Today, we will use context clues to help us choose the word that fits in the blank by using the clues from other words and information in the sentence or sentences. I will read the sentences out loud. Raise your hand when you know which word best completes the sentence. Write the word in the blank. Sometimes the word might require an ending such as -ed, -s, or -ing. Each word will be used only one time.*

 Choose individual students to give answers. Have students point out context clues that helped them to choose the correct answer.

 Say: *Cross out words in the box as we use them. Write your answers in the blank, and write the context clues you used in the space below.*

5 min. Word Wizard

 Say: *As Word Wizards this week, you must always be on the lookout for opportunities to use and demonstrate your word knowledge. Use your Word Wizard Journals to keep track of each time you hear one of this week's vocabulary words used in a sentence at home, school, or even on television. If you don't hear the words used in a sentence, be creative and write original sentences using your new vocabulary knowledge. Next week, each group will read two of their favorite sentences to the class!*

 Say: *Get in your Word Wizard Groups from last week, and share your best sentences.*

 Say: *Which group would like to read two of their sentences using the words from last week's lesson?* Tally the number of sentences per group, and record the amount on the Word Wizard Chart.

Assign At-Home 3

Say: *Tonight you will . . .*

1. *Study your flashcards.*

2. *Complete the Word Wizard Journal.*

3. *Complete the Context Clues Activity.*

Day 4: Expanding Meaning

Prepare for Lesson

 Materials: Student Workbooks

 Read Teacher Tip: Deep Processing (Week 2, page 28)

 (3 min.) ## Vocabulary Review

 Rapid review of vocabulary words (Students use the Week 17 Word List in their Student Workbooks.)

(7 min.) ## Review At-Home 3

 Review the correct answers to At-Home 3.

 Review student work to confirm or clarify responses.

(12 min.) ## Deep Processing

 Say: *Does anyone remember what <u>deep processing</u> is? It is thinking about how words relate to each other.*

 Say: *We have learned the definitions for this week's vocabulary words, but definitions do not really teach everything you need to know to really understand the meaning of a word. Remember, it is important to be able to use these words to describe your own experiences in life and to describe conditions in the world in general.*

 Say: *Open your Student Workbook to Deep Processing: <u>Justin and the Best Biscuits in the World</u>, Part II. We will read each question together and decide what is a reasonable answer and why. Remember, the answers are not in the novel we read but come from your own thinking. Think about the questions and about what would be a reasonable response. Remember, you must be able to explain why you chose your answer.*

Assign At-Home 4

Say: *Tonight you will . . .*

1. *Study your flashcards.*

2. *Complete the Crossword Puzzle.*

Day 5: Keys to Understanding

Prepare for Lesson

 Materials: Student Workbooks, photocopies of Assessment 17

Review At-Home 4

7 min.

 Review the correct answers to At-Home 4.

 Review student work to confirm or clarify responses.

Bingo Game

8 min.

★ Say: *Choose nine words from the Week 17 Word List, and write them on the Bingo Card in your Student Workbook. When I read a definition, raise your hand to identify the word. If you have the word on your card, mark it with an <u>X</u>. The first person who has 3 <u>X</u>s in a row (across, down, diagonally) wins the game.*

★ Read the definitions. As students identify definitions, write the word on the board until someone wins the game.

Synonyms and Antonyms

10 min.

★ Say: *You have learned many new words this week. You might have noticed when using context clues yesterday that some words have the same meaning and some words are opposite in meaning. What do we call words that have the same meaning?* The answer is synonyms. *What do we call words that are opposite in meaning?* The answer is antonyms.

★ Say: *In Week 12, we learned several synonyms for the word <u>preserve</u>. Can anyone tell us a synonym for <u>preserve</u>?* Answers include protect, conserve, and maintain. *Can someone give us an antonym for <u>preserve</u>?* Answers include spoil, decay, deteriorate, and rot.

★ Say: *Today, we will learn to express ideas with words that are the same or opposite in meaning. We will concentrate on four words from our vocabulary list.*

★ Say: *Open your Student Workbook to Week 17: Synonyms and Antonyms. This worksheet has sentences that you took home at the beginning of the week. Let's look at how we can rewrite some of these sentences to express ideas that are opposite or same in meaning.*

★ Say: *I will read the original sentence with the underlined word and the definition. Then, we will read the synonym or antonym sentences together. Remember, not every word has a synonym or antonym.* Read and discuss examples.

★ Say: *Let's read a story about a boy named Sam. In the story, we will use synonyms and antonyms that we have learned today. First, I will read the story out loud. Then, I will read the story again. When you figure out what goes in the blank, raise your hand during the second reading of the story.*

Assessment

10 min.

 Distribute Assessment 17 to each student.

Name: _____ Date: _____

Assessment 17
Justin and the Best Biscuits in the World, Part II

A. Match the word with the appropriate definition.

a)	utensils	d)	clutter	g)	link	j)	herd	m) horizon
b)	dangling	e)	disposition	h)	trail	k)	speckled	n) relieve
c)	gaze	f)	inspection	i)	depend	l)	plains	o) imagine

_____ 1. covered by small marks

_____ 2. hanging loosely

_____ 3. a broad area of level land

_____ 4. useful tools

_____ 5. where the earth and sky seem to meet

B. Circle the word that does not belong.

1.	attitude	disposition	temperament	inspection
2.	herd	pair	dozen	one
3.	think	imagine	conduct	picture
4.	gather	glance	gaze	watch
5.	examination	review	demonstration	inspection

C. Complete the sentence with the best answer.

_____ 1. The famous Oregon Trail probably linked _____.

     a) ranches with markets for selling cattle

     b) Dorothy and the Wizard of Oz

     c) the United Stated with Mexico

_____ 2. A security officer who works a night shift might be relieved by _____ in the morning.

     a) a police woman or a guard

     b) an inventor or a scientist

     c) an optician or a technician

_____ 3. _____ might be used to clutter a desk.

     a) Elephants, tigers, and zebras

     b) Dictionaries, reports, and paper clips

     c) Laboratories, boardinghouses, and counters

_____ 4. Cowboys depend on _____.

     a) contagious fevers

     b) herds with good dispositions

     c) clearly marked trails

_____ 5. On the horizon, you might see _____.

     a) prehistoric mastodons

     b) a setting or rising sun

     c) a herd roaming the plains

Vocabulary Power, Level 1, by Latrice M. Seals, Sharolyn D. Pollard-Durodola, Barbara R. Foorman, and Ashley M. Bradley

Justin and the Best Biscuits in the World, Part III

by Mildred Pitts Walter

DAY 1 Preview of Lesson	DAY 2 Introduction	DAY 3 Using Words in Context	DAY 4 Expanding Meaning	DAY 5 Keys to Understanding
Read New Words Say and Write New Words Read Definitions Assign At-Home 1	Vocabulary Review Review At-Home 1 Predict the Storyline Story Reading (pages 95–109) Identifying Vocabulary in Text Paraphrasing Vocabulary in Text Assign At-Home 2	Vocabulary Review Review At-Home 2 Using Context Clues Word Wizard Assign At-Home 3	Vocabulary Review Review At-Home 3 Morphographic Elements: *Dis-* and *-ful* Assign At-Home 4	Review At-Home 4 Bingo Game Deep Processing Assessment

Words and Definitions

The following are target words for this week. If the word has multiple meanings, we provide only the definition listed in the text. ***Please review the definitions prior to instruction.***

1. **represent**—to serve as a sign or symbol of

2. **bountiful**—given or provided abundantly; plentiful

3. **exhibit**—something shown publicly for competition or demonstration

4. **dare**—to have enough courage, to be bold

5. **festival**—a program of cultural events or entertainment

6. **crate**—an open box of wooden slats

7. **surging**—swelling or sweeping forward

8. **arena**—an enclosed area used for public entertainment

9. **disqualify**—to make ineligible or unfit for a prize or for further competition because of a violation of the rules

10. **shear**—to cut the hair or wool from; clip

11. **events**—contests in a program of sports

12. **alert**—to call to a state of readiness; to warn

13. **preparations**—acts to prepare or make ready in advance

14. **mare**—an adult female horse

15. **rescue**—to free from danger or evil; to save

Day 1: Preview of Lesson

Prepare for Lesson

 Materials: Student Workbooks, *Justin and the Best Biscuits in the World* by Mildred Pitts Walter, display copy of Week 18 Word List

 Read Teacher Tip: Reading New Words (Week 1, page 8)

5 min. Read New Words

 Say: *Today, we will read another chapter from* Justin and the Best Biscuits in the World. *We will read Chapter 11, "Rodeo Time." Remember, on Day 1 we learn to read new words that you will study at home. The words we learn will help you to read this story better and will help you to express your thoughts on paper and when talking to others. Let's see if there are any words that you already know.*

 Display the Week 18 Word List. Cover the bottom box, leaving the word columns at the top of the page exposed. Say: *Which words do you already know?*

 Uncover the bottom box. Say: *Let's read these words. Sound out each syllable as I point to it. Be sure to say each sound clearly. Sound it out.*

 Students sound out each syllable. Say the word. Students repeat the word. Say: *Yes, the word is . . . .*

10 min. Say and Write New Words

 Cover the bottom box and use the word columns at the top of the page.

 Say: *Let's read the words together.* Point to each word and read one time.

 Say: *Take out your pencil and Student Workbook. Find the page that says Week 18: Say and Write New Words. Let's get ready to say and write each word.*

 Point to each word. Say: *What word?* Students say the word. *Write [the word].*

 Students write the word on the appropriate line. Continue until all words are written.

5 min. Read Definitions

 Say: *I will read the definitions so that we will understand what each word means. Some words have more than one meaning; however, these are the definitions that are used in the story.*

 Read the definitions out loud as students read silently. Choose a student to read each sentence.

Definitions

1. **represent** (to serve as a sign or symbol of)
   The new NFL team, the Houston Texans, chose a bull's head as the logo that would <u>represent</u> the team.

2. **bountiful** (given or provided abundantly; plentiful)
   The farmer was pleased with the <u>bountiful</u> harvest because his family would have plenty of food to last them through the winter.

Week 18 Word List

represen**t**	crate	even**ts**
bounti**ful**	surg**ing**	aler**t**
exhib**it**	arena	prepara**tions**
da**re**	disquali**fy**	mare
festi**val**	shea**r**	rescue

1. rep re sen**t**
2. boun **ty**
   bount i **ful**
3. ex hib **it**
4. da**re**
5. fes ti **val**
6. crat**e**
7. surge
   surg **ing**
8. a re **na**

9. qual i fy
   dis qual i **fy**
10. shea**r**
11. e ven**t**
   e ven**ts**
12. a ler**t**
13. pre pare
   prep a ra **tions**
14. mare
15. res cue

Vocabulary Power, Level 1, by Latrice M. Seals, Sharolyn D. Pollard-Durodola, Barbara R. Foorman, and Ashley M. Bradley

3. **exhibit** (something shown publicly for competition or demonstration)
    Diana enjoys quilting and wants to attend the quilt <u>exhibit</u> at the fair to get ideas from other people's handiwork.

4. **dare** (to have enough courage; to be bold)
    I don't <u>dare</u> sneak out of my house at night for fear my parents would ground me for life.

5. **festival** (a program of cultural events or entertainment)
    Our city's International <u>Festival</u> is a celebration of the many cultural groups living here.

6. **crate** (an open box of wooden slats)
    The furniture Hal ordered arrived on his front porch in a large <u>crate</u>.

7. **surging** (swelling or sweeping forward)
    The <u>surging</u> tide crept closer and closer to the sandcastle.

8. **arena** (an enclosed area used for public entertainment)
    The town's new <u>arena</u> will be used to hold basketball games, the rodeo, and concerts.

9. **disqualify** (to make ineligible or unfit for a prize or for further competition because of a violation of the rules)
    If you break the rules, the judges will have to <u>disqualify</u> you from the competition.

10. **shear** (to cut the hair or wool from; clip)
    Don had to hold the lamb around the neck to <u>shear</u> her wool without cutting her.

11. **events** (contests in a program of sports)
    The school planned a field day with 15 different <u>events</u> for the students.

12. **alert** (to call to a state of readiness; to warn)
    The nutritional information posted on all packaged foods is meant to <u>alert</u> the consumer to health facts about the product.

13. **preparations** (acts to prepare or make ready in advance)
    The employees are busy making final <u>preparations</u> for the store's grand opening in the morning.

14. **mare** (an adult female horse)
    The <u>mare</u> and her newborn colt trotted through the pasture, enjoying the crisp morning air.

15. **rescue** (to free from danger or evil; to save)
    Sherry tried to <u>rescue</u> the tiny kitten who was stuck at the top of the huge oak tree.

Assign At-Home 1

Say: *Tonight you will . . .*

1. *Study the vocabulary words with definitions.*

2. *Complete the Riddle Page.*

3. *Do the Matching Activity.*

4. *Make flashcards.*

Day 2: Introduction

Prepare for Lesson

☆ Materials: Student Workbooks, *Justin and the Best Biscuits in the World* by Mildred Pitts Walter

Vocabulary Review
(3 min.)

☆ Rapid review of vocabulary words (Students use the Week 18 Word List in their Student Workbooks.)

Review At-Home 1
(7 min.)

☆ Review the correct answers to At-Home 1.

☆ Review student work to confirm or clarify responses.

Predict the Storyline
(8 min.)

☆ Students look at the illustration on page 105 of *Justin and the Best Biscuits in the World* by Mildred Pitts Walter.

☆ Say: *Today we will read Chapter 11 of <u>Justin and the Best Biscuits in the World</u>. The name of the chapter is "The Rodeo." A rodeo is a show or contest in which cowboys and other people show how well they are able to ride horses, rope and throw cattle on the ground, and ride horses around a barrel or other obstacle. Have you ever attended a rodeo? At a rodeo you can eat hot dogs, chili, and other foods. Sometimes you can visit a petting zoo of farm animals. But most people attend rodeos to watch cowboys and cowgirls perform many stunts and tricks while riding on bulls and horses in a big arena. You can also watch children from different clubs compete in a contest where they try to catch and rope a calf. If they are able to catch the calf, then they can keep him and take him home to their farm.*

☆ Say: *In this chapter, Justin becomes a participant in a rodeo. Justin admires his grandfather and wants to represent him well at the rodeo festival. How many of you have ever been to a rodeo? Let's talk about some exhibits and events that we might see or participate in at a rodeo.*

☆ Say: *Open your Student Workbook to Semantic Web: Rodeo Time. What events can you watch at the rodeo? What events can children participate in at a rodeo? What exhibits can you see?*

☆ Say: *Think of a question that you think the story will answer. Write the question at the bottom of Semantic Web: Rodeo Time.*

Story Reading 1: Identifying Vocabulary in Text
(8–10 min.)

☆ Say: *As I read the story out loud, you will follow along silently. When you see a word from our vocabulary list, give a thumbs up.*

☆ Read pages 95–109.

☆ Discuss what students predicted would happen in the story.

6 min.

Story Reading 2: Paraphrasing Vocabulary in Text

☆ Say: *As I read specific paragraphs of the story out loud again, let's paraphrase what the author has said by using our own words. Let's focus on the first paragraph on page 96. Follow along as I read out loud.* Read the paragraph ("Floats representing the months . . .").

☆ Say: *What's another way of saying, "Floats representing the months of the year passed slowly?" We might say, "Each passing float was a symbol of one month of the year."*

☆ Help students to paraphrase the remaining sentences in the paragraph as appropriate.

Assign At-Home 2

Say: *Tonight you will . . .*

1. *Study your flashcards.*

2. *Complete Word Substitutions.*

3. *Complete Same and Different.*

Day 3: Using Words in Context

Prepare for Lesson

☆ Materials: Student Workbooks

☆ Read Teacher Tip: Word Wizard (Week 1, page 14)

3 min.

Vocabulary Review

☆ Rapid review of vocabulary words (Students use the Week 18 Word List in their Student Workbooks.)

7 min.

Review At-Home 2

☆ Review the correct answers to At-Home 2.

☆ Review student work to confirm or clarify responses.

15 min.

Using Context Clues

☆ Say: *Open your Student Workbook to Week 18: Using Context Clues. Today, we will use context clues to help us choose the word that fits in the blank by using the clues from other words and information in the sentence or sentences. I will read the sentences out loud. Raise your hand when you know which word best completes the sentence. Write the word in the blank. Sometimes the word might require an ending such as -ed, -s, or -ing. Each word will be used only one time.*

☆ Choose individual students to give answers. Have students point out context clues that helped them to choose the correct answer.

☆ Say: *Cross out words in the box as we use them. Write your answers in the blank, and write the context clues you used in the space below.*

5 min.

Word Wizard

☆ Say: *As Word Wizards this week, you must always be on the lookout for opportunities to use and demonstrate your word knowledge. Use your Word Wizard Journals to keep track of each time you hear one of this week's vocabulary words used in a sentence at home, school, or even on television. If you don't hear the words used in a sentence, be creative and write original sentences using your new vocabulary knowledge. Next week, each group will read two of their favorite sentences to the class!*

☆ Say: *Get in your Word Wizard Groups from last week, and share your best sentences.*

☆ Say: *Which group would like to read two of their sentences using the words from last week's lesson?* Tally the number of sentences per group, and record the amount on the Word Wizard Chart.

Assign At-Home 3

Say: *Tonight you will . . .*

1. *Study your flashcards.*

2. *Complete the Word Wizard Journal.*

3. *Complete the Context Clues Activity.*

Day 4: Expanding Meaning

Prepare for Lesson

☆ Materials: Student Workbooks

☆ Read Teacher Tip: Morphographic Elements (Week 1, page 17)

3 min. Vocabulary Review

☆ Rapid review of vocabulary words (Students use the Week 18 Word List in their Student Workbooks.)

7 min. Review At-Home 3

☆ Review the correct answers to At-Home 3.

☆ Review student work to confirm or clarify responses.

20 min. Morphographic Elements: *Dis-* and *-ful*

☆ Say: *Today we will look at prefixes and suffixes that are present in this week's vocabulary words. Find Morphographic Elements:* Dis- *and* -ful *in your Student Workbook.*

☆ Say: *Lets look at the information in the top box. Prefixes are word parts that are added to the beginning of a word. Suffixes are word parts that can be added to the end of a word. Can you think of any prefixes or suffixes that you have studied?* Briefly discuss. *Today, we will look at words that use the prefix* dis- *and the suffix* -ful.

☆ Read the definition for *dis-*. Say: *Let's look in the box and read words that use this prefix.* Read the word, definition, and the sentence that corresponds with the word using the prefix *dis-*.

☆ Read the definition for *-ful*. Say: *Let's look in the box and read words that use this suffix.* Read the word, definition, and the sentence that corresponds with the word using the suffix *-ful*.

☆ Say: *Prefixes and suffixes help us to see relationships between words when we read. Let's read and discuss the word cousins that appear in Part A.* Read the word cousins together.

☆ Say: *Let's look at Part B. Each underlined word is written with a suffix that we have studied today. We will read the word in a sentence and then use context clues and the meaning of the suffix to help us to select the best definition.*

Assign At-Home 4

Say: *Tonight you will . . .*

1. *Study your flashcards.*

2. *Complete the Crossword Puzzle.*

Day 5: Keys to Understanding

Prepare for Lesson

 Materials: Student Workbooks, photocopies of Assessment 18

☆ Read Teacher Tip: Deep Processing (Week 2, page 28)

Review At-Home 4

(7 min.)

☆ Review the correct answers to At-Home 4.

☆ Review student work to confirm or clarify responses.

Bingo Game

(8 min.)

☆ Say: *Choose nine words from the Week 18 Word List, and write them on the Bingo Card in your Student Workbook. When I read a definition, raise your hand to identify the word. If you have the word on your card, mark it with an X. The first person who has 3 Xs in a row (across, down, diagonally) wins the game.*

☆ Read the definitions. As students identify definitions, write the word on the board until someone wins the game.

Deep Processing

(8–10 min.)

☆ Say: *Does anyone remember what deep processing is? It is thinking about how words relate to each other.*

☆ Say: *We have learned the definitions for this week's vocabulary words, but definitions do not really teach everything you need to know to really understand the meaning of a word. Remember, it is important to be able to use these words to describe your own experiences in life and to describe conditions in the world in general.*

☆ Say: *Open your Student Workbook to Deep Processing: Justin and the Best Biscuits in the World, Part III. We will read each question together and decide what is a reasonable answer and why. Remember, the answers are not in the book we read but come from your own thinking. Think about the questions and about what would be a reasonable response. Remember, you must be able to explain why you chose your answer.*

Assessment

(10 min.)

☆ Distribute Assessment 18 to each student.

Name: _____   Date: _____

Assessment 18
Justin and the Best Biscuits in the World, Part III

A. Match the word with the appropriate definition.

a) represent	d) dare	g) surge	j) shear	m) preparation
b) bountiful	e) festival	h) arena	k) events	n) mare
c) exhibit	f) crate	i) disqualify	l) alert	o) rescue

_____ 1. to free from danger

_____ 2. a program that offers entertainment or a cultural event

_____ 3. an open box of wooden slats

_____ 4. to serve as a sign or symbol

_____ 5. contests in a program of sports

B. Circle the word that does not belong.

1.	shear	cut	trim	grow
2.	endanger	risk	protect	dare
3.	warn	hide	notify	alert
4.	disqualify	prohibit	allow	reject
5.	festival	parade	exhibit	hospital

Vocabulary Power, Level 1, by Latrice M. Seals, Sharolyn D. Pollard-Durodola, Barbara R. Foorman, and Ashley M. Bradley   233
© 2007 Paul H. Brookes Publishing Co., Inc. All rights reserved.

C. Complete the sentence with the best answer.

_____ 1.   If you were making preparations for a party, you would _____.

     a)   invite guests to the event

     b)   go on a vacation

     c)   play basketball

_____ 2.   Jessica should feed the mare _____.

     a)   hay and apples

     b)   crates and magazines

     c)   exhibits and games

_____ 3.   If books in the library are bountiful, that means that there are _____ books.

     a)   no

     b)   only a few

     c)   many

_____ 4.   The crowd entering the arena for a festival began to surge, so the mother _____.

     a)   held her little boy close

     b)   sheared her little boy's hair

     c)   showed the exhibits to her little boy

_____ 5.   We attended an art exhibit so that we could _____.

     a)   buy paint brushes and art paper.

     b)   look at the painter's new drawings

     c)   finger-paint with our friends

The Bat Boy and His Violin
by Gavin Curtis

DAY 1 Preview of Lesson	DAY 2 Introduction	DAY 3 Using Words in Context	DAY 4 Expanding Meaning	DAY 5 Keys to Understanding
Read New Words Say and Write New Words Read Definitions Assign At-Home 1	Vocabulary Review Review At-Home 1 Predict the Storyline Story Reading (entire book) Identifying Vocabulary in Text Paraphrasing Vocabulary in Text Assign At-Home 2	Vocabulary Review Review At-Home 2 Using Context Clues Word Wizard Assign At-Home 3	Vocabulary Review Review At-Home 3 Multiple Meanings Assign At-Home 4	Review At-Home 4 Bingo Game AAVE Idiomatic Expressions and Spellings Play Ball! (optional) Assessment

Words and Definitions

The following are target words for this week. If the word has multiple meanings, we provide only the definition listed in the text. ***Please review the definitions prior to instruction.***

1. **pennant**—a triangular flag used for a championship in baseball

2. **recital**—an end-of-year musical performance by a performer or a group of musicians or dancers

3. **performance**—a public presentation of a play, a piece of music, or a movie

4. **skim**—to glide quickly over a surface

5. **bow**—a long, flat piece of wood with strings used for playing stringed instruments (such as the violin)

6. **league**—a group of people with common interests (such as a group of sports teams)

7. **admire**—to like and to respect someone

8. **buff**—to polish something

9. **umpire**—an official who makes official decisions during baseball, tennis, and other sports

10. **massage**—to rub someone's body with fingers and the hands in order to loosen muscles

11. **sprout**—begin to grow

12. **inspire**—to influence and encourage someone to do something

13. **bleachers**—rows of raised seats or benches found in stadiums

14. **measure**—a bar of music

15. **integrate**—to include people of all races

Day 1: Preview of Lesson

Prepare for Lesson

☆ Materials: Student Workbooks, *The Bat Boy and His Violin* by Gavin Curtis, display copy of Week 19 Word List

☆ Read Teacher Tip: Reading New Words (Week 1, page 8)

 5 min.

Read New Words

☆ Say: *Today, we will begin a new story, <u>The Bat Boy and His Violin</u>. Remember, on Day 1 we learn to read new words that you will study at home. The words we learn will help you to read this story better and will help you to express your thoughts on paper and when talking to others. Let's see if there are any words that you already know.*

☆ Display the Week 19 Word List. Cover the bottom box, leaving the word columns at the top of the page exposed. Say: *Which words do you already know?*

☆ Uncover the bottom box. Say: *Let's read these words. Sound out each syllable as I point to it. Be sure to say each sound clearly. Sound it out.*

☆ Students sound out each syllable. Say the word. Students repeat the word. Say: *Yes, the word is . . . .*

 10 min.

Say and Write New Words

☆ Cover the bottom box and use the word columns at the top of the page.

☆ Say: *Let's read the words together.* Point to each word and read one time.

☆ Say: *Take out your pencil and Student Workbook. Find the page that says Week 19: Say and Write New Words. Let's get ready to say and write each word.*

☆ Point to each word. Say: *What word?* Students say the word. *Write [the word].*

☆ Students write the word on the appropriate line. Continue until all words are written.

 5 min.

Read Definitions

☆ Say: *I will read the definitions so that we will understand what each word means. Some words have more than one meaning; however, these are the definitions that are used in the story.*

☆ Read the definitions out loud as students read silently. Choose a student to read each sentence.

Definitions

1. **pennant** (a triangular flag used for a championship in baseball)
   At the baseball game, the Hornets received the championship <u>pennant</u> for the 2003 baseball season.

2. **recital** (an end-of-year musical performance by a performer or a group of musicians or dancers)
   Reginald practiced daily so that he would be prepared to perform his best during the June <u>recital</u> in the church basement.

Vocabulary Power, Level 1

Week 19 Word List

pennan**t**	league	sprou**t**
reci**tal**	admi**r**e	inspi**r**e
performan**ce**	bu**ff**	bleach**ers**
ski**m**	umpi**r**e	mea**sure**
bow	massa**ge**	integra**t**e

1. pen nan**t**
2. re cite
   re ci **tal**
3. per form
   per form an**ce**
4. ski**m**
5. bow
6. league
7. ad mir**e**
8. bu**ff**

9. um pir**e**
10. mas sa**ge**
11. sprou**t**
12. in
    in spir**e**
13. bleach
    bleach **ers**
14. mea **sure**
15. in
    in te grat**e**

3. **performance** (a public presentation of a play, a piece of music, or a movie)
   We paid $60 a ticket in order to acquire good seats at the <u>performance</u> of the Bolshoi Ballet.

4. **skim** (to glide quickly over a surface)
   The dragonfly <u>skim</u>med over the surface of the glistening lake.

5. **bow** (a long, flat piece of wood with strings used for playing stringed instruments such as the violin)
   When learning to play the cello, it is crucial or important that one holds the <u>bow</u> at an angle so that the appropriate strings are touched.

6. **league** (a group of people with common interests [such as a group of sports teams])
   The Westbank Softball <u>League</u> decided to initiate a fundraiser to raise money for new uniforms for the five teams within its division.

7. **admire** (to like and to respect someone)
   Reginald <u>admire</u>d his father for the time and effort he dedicated to the Dukes baseball team.

8. **buff** (to polish something)
   Before we set out the china, everyone is responsible for <u>buff</u>ing the silver water pitcher and serving platters.

9. **umpire** (an official who makes official decisions during baseball, tennis, and other sports)
   The <u>umpire</u> spread his arms out straight and shouted, "Safe!" as the player slid across home plate.

10. **massage** (to rub someone's body with fingers and the hands in order to loosen muscles)
    Before bed, Dad <u>massage</u>s my arms and legs that are sore from playing tennis.

11. **sprout** (begin to grow)
    After much watering, the sunflowers began to <u>sprout</u> during the early part of summer.

12. **inspire** (to influence and encourage someone to do something)
    Marian Anderson <u>inspire</u>d many when she decided to sing at the steps of the Jefferson Memorial.

13. **bleachers** (rows of raised seats or benches found in stadiums)
    There was boisterous cheering from the <u>bleachers</u> when David hit the ball out of the park with the bases loaded.

14. **measure** (a bar of music)
    In the song, the pianist counted 15 <u>measure</u>s total, with each measure receiving four beats.

15. **integrate** (to include people of all races)
    During the 1960s, many public schools made attempts to <u>integrate</u> their campuses.

Assign At-Home 1

Say: *Tonight you will . . .*

1. *Study the vocabulary words with definitions.*

2. *Complete the Riddle Page.*

3. *Do the Matching Activity.*

4. *Make flashcards.*

Day 2: Introduction

Prepare for Lesson

 Materials: Student Workbooks, *Bat Boy and the Violin* by Gavin Curtis

3 min. ## Vocabulary Review

 Rapid review of vocabulary words (Students use the Week 19 Word List in their Student Workbooks.)

7 min. ## Review At-Home 1

 Review the correct answers to At-Home 1.

☆ Review student work to confirm or clarify responses.

8 min. ## Predict the Storyline

☆ Students look at the illustration on the cover of *The Bat Boy and His Violin* by Gavin Curtis.

☆ Say: *Today we will read the book* <u>The Bat Boy and His Violin</u>. *What do you know about the sport of baseball? Let's think of words that we associate with playing baseball.* If desired, write the words on the board.

☆ Say: *Open your Student Workbook to Semantic Web: Baseball. Are there any words that we didn't already think of?* Discuss the words in terms of how they are related to baseball.

☆ Say: *What categories could we create to classify some of the words on the list? For example, what do these words have in common: glove, caps, uniform, metal cleats (on shoes)? Yes, these are kinds of things that you wear when playing baseball. What other categories could we create?* Examples include members of a baseball team and awards.

☆ Say: *This book is not just about a boy who wants to play baseball. Look at the front cover. How do you think the main character, Reginald, really wants to spend his leisure time? Yes, instead of playing a sport, it appears that he would rather play a musical instrument, the violin. Maybe the theme of this book is about overcoming obstacles. Maybe someone or something is preventing him from being a musician. What do you think?*

☆ Say: *What are some ways in which playing a musical instrument is the same as playing a sport?* Possible answers are that both require much practice and that the outcome of both is a public performance.

☆ Say: *Think of a question that you think the story will answer. Write the question at the bottom of Semantic Web: Baseball.*

8–10 min. ## Story Reading 1: Identifying Vocabulary in Text

 Say: *As I read the story out loud, you will follow along silently. When you see a word from our vocabulary list, give a thumbs up.*

☆ Read the entire book.

☆ Discuss what students predicted would happen in the story.

Story Reading 2: Paraphrasing Vocabulary in Text

☆ Say: *As I read specific paragraphs of the story out loud again, let's paraphrase what the author has said by using our own words. Let's focus on the last paragraph on the first page. Follow along as I read out loud.* Read the paragraph ("I try to play louder . . .").

☆ Say: *What's another way of saying, ". . . by sawing the music hard"? We might say, "Reginald would play the music loudly so that he couldn't hear his father's voice. He played loudly to drown out his father's voice when Papa was in a bad mood."*

☆ Help students to paraphrase the remaining sentences in the paragraph as appropriate.

Assign At-Home 2

Say: *Tonight you will . . .*

1. *Study your flashcards.*

2. *Complete Word Substitutions.*

3. *Complete Same and Different.*

Day 3: Using Words in Context

Prepare for Lesson

☆ Materials: Student Workbooks

☆ Read Teacher Tip: Word Wizard (Week 1, page 14)

3 min. Vocabulary Review

☆ Rapid review of vocabulary words (Students use the Week 19 Word List in their Student Workbooks.)

7 min. Review At-Home 2

☆ Review the correct answers to At-Home 2.

☆ Review student work to confirm or clarify responses.

15 min. Using Context Clues

☆ Say: *Open your Student Workbook to Week 19: Using Context Clues. Today, we will use context clues to help us choose the word that fits in the blank by using the clues from other words and information in the sentence or sentences. I will read the sentences out loud. Raise your hand when you know which word best completes the sentence. Write the word in the blank. Sometimes the word might require an ending such as -ed, -s, or -ing. Each word will be used only one time.*

☆ Choose individual students to give answers. Have students point out context clues that helped them to choose the correct answer.

☆ Say: *Cross out words in the box as we use them. Write your answers in the blank, and write the context clues you used in the space below.*

5 min. Word Wizard

☆ Say: *As Word Wizards this week, you must always be on the lookout for opportunities to use and demonstrate your word knowledge. Use your Word Wizard Journals to keep track of each time you hear one of this week's vocabulary words used in a sentence at home, school, or even on television. If you don't hear the words used in a sentence, be creative and write original sentences using your new vocabulary knowledge. Next week, each group will read two of their favorite sentences to the class!*

☆ Say: *Get in your Word Wizard Groups from last week, and discuss which of the sentences you have written is the best.*

☆ Say: *Which group would like to read two of their favorite sentences using the words from last week's lesson?* Tally the number of sentences per group, and record the amount on the Word Wizard Chart.

Assign At-Home 3

Say: *Tonight you will . . .*

1. *Study your flashcards.*

2. *Complete the Word Wizard Journal.*

3. *Complete the Context Clues Activity.*

Day 4: Expanding Meaning

Prepare for Lesson

☆ Materials: Student Workbooks

3 min. ## Vocabulary Review

☆ Rapid review of vocabulary words (Students use the Week 19 Word List in their Student Workbooks.)

7 min. ## Review At-Home 3

☆ Review the correct answers to At-Home 3.

☆ Review student work to confirm or clarify responses.

20 min. ## Multiple Meanings

☆ Say: *Sometimes words have several meanings. For example, in Week 11, we studied different definitions for the words <u>relief</u>, <u>security</u>, and <u>exchange</u>. For example, the word <u>relief</u> may mean freedom from worrying about pain or it could refer to raised figures on a map.*

☆ Say: *Some of the words in this week's story also have multiple meanings. These words are <u>skim</u>, <u>bow</u>, <u>measure</u>, <u>performance</u>, and <u>integrate</u>. Turn to Week 19: Multiple Meanings in your Student Workbook. Let's read the definitions for these words.*

☆ Say: *Let's read sentences using these words and look for context clues that can help us to choose the correct definition.*

☆ Read the first sentence out loud. Say: *Which definition for <u>skim</u> are we using in this sentence?* The correct answer is c, to read through something quickly to get the main idea.

☆ Say: *What context clues helped us to understand the meaning of the word?* Answers include magnifying glass and letters.

☆ Say: *I will read each sentence out loud, and you will choose the letter of the definition that describes how the word is used in the sentence.*

☆ *Note:* When reading the definition for *bow*, the front of a ship, the pronunciation changes to /ow/ as in the word *cow*. Have students practice reading the sentence out loud.

Assign At-Home 4

Say: *Tonight you will . . .*

1. *Study your flashcards.*

2. *Complete the Crossword Puzzle.*

Day 5: Keys to Understanding

Prepare for Lesson

 Materials: Student Workbook, photocopies of Assessment 19

Read Teacher Tip: African American Vernacular English (Week 6, page 81)

Review At-Home 4

7 min.

Review the correct answers to At-Home 4.

 Review student work to confirm or clarify responses.

Bingo Game

8 min.

Say: *Choose nine words from the Week 19 Word List, and write them on the Bingo Card in your Student Workbook. When I read a definition, raise your hand to identify the word. If you have the word on your card, mark it with an X. The first person who has 3 Xs in a row (across, down, diagonally) wins the game.*

Read the definitions. As students identify definitions, write the word on the board until someone wins the game.

AAVE Idiomatic Expressions and Spellings

15 min.

 Say: *Sometimes authors write the way we speak. That means that the author's written language will contain elements that we only hear when people are talking. For example, when talking, we might leave off the endings of some words, such as comin' for coming and talkin' for talking, or we may change the sounds in a word when speaking. We may say dis instead of this.*

Say: *Open your Student Workbook to Idiomatic Expressions and Spellings. Let's read these expressions and think of a different way to express the same thought. Ask students to read each idiomatic expression aloud. Discuss.*

Say: *Now that we have discussed how the characters talked in the story, let's match these phrases with the way the characters might speak or write at school. In Part B, Spelling, we see examples of words that are spelled without the final g for the -ing pattern. These words represent how we might say the word at home. Rewrite the word and make sure you add the -ing ending.*

Say: *Read the sentences in Part C, Writing Practice, and rewrite them using the language you would use at school.*

Say: *Is either way of speaking better than the other? No! Remember, you may speak or write differently depending on where you are and your purpose in communicating.*

Play Ball! (optional)

☆ Students match names of famous African American baseball players with biographical information.

Assessment

☆ Distribute Assessment 19 to each student.

Name: _____ Date: _____

Assessment 19
The Bat Boy and His Violin

A. Match the word with the appropriate definition.

a) pennant	d) skim	g) admire	j) massage	m) bleachers
b) recital	e) bow	h) buff	k) sprout	n) measure
c) performance	f) league	i) umpire	l) inspire	o) integrate

_____ 1. a long, wooden piece used to play a string instrument

_____ 2. a group of people with common interests

_____ 3. an official who makes decisions at baseball games

_____ 4. to polish or make something shine

_____ 5. a triangular flag used for a championship in baseball

B. Circle the word that does not belong.

1.	sprout	grow	germinate	wither
2.	observation	performance	recital	concert
3.	admire	dislike	respect	revere
4.	discourage	inspire	encourage	motivate
5.	rub	cut	press	massage

C. Complete the sentence with the best answer.

_____ 1. After an inspiring cello recital, members of the audience _____.

    a) admired and applauded the cello player

    b) formed a league against cellos

    c) were relieved to leave the performance

_____ 2. On a regular basis, _____ must be buffed or it might tarnish and become dull.

    a) a velvet purse

    b) a plastic plate

    c) a silver bracelet

_____ 3. During a soccer competition, an umpire might _____.

    a) skim through a book about massage

    b) ignore measures established in a book of rules

    c) award the winning league with a pennant

_____ 4. The vegetarian shared ideas from top performance cooks that are expert in using _____.

    a) buffed soap in soups

    b) bean sprouts in salads

    c) pennants as lettuce

_____ 5. The musician skimmed the strings of the violin with his bow and frowned because _____.

    a) the bleachers were covered with ice

    b) the recital was not going well

    c) the measures were inspiring

Review Unit 4

REVIEW DAY 1	REVIEW DAY 2	REVIEW DAY 3	REVIEW DAY 4	REVIEW DAY 5
Introduce Unit Review "I Spy" Game Assign At-Home 1	Semantic Feature Analysis Assign At-Home 2	Multiple Meanings Find It, Say It! Game Assign At-Home 3	Clueless Game Assign At-Home 4	Assessment

Words and Definitions

The following are target words for this week. If the word has multiple meanings, we provide only the definition listed in the text. *Please review the definitions prior to instruction.*

1. **weakness**—object of special desire or fondness
2. **strain**—to stretch beyond a natural limit
3. **exhausted**—a state in which all of one's mental or physical energy has been used up
4. **buff**—to polish something
5. **ground**—to prohibit from participating in an activity
6. **trail**—a path marked to show a route through a wilderness region
7. **relieve**—to release from a post or duty
8. **depend**—to rely on for support
9. **horizon**—the line where the earth or sea and the sky seem to meet
10. **shear**—to cut the hair or wool from; clip
11. **disqualify**—to make ineligible or unfit for a prize or for further competition because of a violation of the rules
12. **crate**—an open box of wooden slats
13. **measure**—a bar of music
14. **integrate**—to include people of all races
15. **exhibit**—something shown publicly for competition or demonstration
16. **glance**—to look at quickly or hastily
17. **gaze**—to fix the eyes in a steady and intent look
18. **inspire**—to influence and encourage someone to do something
19. **bow**—a long, flat piece of wood used for playing instruments
20. **admire**—to like and respect someone
21. **recital**—an end-of-year musical performance by a performer or a group of musicians or dancers
22. **bountiful**—given or provided abundantly; plentiful
23. **alert**—to call to a state of readiness; to warn
24. **dare**—to have enough courage; to be bold
25. **plains**—a broad area of level or rolling treeless country

Review Day 1

Prepare for Lesson

☆ Materials: Student Workbooks, display copy of Unit 4 Word List (optional)

Introduce Unit Review

☆ Say: *Last week we completed the last story in our unit. We have read four stories and learned many new words each week. This week, we will review some key words that we learned in Unit 4. At the end of the week, you will have an opportunity to demonstrate just how much you've learned.*

"I Spy" Game

☆ Say: *How many of you remember playing "I Spy?" When we play "I Spy" we use clues to help us identify words.*

☆ Say: *Turn to Unit 4 "I Spy" in your Student Workbook. Today, we will work as word detectives and use a list of clues to determine the review word. Let's read the clues and decide which word is being described. Write the word next to the appropriate clue. Remember, a good detective never gives up!*

☆ Read the sentences out loud, and call on students for answers. Say: *I am looking for a word that means . . . ,* then read the definition. Students should respond in the form, "I spy . . ." then say the vocabulary word.

Assign At-Home 1

Say: *Tonight at home you will . . .*

1. *Study the Unit 4 vocabulary words with definitions.*

2. *Make flashcards.*

Unit 4 Word List

weakness	strain	buff
exhausted	ground	trail
relieve	depend	horizon
shear	disqualify	crate
measure	integrate	exhibit
glance	gaze	inspire
bow	admire	recital
bountiful	alert	dare
plains		

Vocabulary Power, Level 1, by Latrice M. Seals, Sharolyn D. Pollard-Durodola, Barbara R. Foorman, and Ashley M. Bradley

Prepare for Lesson

☆ Materials: Student Workbooks, display copy of Semantic Feature Analysis: To Look At

☆ Read Teacher Tip: Semantic Feature Analysis (Week 5, page 62)

Semantic Feature Analysis

☆ Say: *The objective of today's activity is to compare different words and to decide how words are similar and different. The purpose of this activity is to help you to see how words are related to each other.*

☆ Say: *In Review Unit 3, we categorized words that describe different kinds of stores. This week, we will focus on words that mean "to look at." For example,* gaze *and* glance *both mean to look at something, but they are used in different ways. Can you think of other words that mean "to look at something?"*

☆ Say: *Open your Student Workbook to Semantic Feature Analysis: To Look At. Let's look at the words listed in the left column of the matrix. Does the list contain the words meaning "to look at" that we have just discussed in class?* Read through the list with students. Add any words that were discussed in class but that are not on the list.

☆ Say: *Let's look at some features of these words. Look at the top row of the matrix. Can you think of any other features that should be listed here?* Any additional features may be added.

☆ Say: *Let's discuss the features of different words that mean to look at something. We will fill in the matrix with a plus or minus to indicate the presence or absence of each feature. If we can't agree, we will place a zero in the matrix.*

☆ After the matrix is complete, say: *Let's look at the matrix and compare different kinds of words that mean to look at.* Discuss similar and different features.

☆ Help students discover that no two words have exactly the same pattern of pluses (similiarities) and minuses (differences): none are identical. Even the categories that are most alike will reveal their differences if enough features are added.

Assign At-Home 2

Say: *Tonight at home you will study the vocabulary words on your flashcards.*

Semantic Feature Analysis: To Look At

	To look at quickly	To look at for a long time	To look at secretly	To look, study, and think	To look at closely	To look at with positive emotions	To look at with negative emotions			
Glance										
Stare										
Peek										
Examine										
Scrutinize										
View										
Gaze										

Prepare for Lesson

 Materials: Student Workbooks

15 min.

Multiple Meanings

 Say: *Today we are going to work with some of the words from the past 4 weeks that have more than one meaning. In the first part of the activity, we will quickly review the different meanings for each word.*

☆ Say: *Who remembers one of the meanings for the word <u>settle</u>? Continue until the students have identified as many definitions as they can for settle. Do the same for weakness, horizon, and ground.*

☆ Say: *Open your Student Workbook to Week 20: Multiple Meanings. Let's see how many meanings we know for these words.*

15 min.

Find It, Say It! Game

☆ Say: *Next, we will play Find It, Say It! Turn to Week 20: Find It, Say It!*

☆ Say: *Remember, when we play Find It, Say It! I first read the sentence with the underlined word and say, "Find It!" You then go to the box of the underlined word and find the definition that best fits the way the word is used in each sentence. Without talking, you write the letter for that definition in the space at the beginning of the sentence. When I say, "Say It," everyone will say the answer out loud together.*

☆ After asking students to find the answer, allow them approximately 7 seconds before asking them to say it.

Assign At-Home 3

Say: *Tonight at home you will study the vocabulary words on your flashcards.*

Review Day 4

Prepare for Lesson

☆ Materials: Clue Cards, photocopies of Score Keeper Card

 Clueless Game

☆ Write the words "Class Score Keeper" and the numbers 1–10 on the board.

☆ Say: *Today, we will play Clueless. As you may recall from the last unit review, the objective of this game is to focus on single word clues that can help you to remember the words that you have learned. Remember, you may not use your Student Workbook to help you.*

☆ Say: *Do you remember your groups from last time?* If necessary, create new groups.

☆ Say: *We will appoint a new score keeper for each team. We will use the part of the Score Keeper Card for Review Unit 4.* Assign a person from each group to be the score keeper or allow teams to choose their own score keepers.

☆ Say: *Let's review the rules. I will place a marker on 10 on the Class Score Keeper. Then, I will flash a Clue Card with a one-word clue. I will start with Team A. If Team A correctly identifies the word, they get the points indicated on the Class Score Keeper. If the marker is on 10, they get 10 points, and the team's score keeper records the value on the Score Keeper Card.*

☆ Say: *If the word is not guessed from the Clue Card, the marker on the Class Score Keeper is moved to 9, and it becomes the other team's turn. If they guess the word, they receive the points indicated by the Class Score Keeper.*

☆ Say: *Remember, if the word is not guessed from the first clue, the marker on the Class Score Keeper is moved to 9, and it becomes the other team's turn. If the next team cannot guess the word, the marker is moved to 8, and so forth. Each time the word is not guessed the marker is moved one number lower.*

☆ Say: *Each time we read a new clue, the marker is placed back on 10, and the other team tries to identify the word from the next clue card.*

☆ Say: *We continue to play until we have identified all the clue words. The team with the highest total score is the winner.*

☆ Distribute the Score Keeper Cards for each team. After playing the game, collect the Score Keeper Cards so that they can be used with the next review unit.

Assign At-Home 4

Say: *Tonight at home you will study for Friday's test.*

clip	ineligible	tired	performance	challenge
warn	punish	stretched	instrument	rely
land	encourage	container	path	plenty
sunset	look	release	respect	polish
mix	stare	bar	show	fondness

Vocabulary Power, Level 1, by Latrice M. Seals, Sharolyn D. Pollard-Durodola, Barbara R. Foorman, and Ashley M. Bradley

Review Day 5

Prepare for Lesson

☆ Materials: photocopies of Assessment 20

Assessment

☆ Distribute Assessment 20 to each student.

☆ Read the directions out loud.

☆ Read each vocabulary word out loud along with the answer choices. Allow students a few seconds to choose and write the letter for a definition.

☆ Collect assessments.

Name: _____ Date: _____

Assessment 20
Unit 4

Choose the letter that represents the best definition for each word.

____ 1. exhausted
   a. daring and brazen
   b. strong and flexible
   c. weak and weary

____ 2. recital
   a. a final performance
   b. a final rehearsal
   c. a final try out

____ 3. crate
   a. a blender
   b. a box
   c. a vase

____ 4. alert
   a. to warn someone about danger
   b. to give someone a party
   c. to challenge someone to a contest

____ 5. shear
   a. to slice evenly with a knife
   b. to cut vertically with scissors
   c. to cut closely with clippers

____ 6. plains
   a. flat land
   b. rolling hills
   c. steep mountains

____ 7. ground
   a. to walk around
   b. to keep from participating
   c. to place in a box

____ 8. dare
   a. to be confident
   b. to be contagious
   c. to be courageous

____ 9. bountiful
   a. secret
   b. plenty
   c. scarce

____ 10. strain
   a. stretch tight
   b. pull back
   c. loosen up

____ 11. horizon
   a. a crooked line between earth and sky.
   b. an imaginary line between earth and sky
   c. an line between the northern and southern hemispheres

____ 12. bow
   a. a wooden stick
   b. a shiny object
   c. a paper airplane

____ 13. trail
   a. a winding street
   b. a dirt path
   c. a wide road

____ 14. weakness
   a. a defect or fault
   b. an energy or force
   c. a strength or asset

____ 15. glance

    a. to look for a long time

    b. to look for a short time

    c. to look around

____ 16. measure

    a. a bar of chocolate with nuts

    b. a bar of soap with bubbles

    c. a bar of music with notes

____ 17. integrate

    a. separate

    b. include

    c. intercept

____ 18. relieve

    a. to free

    b. to bind

    c. to outlaw

____ 19. disqualify

    a. to make illegible

    b. to make ineligible

    c. to make illegal

____ 20. depend

    a. to free from

    b. to rely on

    c. to stand above

____ 21. buff

    a. to make something shine

    b. to make something sing

    c. to make something settle

____ 22. gaze

    a. to look away

    b. to peer quickly

    c. to stare steadily

____ 23. recital

    a. a musical score

    b. a musical instrument

    c. a musical performance

____ 24. inspire

    a. to urge

    b. to discourage

    c. to instruct

____ 25. exhibit

    a. a shower

    b. a show

    c. a sheep

Vocabulary Power, Level 1, by Latrice M. Seals, Sharolyn D. Pollard-Durodola, Barbara R. Foorman, and Ashley M. Bradley

Answer Key

Use these scoring grids to grade the At-Home assignments and Assessments.

At-Home 1

– 1 95%	– 2 90%	– 3 85%	– 4 80%	– 5 75%	– 6 70%	– 7 65%	– 8 60%	– 9 55%	– 10 50%
– 11 45%	– 12 40%	– 13 35%	– 14 30%	– 15 25%	– 16 20%	– 17 15%	– 18 10%	– 19 5%	– 20 0%

At-Home 2

– 1 90%	– 2 80%	– 3 70%	– 4 60%	– 5 50%	– 6 40%	– 7 30%	– 8 20%	– 9 10%	– 10 0%

At-Home 3, At-Home 4, and weekly Assessments

– 1 93%	– 2 87%	– 3 80%	– 4 73%	– 5 67%	– 6 60%	– 7 53%	– 8 47%
– 9 40%	– 10 33%	– 11 27%	– 12 20%	– 13 13%	– 14 7%	– 15 0%	

Review Unit Assessments

– 1 96%	– 2 92%	– 3 88%	– 4 84%	– 5 80%	– 6 76%	– 7 72%	– 8 68%	– 9 64%
– 10 60%	– 11 56%	– 12 52%	– 13 48%	– 14 44%	– 15 40%	– 16 36%	– 17 32%	– 18 28%
– 19 24%	– 20 20%	– 21 16%	– 22 12%	– 23 8%	– 24 4%	– 25 0%		

Answer Key

For some activities, such as Semantic Web, suggested answers are provided; other answers may be acceptable. For multiple-choice questions with long answers, the letter of the correct choice is given, along with a few key words for clarification.

AT-HOME 1

Riddle Page: "What am I?"

1. boardinghouse
2. troop
3. master
4. wealthy
5. stacks

Matching Activity

1. troop
2. cautious
3. wealthy
4. approach
5. bend
6. boardinghouse
7. optician
8. suspicious
9. powerful
10. borrow
11. stacks
12. rebel
13. roam
14. ignore
15. master

SEMANTIC WEB: LIBRARY

1. *What were Richard's experiences in the library?*—people looked at him suspiciously; Richard spent his time in the stacks, amazed at so many books
2. *How can a trip to the library change one's life?*—exposure to new ideas, read about characters in books who are like yourself (same goals), read about solutions to difficult situations or problems (like your own.)
3. *Why do people go to the library?*—conduct research, borrow books, read books and other materials

AT-HOME 2

Word Substitutions

1. a) troops
2. b) careful
3. b) draws near
4. a) person in charge
5. a) authoritative

Same and Different

1. lagoon
2. underprivileged
3. follower
4. attorney
5. borrow

USING WORDS IN CONTEXT

1. master
2. wealthy
3. cautious
4. powerful
5. roam
6. borrow
7. suspicious
8. boardinghouse
9. ignored
10. bend
11. stacks
12. approached
13. optician
14. troops
15. Rebels

Answer Key

AT-HOME 3

Context Clues Activity

1.	a) borrow	6.	b) suspicious	11.	b) master
2.	b) boardinghouse	7.	a) wealthy	12.	a) a level surface
3.	a) troop	8.	b) ignore	13.	b) hole
4.	a) rebels	9.	b) optician	14.	a) set free
5.	b) powerful	10.	a) roamed	15.	b) utensil that blends

MULTIPLE MEANINGS: *MASTER* AND *APPROACH*

1.	f	4.	c	7.	h
2.	b	5.	e	8.	i
3.	a	6.	d	9.	g

AT-HOME 4

Across

2.	borrow	9.	rebel	13.	optician
5.	suspicious	10.	cautious	14.	stacks
7.	bend	12.	roam		

Down

1.	powerful	6.	wealthy	15.	approach
3.	master	8.	troop		
4.	boardinghouse	11.	ignore		

Get Ready to Read!

There is no one answer.

James Baldwin	1924–1987		*If Beale Street Could Talk*
Paul Laurence Dunbar	1872–1906		*Oak and Ivy: Complete Poems of Paul Laurence Dunbar*
Ida B. Wells Barnett	1862–1931		*Crusade for Justice*
W.E.B. DuBois	1868–1938		*The Souls of Black Folks*
Phyllis Wheatley	1753–1784		*Poems on Various Subjects*
Langston Hughes	1902–1967		*Not Without Laughter*
Dorothy West	1907–1998		*The Living is Easy*
Ann Petry	1908–1997		*The Street*
William Wells Brown	1814–1884		*Clotel*

MORPHOGRAPHIC ELEMENTS: *-IAN*

1. b) one who makes music
2. a) one who performs magic
3. b) ordinary citizens
4. a) works in clinic
5. a) member in school of study
6. b) one who lives in Boston

ASSESSMENT 1

Part A

1. c) rebel
2. e) wealthy
3. f) borrow
4. o) stacks
5. h) boardinghouse

Part B

1. notice
2. sit
3. Cautious
4. comfortable
5. helpless

Part C

1. a) plan cautiously
2. c) all of the above
3. b) a bend in the road
4. b) a powerful rebel
5. c) all of the above

AT-HOME 1

Riddle Page: "What am I?"

1. booming
2. crater
3. beater
4. counter
5. guard

Matching Activity

1. counter
2. press
3. loosen
4. booming
5. crater
6. guard
7. pudding
8. beater
9. straight
10. thick
11. whip
12. crack
13. smooth
14. even
15. leave

SEMANTIC WEB: SPECIAL FOODS

1. *What are some special foods that people prepare for special occasions?*—wedding cake, birthday cake, cookies, pies, BBQ, Valentine's Day cookies, puddings, custards, cupcakes
2. *Why do people prepare special foods?*—celebrate special occasions, make people feel appreciated, try something new
3. *What kinds of cooking utensils or instruments are used to prepare special foods?*—beaters, mixers, blenders, spatulas, cake pans, bowls, spoons, whisks

AT-HOME 2

Word Substitutions

1. b) guarded
2. a) leave
3. b) craters
4. b) press
5. a) whip

Same and Different

1. tie
2. curved
3. thick
4. speechless
5. smooth

USING CONTEXT CLUES

1. craters
2. smooth
3. guarded
4. pressed
5. booming
6. leave
7. pudding
8. thicker
9. counter
10. beater
11. even
12. whipped
13. cracked
14. loosen
15. straight

AT-HOME 3

Context Clues Activity

1. a) work free, unbind
2. a) even
3. b) flattened
4. a) booming
5. b) crack

6. a) smooth
7. b) guarded
8. a) craters
9. b) thick
10. a) straight

11. a) leave
12. a) before written history
13. a) system, way
14. b) type of elephant
15. a) sound made by pigs

AT-HOME 4

Across

2. whip
7. booming
8. press

9. crack
10. thick
12. even

13. guard
14. leave

Down

1. straight
3. pudding
4. beater

5. loosen
6. smooth
9. counter

11. crater

PERSONIFICATION AND SIMILE

Part A

1. p
2. p
3. s

4. s
5. s
6. s

7. s
8. s
9. s

Part B

1. a
2. b
3. b

4. a
5. a
6. b

7. b
8. b

ASSESSMENT 2

Part A

1. h) crater
2. d) beater

3. n) booming
4. b) whip

5. k) press

Part B

1. crackers
2. destroy

3. enter
4. even

5. circular

Part C

1. c) marble
2. a) hammer

3. c) stuffed and overpacked
4. a) plastic knife

5. b) smooth and flat

Answer Key

AT-HOME 1

Riddle Page: "What am I?"

1. caveman
2. method
3. mastodon
4. pliers
5. decide

Matching Activity

1. either
2. grunt
3. saber-toothed tiger
4. caveman
5. special
6. decide
7. strange
8. thread
9. pliers
10. method
11. suddenly
12. unusual
13. prehistoric
14. twist
15. mastodon

SEMANTIC WEB: PULLING TEETH

1. *How do people feel when a tooth is pulled?*—strange, hurt
2. *Who are some people who can pull a loose tooth?*—dentist, relatives, orthodontist
3. *What are some ways to pull a loose tooth?*—thread, pliers, fingers, dental tools
4. *What do people do when their teeth are pulled?*—grunt, twist, yell

AT-HOME 2

Word Substitutions

1. a) unexpectedly
2. b) choose
3. a) different
4. b) a tool
5. b) plan

Same and Different

1. new
2. elephant
3. tape
4. crater
5. straighten

USING CONTEXT CLUES

1. saber-toothed tiger
2. prehistoric
3. suddenly
4. decide
5. unusually
6. pliers
7. either
8. thread
9. cavemen
10. twist
11. special
12. method
13. mastodon
14. grunt
15. strange

AT-HOME 3

Context Clues Activity

1. b) saber-toothed tiger
2. a) strange
3. b) suddenly
4. a) grunted
5. b) special
6. a) prehistoric
7. a) decide
8. a) twist
9. b) pliers
10. a) ancestor of elephant
11. a) method
12. b) thread
13. a) unusual
14. b) caveman
15. b) either

MORPHOGRAPHIC ELEMENTS: *PRE-, UN-, -IC,* AND *-LY*

1. b) to empty the sink
2. a) before elementary school
3. a) related to are
4. a) every 7 days
5. a) being nervous
6. b) uncaring/unfeeling
7. a) not part of the routine
8. a) before season begins
9. b) choose based on majority
10. a) kind spirit

AT-HOME 4

Across

1. twist
5. either
6. prehistoric
7. caveman
8. method
10. suddenly
11. strange
12. decide
14. mastodon

Down

2. thread
3. saber-toothed
4. grunt
9. pliers
10. special
13. unusually

SYNONYMS AND ANTONYMS

Any reasonable answer is correct.

ASSESSMENT 3

Part A

1. b) pliers
2. m) either
3. a) thread
4. e) mastodon
5. l) grunt

Part B

1. common
2. slowly
3. sloppy
4. prehistoric
5. straighten

Part C

1. b) house made of wood
2. b) a hunting tool
3. c) a tiger that talks
4. a) plate falling
5. b) red ribbons

Answer Key

AT-HOME 1

Riddle Page: "What am I?"

1. field
2. catalog
3. seriously
4. collection
5. branch

Matching Activity

1. braided
2. collection
3. squawk
4. branch
5. cartwheel
6. tease
7. practice
8. mustache
9. giggle
10. catalog
11. knot
12. fasten
13. seriously
14. piece
15. field

SEMANTIC WEB: MAKING FRIENDS

1. *What are some qualities of a good friend?*—can keep secrets, compassionate, shares, generous, fun-loving
2. *What are some things that friends share?*—collections (sports cards, rocks), good jokes, books, hobbies, sports, kite flying
3. *Describe some places you might make a new friend*—school, neighborhood, playground, at an event

AT-HOME 2

Word Substitutions

1. b) button
2. a) scraps
3. b) seriously
4. b) rehearsed
5. b) knot

Same and Different

1. forest
2. eyeball
3. one
4. please
5. squawk

USING CONTEXT CLUES

1. mustache
2. cartwheel
3. knots
4. practice
5. braided
6. collection
7. catalog
8. fasten
9. tease
10. field
11. branch
12. squawk
13. seriously
14. giggle
15. pieces

AT-HOME 3

Context Clues Activity

1. a) collection
2. b) pieces
3. b) fields
4. b) joyful
5. a) branches

6. b) teases
7. b) knot
8. a) catalog
9. b) fasten
10. a) practiced

11. b) braided
12. a) squawking
13. b) mustache
14. a) giggled
15. a) cartwheels

MORPHOGRAPHIC ELEMENTS: *-TION*

1. a) moving locations
2. b) quantity of food
3. b) group of people

4. a) injecting live material
5. b) becoming developed
6. b) governing people

7. a) large farm

AT-HOME 4

Across

2. knot
6. braided
7. tease

9. collection
11. practice
12. serious

13. field
14. catalog

Down

1. mustache
3. fasten
4. giggle

5. branch
8. piece
9. cartwheel

10. squawk

ASSESSMENT 4

Part A

1. i) cartwheel
2. n) knot

3. e) fasten
4. m) piece

5. j) mustache

Part B

1. lake
2. crop

3. tease
4. serious

5. whisper

Part C

1. b) group of clowns
2. b) list of seasonal crops

3. a) thick threads
4. b) guarding a player

5. c) golf

Answer Key

"I SPY" GAME

1. catalog
2. squawk
3. grunt
4. ignore
5. prehistoric
6. practice
7. collection
8. thick
9. decide
10. optician
11. counter
12. powerful
13. strange
14. unusually
15. twist
16. field
17. piece
18. crater
19. leave
20. branch
21. method
22. mastodon
23. loosen
24. even
25. guard

SEMANTIC FEATURE ANALYSIS: ACTION WORDS

	Directed toward objects	Directed toward people	Directed toward places	Sounds	Physical	Mental	Positive	Negative	Much effort	Little effort
Ignore	+	+	+	+	+	0	–	+	+	+
Twist	+	+	–	–	+	–	+	+	+	+
Practice	+	–	–	0	+	+	+	+	+	+
Guard	+	+	+	–	+	–	+	+	+	+
Leave	+	+	+	–	+	0	+	+	+	+
Decide	–	–	–	–	–	+	+	+	0	0
Grunt	–	0	–	+	+	–	–	+	0	0
Loosen	+	–	–	–	+	–	+	+	+	+
Even	+	–	0	–	+	–	+	+	+	+

FIND IT, SAY IT! GAME

1. c
2. a
3. b
4. e
5. d
6. f
7. g
8. h
9. i
10. j
11. k
12. l
13. m
14. hold
15. whole
16. hole

CLUELESS GAME

Answers in parentheses.

1. level (even)
2. list (catalog)
3. untie (loosen)
4. group (collection)
5. scream (squawk)
6. tree (branch)
7. land (field)
8. rare (unusual)
9. different (strange)
10. pigs (grunt)
11. decision (decide)
12. teeth (mastodon)
13. history (prehistoric)
14. process (method)
15. surface (counter)
16. discontinue (leave)
17. holes (crater)
18. protect (guard)
19. crowded (thick)
20. habit (practice)
21. bend (twist)
22. part (piece)
23. overlook (ignore)
24. eyes (optician)
25. mighty (powerful)

ASSESSMENT 5

1. b) written or printed
2. a) close one's eyes
3. c) make smooth
4. c) makes eyeglasses
5. b) free from pressure
6. b) divided into parts
7. b) a group of things
8. c) wind, turn, weave
9. a) woody stem of limb
10. b) to repeat a drill
11. c) make a loud protest
12. a) before written accounts
13. c) shield from danger
14. b) odd, peculiar, uncommon
15. a) packed, crammed
16. b) bizarre, different
17. b) hole in the ground
18. a) settle on a choice
19. a) stop bothering
20. b) extinct animal
21. a) surface money counted
22. b) orderly and planned way
23. a) make a deep sound
24. b) expansive, wide area
25. b) full of strength
26. b) stream that flows
27. c) award with medal
28. a) division of a family

Answer Key

AT-HOME 1

Riddle Page: "What am I?"

1. britches
2. furnace
3. basement
4. pneumonia
5. Depression

Matching Activity

1. desperate
2. impatient
3. pneumonia
4. bare-waisted
5. furnace
6. basement
7. decent
8. Depression
9. Reconstruction
10. britches
11. fancy
12. Congress
13. plank
14. quilt
15. downstream

SEMANTIC WEB: COLLECTIONS

1. *What are some objects that people collect?*—rare coins, marbles, sports cards, books, paintings, antiques, sports cars, dolls, relics from the past (e.g., arrow heads, photographs)
2. *Why do people collect objects?*—for a hobby, in order to trade items, as an investment
3. *Where do people store their special collections?*—counters, shelves, special boxes, scrapbooks, trunks, attic, safe-deposit box, glass case, museums, libraries

AT-HOME 2

Word Substitutions

1. b) britches
2. a) desperate
3. a) adequate
4. a) impatient
5. b) basement

Same and Different

1. tranquil
2. fan
3. patient
4. skirt
5. clothed

USING CONTEXT CLUES

1. Depression
2. impatiently
3. bare-waisted
4. britches
5. basement
6. desperate
7. Reconstruction
8. furnace
9. pneumonia
10. adequate
11. quilt
12. plank
13. downstream
14. Congress
15. fancy

AT-HOME 3

Context Clues Activity

1. b) fancy
2. b) quilt
3. a) impatient
4. a) reconstruct
5. a) decent

6. b) desperate
7. b) basement
8. a) britches
9. b) planks
10. a) downstream

11. b) bare-waisted
12. a) shipment of goods
13. b) reddish wood
14. a) weak, sickly
15. b) stream

AT-HOME 4

Across

3. decent
5. plank

9. pneumonia
11. Reconstruction

13. britches
14. furnace

Down

1. basement
2. impatient
3. desperate

4. bare-waisted
6. depression
7. fancy

8. quilt
10. downstream
12. congress

AAVE IDIOMS AND FIGURATIVE SPEECH

A.   Matching

1. d) You look exactly like John.
2. a) He preferred to live in the city.
3. e) It didn't make any difference to them.
4. b) The boat was old.
5. c) What is your mamma's name?

B.   Writing Practice

1. Those calves look like the mother cow.
2. My dad loves the country.
3. It doesn't matter to me if we go to the movies or stay home.
4. That dress is old.

Answer Key

ASSESSMENT 6

Part A

1. f) bare-waisted
2. h) decent
3. j) impatient
4. i) Reconstruction
5. e) pneumonia

Part B

1. refrigerator
2. open-air market
3. desperate
4. reconstruct
5. skirt

Part C

1. c) didn't have enough
2. b) his shirt was not dry
3. c) said they were warm
4. a) in the rain
5. b) suffered from earthquake

Bonus

1. b) look like their mom
2. a) liked to live in city

AT-HOME 1

Riddle Page: "What am I?"

1. disappear
2. freight
3. murmur
4. mahogany
5. stubborn

Matching Activity

1. freight
2. disappear
3. woodshop
4. murmur
5. perspiration
6. plain
7. protect
8. stiff
9. stubborn
10. creek
11. irritable
12. frail
13. mahogany
14. dresser
15. stuffing

SEMANTIC WEB: GROWING OLD

1. *Which characters in the story are growing old?*—Aunt Dew, everyone eventually grows old
2. *What are some characteristics of old age?*—forgetfulness, irritability, nostalgia (relive events from the past), gray hair, false teeth, frailty, physical weakness
3. *Where do people live when they grow old?*—home for the elderly, a relative's home, a hospice
4. *Do you know anyone who is growing old?*—grandparents, neighbor

AT-HOME 2

Word Substitutions

1. b) rigid
2. a) delicate
3. a) willful
4. b) faded
5. b) bad-tempered

Same and Different

1. lightweight
2. ice
3. murmur
4. muscular
5. stubborn

USING CONTEXT CLUES

1. freight
2. stuffing
3. frail
4. murmur
5. stiff
6. perspiration
7. irritable
8. disappear
9. plain
10. creek
11. dresser
12. woodshop
13. mahogany
14. protect
15. stubborn

Answer Key

AT-HOME 3

Context Clues Activity

1. a) kept safe
2. b) angry
3. a) weak
4. b) stream
5. a) fade away

6. b) sweat
7. b) whispered
8. a) goods to be carried
9. b) not easily moved
10. a) material that fills

11. a) bedroom furniture
12. a) study of the stars
13. b) instrument appear closer
14. a) existing in former times
15. b) judge the value

SYNONYMS AND ANTONYMS

Any reasonable answer is correct.

AT-HOME 4

Across

2. disappear
5. woodshop
9. irritable

10. stuffing
12. murmur
13. protect

14. stubborn

Down

1. frail
2. dresser
3. plain

4. mahogany
6. perspiration
7. creek

8. stiff
11. freight

AAVE IDIOMS AND FIGURATIVE SPEECH

A. Matching

1. c) I have been asleep all day.
2. d) What is your name?
3. a) He was almost bitten.
4. b) I pretended that I didn't see her.

B. Writing Practice

1. Don't pretend that you want to go if you really do not want to.
2. We have been waiting for the bus for a long time.
3. We almost got on the wrong train.
4. What kind of dog do you have?

THE BEAUTY OF CONVERSATIONAL SPEECH

What are signs of the approaching holiday?

1. The air is getting cooler and cooler.
2. Frost comes at night.
3. The hickory nuts and walnuts are falling [from the trees].
4. The opossum is keeping out of sight [hiding out of fear].
5. The turkey is strutting in the barnyard.
6. The pumpkin is getting good and yellow.
7. Seems like the pumpkin is looking at me and saying, "Pies."
8. The turkey is going around, showing off.
9. There is chopping going on in the kitchen.
10. There is crushing of raisins in the hall.
11. Beef is cooking for the mince meat [pie].
12. Spices are being ground.

ASSESSMENT 7

Part A

1. k) woodshop
2. f) frail
3. i) creek
4. d) perspiration
5. h) freight

Part B

1. stiff
2. bathtub
3. cooperative
4. disappear
5. damage

Part C

1. a) expensive prices
2. a) crumpled newspaper
3. c) reaching for water
4. b) lifting freight
5. b) jumping into creek

Answer Key

AT-HOME 1

Riddle Page: "What am I?

1. nutrition
2. extraterrestrial
3. boutique
4. orchestral
5. hieroglyphics

Matching Activity

1. billboard
2. property
3. warrior
4. squabble
5. private
6. solidarity
7. orchestral
8. cuddle
9. collect
10. hieroglyphics
11. boutique
12. extraterrestrial
13. profound
14. nutrition
15. discovery

SEMANTIC WEB: WORDS, WORDS, WORDS

1. *How can words be magic?*—words make you feel many emotions, such as angry, happy, resentful, ashamed, grateful, curious, fearful, and secure.
2. *Where can we find interesting words?*—dictionaries, books, conversations, television, billboards, magazines
3. *What different kinds of words are there?*—nouns, adjectives, verbs, one syllable, multi-syllable, singular, plural
4. *Why do you think Donovan believes that words can be powerful?*—words can change how you feel about yourself and how you feel about others

AT-HOME 2

Word Substitutions

1. b) quarreled angrily
2. a) unity
3. b) not public
4. b) snuggling
5. a) sign

Same and Different

1. peacemaker
2. factory
3. shallow
4. misplace
5. candy

USING CONTEXT CLUES

1. private
2. solidarity
3. extraterrestrial
4. boutique
5. profound
6. warriors
7. discovery
8. property
9. squabble
10. collect
11. orchestral
12. nutrition
13. cuddled
14. billboard
15. hieroglyphics

AT-HOME 3

Context Clues Activity

1. b) extraterrestrial
2. a) profound
3. b) to argue loudly
4. a) discovered
5. b) property
6. a) solidarity
7. a) collect
8. b) boutiques
9. a) warrior
10. b) cuddle
11. b) common
12. a) a suggestion
13. b) choice
14. b) strong cotton cloth
15. a) focus one's mind

AT-HOME 4

Across

2. property
5. cuddle
6. extraterrestrial
9. solidarity
11. squabble
12. profound
13. private
14. billboard
15. discovery

Down

1. warrior
3. orchestral
4. collect
7. boutique
8. hieroglyphics
10. nutrition

ASSESSMENT 8

Part A

1. k) extraterrestrial
2. l) billboard
3. e) hieroglyphics
4. o) orchestral
5. c) nutrition

Part B

1. communal
2. superficial
3. reject
4. agree
5. Earth

Part C

1. a) electricity
2. b) spears and knives
3. c) a glass of milk
4. c) all of the above
5. a) dream about future

Answer Key

AT-HOME 1

Riddle Page: "What am I?"

1. partner
2. canvas
3. file
4. steady, firm
5. patterned

Matching Activity

1. partner
2. file
3. concentrate
4. patterned
5. interruption
6. dilemma
7. decision
8. firm
9. solution
10. advice
11. suggestion
12. gather
13. canvas
14. steady
15. definitive

SEMANTIC WEB: DIFFICULT CHOICES

1. *What vocabulary words do we associate with difficult choices?*—dilemma, solution, advice, decision
2. *What kinds of people make difficult choices?*—surgeons, jurors, judges, attorneys, teachers, soldiers, pilots
3. *How do you feel when faced with a difficult decision?*—afraid, vulnerable, anxious, alone, fretful
4. *What are some places where difficult decisions are made?*—courtrooms, emergency rooms, schools, air traffic control towers

AT-HOME 2

Word Substitutions

1. a) collect
2. a) recommendation
3. b) problem
4. a) focus
5. b) disruptions

Same and Different

1. device
2. enemy
3. creation
4. incomplete
5. wander

USING CONTEXT CLUES

1. concentrate
2. file
3. partners
4. patterns
5. gathered
6. canvas
7. interruption
8. steady
9. advice
10. definitive
11. suggestion
12. dilemma
13. solution
14. decision
15. firm

AT-HOME 3

Context Clues Activity

1. a) recommendation
2. b) concentrate
3. b) file
4. a) final and absolute
5. b) suggestion

6. b) interruption
7. a) dilemma
8. b) person on my side
9. b) bring together
10. a) strong white cloth

11. a) solution
12. b) loud, noisy
13. a) shy
16. b) leisure
17. a) perseverance

MULTIPLE MEANINGS: *SOLUTION, SUGGESTION, FIRM,* AND *GATHER*

1. b
2. a
3. d
4. c

5. h
6. f
7. g
8. e

9. l
10. j
11. i
12. k

AT-HOME 4

Across

6. suggestion
7. definitive
8. firm

10. dilemma
11. interruption
12. concentrate

13. decision

Down

1. canvas
2. solution
3. gather

4. advice
5. partner
6. steady

8. file
9. patterned

ASSESSMENT 9

Part A

1. o) partner
2. e) file

3. j) canvas
4. m) gather

5. k) interruption

Part B

1. decision
2. flimsy

3. solution
4. beginning

5. drift

Part C

1. a) a parent
2. b) eyesight

3. b) threat of war
4. c) disconnection

5. c) gathering veggies

Answer Key

"I SPY" GAME

1. basement
2. impatient
3. profound
4. creek
5. firm
6. disappear
7. mahogany
8. freight
9. canvas
10. solution
11. warrior
12. concentrate
13. file
14. extraterrestrial
15. irritable
16. solidarity
17. frail
18. discovery
19. furnace
20. suggestion
21. private
22. nutrition
23. depression
24. reconstruction
25. partner

SEMANTIC FEATURE ANALYSIS: HEATING SYSTEMS

	Heats the building	Makes faucet water hot	Cooks food	Bakes pottery	Uses water	Uses coal	Heats a room	Uses oil
Radiator	+	–	–	–	+	–	+	–
Heater	+	–	–	–	0	0	+	–
Oven	0	–	+	–	–	–	0	–
Boiler	+	+	–	–	+	–	0	–
Furnace	+	–	–	–	–	+	0	+
Central heat	+	–	–	–	–	0	+	0
Kiln	–	–	–	+	–	–	–	–

FIND IT, SAY IT! GAME

1. b
2. a
3. c
4. d
5. e
6. h
7. g
8. f
9. j
10. i
11. l
12. k

CLUELESS GAME

Answers in parentheses.

1. individual (private)
2. anxious (impatient)
3. health (nutrition)
4. wood (mahogany)
5. answer (solution)
6. heat (furnace)
7. rebuild (reconstruction)
8. cargo (freight)
9. paintings (canvas)
10. papers (file)
11. finding (discovery)
12. agreement (solidarity)
13. focus (concentrate)
14. co-worker (partner)
15. deep (profound)
16. underground (basement)
17. vanish (disappear)
18. stream (creek)
19. idea (suggestion)
20. soldier (warrior)
21. feeble (frail)
22. angry (irritable)
23. sadness (depression)
24. space (extraterrestrial)
25. secure (firm)

ASSESSMENT 10

1. c) healthy food
2. b) a small stream
3. a) an explanation
4. b) from outer space
5. a) anxious
6. b) a heating system
7. a) a co-worker
8. a) room underground
9. c) stable
10. a) strong cloth
11. b) unity
12. a) soldier
13. b) to build again
14. b) a red wood
15. a) to focus on
16. a) one group
17. c) cabinet with papers
18. a) tired
19. a) to feel deeply
20. c) leave one's sight
21. a) a plan
22. b) a shipment
23. a) something unearthed
24. b) feeling unhappy
25. a) feeling angry

Answer Key

AT-HOME 1

Riddle Page: "What am I?"

1. hassock
2. security
3. leisure
4. boisterous
5. exchange

Matching Activity

1. lounge
2. perseverance
3. timid
4. leisure
5. diplomacy
6. hassock
7. gruff
8. delight
9. security
10. boisterous
11. compromise
12. exchange
13. serendipity
14. relief
15. stern

AT-HOME 2

Word Substitutions

1. b) compromise
2. a) rowdy
3. b) relief
4. b) certainty
5. a) substitute

Same and Different

1. bold
2. workday
3. weakness
4. plan
5. displeasure

USING CONTEXT CLUES

1. Compromise
2. diplomacy
3. lounge
4. delight
5. relief
6. Security
7. timid
8. gruff
9. boisterous
10. perseverance
11. leisure
12. exchange
13. hassocks
14. serendipity
15. stern

AT-HOME 3

Context Clues Activity

1. a) perseverance
2. b) not courageous
3. b) exchanged
4. a) plush pad
5. a) delight
6. a) sternly
7. b) nothing to do
8. a) reach agreement
9. b) serendipity
10. a) poise and finesse
11. a) waiting room
12. a) people, minerals
13. b) worth a good price
14. a) one who digs
15. a) damp and sticky

MULTIPLE MEANINGS: *RELIEF, SECURITY,* AND *EXCHANGE*

1. a
2. d
3. b
4. c
5. f
6. e
7. g
8. j
9. i
10. h

AT-HOME 4

Across

3.	leisure	10.	diplomacy	13.	stern
6.	delight	11.	gruff	15.	hassock
8.	compromise	12.	security		

Down

1.	serendipity	5.	timid	14.	lounge
2.	perseverance	7.	relief		
4.	exchange	9.	boisterous		

ASSESSMENT 11

Part A

1.	b) lounge	3.	o) relief	5.	h) delight
2.	m) hassock	4.	n) gruff		

Part B

1.	loose	3.	tactlessness	5.	boisterous
2.	feeble	4.	pleasant		

Part C

1.	c) all of the above	3.	a) national security	5.	a) two quarters
2.	c) Leisure activities	4.	c) practice diplomacy		

Answer Key

AT-HOME 1

Riddle Page: "What am I?"

1. desert
2. complain
3. miner
4. reinforcement
5. mica

Matching Activity

1. reinforcement
2. desert
3. prospector
4. miner
5. engineer
6. treasure
7. valuable
8. stake
9. clammy
10. mica
11. complain
12. yardstick
13. preserve
14. rot
15. figure

SEMANTIC WEB: TREASURES

1. *What kinds of treasures are there?*—gold, silver, diamonds, coins
2. *Who searches for treasure?*—miners, prospectors, pirates, kids
3. *What equipment do they need?*—pick, shovel, miner's hat, stake, reinforcements
4. *Where do they look for treasure?*—mines, mountains, ground, caves
5. *Who are some people in your life who are treasures?*—parents, family, friends

AT-HOME 2

Word Substitution

1. a) supports
2. b) save
3. b) decay
4. a) pointed stick
5. a) concluded

Same and Different

1. homebody
2. praise
3. rose
4. worthless
5. baseball

USING CONTEXT CLUES

1. yardstick
2. reinforcements
3. valuable
4. complain
5. stake
6. figured
7. preserve
8. prospectors
9. miner
10. engineer
11. clammy
12. rot
13. mica
14. treasure
15. desert

AT-HOME 3

Context Clues Activity

1. b) complain
2. a) miner
3. a) prospectors
4. b) preserve
5. a) translucent mineral

6. b) worth a great price
7. a) stakes
8. a) rot
9. b) precious person
10. a) damp and sticky

11. a) hot landscape
12. a) one who controls
13. b) employ, give a job to
14. a) undersurface of shoe
15. b) small version

SYNONYMS AND ANTONYMS

Any reasonable answer is correct.

AT-HOME 4

Across

2. clammy
4. stake
7. reinforcement

8. valuable
9. figure
11. desert

12. mica
13. prospector
14. yardstick

Down

1. preserve
2. complain

3. miner
5. treasure

6. rot
10. engineer

BE A MINER

1. Red (ruby, garnet)
2. Pink (topaz)
3. Blue (sapphire, aquamarine, turquoise, topaz)

4. Green (emerald, jade, peridot)
5. Violet (amethyst)
6. Yellow/gold (amber, topaz, zircon)

ASSESSMENT 12

Part A

1. i) mica
2. b) rot

3. c) treasure
4. g) stake

5. h) figure

Part B

1. inches
2. praise

3. preserve
4. dry

5. worthless

Part C

1. b) maps, books
2. a) signs and tents

3. c) use right materials
4. b) torn elbows of jacket

5. a) a hot desert

Answer Key

AT-HOME 1

Riddle Page: "What am I?"

1. union
2. pair
3. finished
4. patent
5. model

Matching Activity

1. finished
2. inventor
3. operator
4. metal
5. model
6. patent
7. pair
8. sole
9. share
10. scrap
11. factory
12. shop
13. union
14. hire
15. industry

SEMANTIC WEB: SHOES

1. *Kinds of shoes*—dress, tennis, athletic, sandals, high heels, topsiders, penny loafers
2. *Who makes shoes?*—cobblers, big companies (Nike, Adidas)
3. *Parts of a shoe*—sole, tongue, laces, heel
4. *Equipment needed for shoemaking*—lasting machine, sewing machine, nails, hammer, leather

AT-HOME 2

Word Substitutions

1. a) model
2. b) hired for
3. a) patient
4. b) sole
5. a) unions

Same and Different

1. copier
2. alone
3. hat
4. whole
5. beach

USING CONTEXT CLUES

1. finished
2. soles
3. operator
4. industry
5. inventor
6. factory
7. pair
8. metal
9. model
10. hire
11. scrap
12. shop
13. patent
14. shares
15. union

AT-HOME 3

Context Clues Activity

1. a) industry
2. b) factories
3. b) inventor
4. a) patent
5. a) operator
6. a) shop
7. a) scrap
8. b) finished
9. b) hired
10. a) union
11. a) shares
12. b) gathering
13. b) parts
14. a) recovery from disease
15. b) gave to a charity

AT-HOME 4

Across

5.	union	9.	hire	12.	shop
6.	patent	10.	metal	13.	inventor
7.	sole	11.	factory	14.	pair

Down

1.	share	3.	model	8.	operator
2.	finished	4.	industry	12.	scrap

ASSESSMENT 13

Part A

1.	l) industry	3.	a) inventor	5.	i) patent
2.	c) operator	4.	b) pair		

Part B

1.	one	3.	begin	5.	original
2.	restaurant	4.	hire		

Part C

1.	a) remained glued	3.	b) design a new go cart	5.	a) health insurance
2.	c) our relatives	4.	c) money		

Answer Key

AT-HOME 1

Riddle Page: "What am I?"

1. treatment, cure
2. donate
3. common
4. demonstration
5. ingredients

Matching Activity

1. attic
2. cure
3. training
4. common
5. product
6. treatment
7. harvest
8. ingredients
9. laboratory
10. establish
11. object
12. fever
13. donate
14. demonstration
15. mixture

SEMANTIC WEB: MILLIONAIRES

1. *Famous millionaires*—Rockefellers, Madam C. J. Walker, Bill Gates, movie stars, sports stars
2. *Ways people become millionaires*—inventing products, establishing a business, finding a cure, creating unusual treatments, making a recipe with secret ingredients
3. *Millionaires donate money to*—churches, schools, favorite charities, organizations, hospitals, museums
4. *Words that describe millionaires*—entrepreneur, philanthropist, wealthy

AT-HOME 2

Word Substitutions

1. a) common
2. b) harvest
3. a) establish
4. a) mixture
5. b) object

Same and Different

1. disease
2. unusual
3. ingredient
4. individual
5. piano

USING CONTEXT CLUES

1. common
2. establish
3. mixture
4. cure
5. product
6. training
7. harvest
8. laboratory
9. fever
10. ingredients
11. donate
12. attic
13. treatment
14. demonstration
15. object

AT-HOME 3

1. a) common
2. a) a treatment
3. b) training
4. a) attic
5. a) demonstration

6. a) donate
7. b) harvest
8. b) ingredients
9. a) establish
10. b) cure

11. a) object
12. b) invited to take part
13. a) object of desire
14. b) to separate widely
15. a) to look at quickly

MORPHOGRAPHIC ELEMENTS: *-MENT*

1. a) becoming larger
2. b) food

3. a) making a promise
4. b) process of providing

5. a) a sum of money

AT-HOME 4

Across

5. establish
6. fever
7. common

11. mixture
12. attic
13. donate

14. ingredients
15. training

Down

1. harvest
2. cure
3. demonstration

4. treatment
8. object
9. product

10. laboratory

ASSESSMENT 14

Part A

1. i) laboratory
2. f) mixture

3. e) fever
4. g) attic

5. a) common

Part B

1. disease
2. confusion

3. plant
4. explosion

5. take

Part C

1. a) new products
2. a) establish a business

3. c) vaccines, medicines
4. c) develop a cure

5. b) common medicines

Answer Key

"I SPY" GAME

1. clammy
2. hire
3. compromise
4. scrap
5. cure
6. perseverance
7. preserve
8. harvest
9. union
10. shop
11. figure
12. factory
13. treasure
14. complain
15. treatment
16. donate
17. patent
18. yardstick
19. fever
20. demonstration
21. common
22. reinforcement
23. relief
24. mixture
25. training

SEMANTIC FEATURE ANALYSIS: SHOPS

	Sells food	Sells clothing	Sells something besides food or clothes	Is privately owned	Inexpensive	Expensive	Chic atmosphere	Ordinary atmosphere	Inner-city	Rural	Single store	Multiple stores	Single employee	Multiple employees	Accepts cash	Accepts credit
Shop	+	+	+	+	+	+	0	0	+	+	+	−	0	0	+	+
Boutique	−	+	+	+	0	+	+	−	+	+	+	−	0			
Chain	+	+	+	0	+	+	0	+	+	+	−	+				
Deli	+	−	−	0	0	0	0	0	+	+	+	−	0	+	+	0
Department store	0	+	+	−	+	+	+	+	+	0	+	−	−	+	+	+
Emporium	+	+	+	0	0	0	+	0	+	0	+	−	−	+	+	+
Five-and-dime	−	+	+	−	+	−	−	+	+	+	+	−	−	+	+	+
Market	+	0	+	+	+	0	−	+	+	+	+	+	+	+	+	0
Outlet	−	+	+	−	+	−	−	+	+	+	+	+	−	+	+	+
Stand	+	−	−	+	+	−	−	+	+	+	+	−	+	+	+	−
Supermarket	+	+	+	+	+	+	0	+	+	+	+	−	−	+	+	+
Store	+	+	+	0	+	+	+	+	+	+	+	+	+	+	+	+

FIND IT, SAY IT! GAME

1. b
2. d
3. c
4. a

5. f
6. e
7. g
8. h

9. i
10. j
11. k

CLUELESS GAME

Answers in parentheses.

1. employ (hire)
2. teaching (training)
3. settlement (compromise)
4. crop (harvest)
5. support (reinforcement)
6. valuable (treasure)
7. sweaty (clammy)
8. decide (figure)
9. care (treatment)

10. often (common)
11. organization (union)
12. willpower (perseverance)
13. business (shop)
14. combination (mixture)
15. freedom (relief)
16. pieces (scraps)
17. healing (cure)
18. building (factory)

19. save (preserve)
20. grumble (complain)
21. inventor (patent)
22. gift (donate)
23. measurement (yardstick)
24. temperature (fever)
25. showing (demonstration)

ASSESSMENT 15

1. b) therapy or care
2. a) gripe or grumble
3. c) familiar
4. a) teaching, instruction
5. c) displaying a product
6. b) determination
7. a) establishes ownership
8. b) building
9. b) experience less pain

10. a) a combination
11. c) for measuring objects
12. b) season for gathering
13. b) sweaty and sticky
14. a) wealth of any kind
15. b) organization
16. a) rise in temperature
17. b) to pay someone
18. c) give to a charity

19. b) thrown away
20. b) a business
21. a) an agreement
22. b) recovery from disease
23. c) to conclude or decide
24. b) gives support
25. a) keep from rotting

Answer Key

AT-HOME 1

Riddle Page: "What am I?"

1. challenge
2. aggressive
3. exhausted
4. scatter
5. mimic

Matching Activity

1. exhausted
2. challenge
3. rebound
4. weakness
5. organize
6. strain
7. aggressive
8. ground
9. glance
10. mimic
11. scatter
12. rebound
13. experiment
14. reek
15. retort

SEMANTIC WEB: WORK

1. *Housework*—sweeping, vacuuming, dusting, mowing, cleaning your room, washing dishes
2. *Schoolwork*—worksheets, tests, studying, making flashcards, special projects, reports, experiments
3. *Places where people work*—factories, offices, training schools, laboratories, shops, various industries, mines, freight trains, Congress

AT-HOME 2

Word Substitutions

1. a) urge
2. a) retorted
3. b) stretched
4. a) mimicked
5. b) organized

Same and Different

1. avoid
2. relax
3. dislike
4. scatter
5. energetic

USING CONTEXT CLUES

1. exhausted
2. strain
3. ground
4. mimic
5. reeks
6. challenge
7. glanced
8. aggressive
9. retorted
10. experiment
11. weakness
12. organize
13. scattered
14. urge
15. rebound

AT-HOME 3

Context Clues Activity

1. a) dared
2. b) strained
3. a) grounded
4. a) weakness
5. b) organized

6. b) scattered
7. a) glance
8. b) replied harshly
9. b) experiments
10. b) mimicking

11. a) reeks of
12. a) useful tools
13. b) fixed his eyes
14. a) path through
15. a) covered

MORPHOGRAPHIC ELEMENTS: *-NESS*

1. a) no expectation
2. b) finding enjoying

3. a) being pleasing
4. a) containing nothing

5. b) being happy

AT-HOME 4

Across

5. aggressive
9. glance
10. ground

11. scatter
13. exhausted
14. retort

15. strain

Down

1. weakness
2. rebound
3. urge

4. mimic
6. reek
7. experiment

8. organize
12. challenge

ASSESSMENT 16

Part A

1. k) retort
2. e) glance

3. a) challenge
4. f) experiment

5. g) reek

Part B

1. dislike
2. create

3. messy
4. friendly

5. gather

Part C

1. c) don't do chores
2. a) catch in glove

3. a) take a hot shower
4. b) lift a bookcase

5. a) Hershey's bar

Answer Key

AT-HOME 1

Riddle Page: "What am I?"

1. clutter
2. horizon
3. speckled
4. link
5. dangling

Matching Activity

1. link
2. dangling
3. plains
4. utensils
5. herd
6. clutter
7. imagine
8. depend
9. relieve
10. gaze
11. trail
12. disposition
13. horizon
14. inspection
15. speckled

SEMANTIC WEB: LIFE ON A RANCH WITH COWBOYS

1. *People and animals on a ranch*—cowboys, ranch hands, cattle, sheep, sheepdogs, mares, stallions
2. *Types of work*—horse breaking, putting herds out to graze, lassoing escaped animals, mending fences, taking cattle to market
3. *What cowboys eat*—beans, beef jerky, anything cooked in the chuck wagon over a fire, biscuits
4. *Where and how cowboys travel*—on horseback, trail rides, cattle drives, over plains, camping out on the trail, with families in covered wagons to settle in a new area
5. *What cowboys wear*—chaps, hats, boots, vests, spurs, lassoes attached to belts

AT-HOME 2

Word Substitutions

1. a) dangling from
2. a) linked
3. b) depend on
4. a) imagine
5. b) inspection

Same and Different

1. sniff
2. organize
3. kitchen
4. individual
5. imagine

USING CONTEXT CLUES

1. disposition
2. utensils
3. gazing
4. plains
5. imagined
6. speckled
7. cluttered
8. relieved
9. link
10. inspection
11. depend
12. horizon
13. herd
14. trails
15. dangling

AT-HOME 3

Context Clues Activity

1. a) utensils
2. b) imagine
3. b) link
4. a) dangling
5. a) plains

6. a) gazed
7. a) speckled
8. a) trail
9. a) depend
10. b) herd

11. b) disposition
12. b) save from danger
13. a) acts to prepare
14. a) call to a state
15. b) open boxes

AT-HOME 4

Across

3. clutter
6. disposition
8. link

10. relieve
12. herd
13. trail

14. dangling
15. gaze

Down

1. inspection
2. plains
4. horizon

5. utensils
7. speckled
9. depend

11. imagine

SYNONYMS AND ANTONYMS

Any reasonable answer is correct.

ASSESSMENT 17

Part A

1. k) speckled
2. b) dangling

3. l) plains
4. a) utensils

5. m) horizon

Part B

1. inspection
2. one

3. conduct
4. gather

5. demonstration

Part C

1. a) ranches with markets
2. a) a police woman

3. b) Dictionaries, reports
4. c) clearly marked trails

5. b) setting or rising sun

Answer Key

AT-HOME 1

Riddle Page: "What am I?"

1. festival
2. mare
3. crate
4. rescue
5. alert

Matching Activity

1. rescue
2. arena
3. represent
4. events
5. exhibit
6. preparations
7. festival
8. disqualify
9. mare
10. bountiful
11. crate
12. surging
13. shear
14. dare
15. alert

SEMANTIC WEB: RODEO TIME

1. *What events can you watch at a rodeo?*—barrel racing, bronco busting, calf roping, bull riding, covered wagon races, clowns playing
2. *What events can kids participate in?*—sack race, greased pig chase, calf catching, sheep shearing, roping animals, riding horses
3. *What exhibits can you see?*—farm animals, cattle, sheep, chickens, quilts, art, tractor and farm equipment

AT-HOME 2

Word Substitutions

1. a) represent
2. a) bountiful
3. b) disqualified
4. a) events
5. b) shear

Same and Different

1. bare
2. endanger
3. calf
4. arena
5. dare

USING CONTEXT CLUES

1. represent
2. events
3. preparations
4. exhibit
5. festival
6. mare
7. arena
8. bountiful
9. dare
10. surging
11. shear
12. crate
13. disqualify
14. alert
15. rescue

AT-HOME 3

Context Clues Activity

1. a) pushing forward
2. b) events
3. a) have enough
4. b) represent
5. a) bountiful

6. b) exhibit
7. a) mares
8. b) rescue
9. a) alert
10. b) shear

11. b) removed
12. a) first settlers
13. a) anxious, enthusiastic
14. b) wilted from heat
15. a) group

MORPHOGRAPHIC ELEMENTS: *DIS-* AND *-NESS*

1. a) no longer connected
2. b) no longer having

3. a) not liking or enjoying
4. a) dangerous ingredients

5. a) delight or enjoyment

AT-HOME 4

Across

1. festival
6. arena
7. represent

10. rescue
11. disqualify
14. surging

15. exhibit

Down

2. events
3. dare
4. mare

5. shear
8. preparations
9. bountiful

12. alert
13. crate

ASSESSMENT 18

Part A

1. o) rescue
2. e) festival

3. f) crate
4. a) represent

5. k) events

Part B

1. grow
2. protect

3. hide
4. allow

5. hospital

Part C

1. a) invite guests
2. a) hay and apples

3. c) many
4. a) held close

5. b) look at

Answer Key

AT-HOME 1

Riddle Page: "What am I?"

1. pennant
2. buff
3. sprout
4. bow
5. umpire

Matching Activity

1. sprout
2. skim
3. bleachers
4. buff
5. measure
6. pennant
7. bow
8. performance
9. integrate
10. admire
11. umpire
12. massage
13. recital
14. inspire
15. league

AT-HOME 2

Word Substitutions

1. a) sprout
2. a) bleachers
3. b) inspired
4. a) skim
5. a) integrate

Same and Different

1. individual
2. spoons
3. metal
4. disapprove
5. tarnish

USING CONTEXT CLUES

1. bleachers
2. measure
3. sprouted
4. skim
5. buffed
6. umpire
7. League
8. bow
9. massage
10. recital
11. integrated
12. admire
13. inspired
14. pennant
15. performance

AT-HOME 3

Context Clues Activity

1. b) skims
2. b) performances
3. a) league
4. a) umpires
5. b) sprouting
6. a) recital
7. a) admired
8. b) inspire
9. a) bleachers
10. b) pennants
11. a) buff
12. b) massaged
13. a) wooden arc
14. a) integrate
15. b) measures

MULTIPLE MEANINGS

1. c
2. b
3. a
4. e
5. f
6. d
7. h
8. i
9. j
10. g
11. l
12. k
13. n
14. m

AT-HOME 4

Across

1.	umpire	5.	integrate	11.	skim
3.	inspire	7.	admire	13.	league
4.	bow	10.	bleachers	14.	pennant

Down

2.	performance	8.	measure	10.	buff
6.	massage	9.	sprout	12.	recital

AAVE IDIOMATIC EXPRESSIONS AND SPELLINGS

A. Matching

1.	b	3.	f	5.	d
2.	e	4.	a	6.	c

B. Spelling

1.	helping	4.	reading	7.	afford
2.	swimming	5.	around		
3.	driving	6.	adopt		

C. Writing Practice

1. Going to the circus is not important.
2. Why are you excited about something that does not matter?
3. Christmas is coming soon.
4. The strawberries are not sprouting or growing yet.
5. Where are we going?

PLAY BALL! (OPTIONAL)

1.	a	4.	e	7.	d
2.	g	5.	c	8.	h
3.	f	6.	b		

ASSESSMENT 19

Part A

1.	e) bow	3.	i) umpire	5.	a) pennant
2.	f) league	4.	h) buff		

Part B

1.	wither	3.	dislike	5.	cut
2.	observation	4.	discourage		

Part C

1.	a) admired	3.	c) award winning	5.	b) recital not going well
2.	c) silver bracelet	4.	b) bean sprouts		

Answer Key

"I SPY" GAME

1. trail	10. weakness	19. glance
2. dare	11. shear	20. bow
3. bountiful	12. gaze	21. recital
4. integrate	13. crate	22. firm
5. alert	14. exhausted	23. depend
6. measure	15. relieve	24. settle
7. disqualify	16. horizon	25. ground
8. plains	17. strain	
9. inspire	18. admire	

SEMANTIC FEATURE ANALYSIS: TO LOOK AT

	To look at quickly	To look at for a long time	To look secretly	To look, study, and think	To look at closely	To look at with positive emotions	To look at with negative emotions
Glance	+	–	0	–	–	0	0
Stare	–	+	0	0	+	–	+
Peek	+	–	+	–	–	0	0
Examine	–	+	0	+	+	+	+
Scrutinize	–	+	-	+	+	–	+
View	–	+	0	0	+	+	–
Gaze	–	+	0	+	+	0	–

FIND IT, SAY IT! GAME

1. a	4. c	7. h
2. b	5. e	8. f
3. d	6. i	9. g

CLUELESS GAME

Answers in parentheses.

1. clip (shear)
2. ineligible (disqualify)
3. tired (exhausted)
4. performance (recital)
5. challenge (dare)
6. warn (alert)
7. punish (ground)
8. stretched (strained)
9. instrument (bow)
10. rely (depend)
11. land (plains)
12. encourage (inspire)
13. container (crate)
14. path (trail)
15. plenty (bountiful)
16. sunset (horizon)
17. look (glance)
18. release (relieve)
19. respect (admire)
20. polish (buff)
21. mix (integrate)
22. stare (gaze)
23. bar (measure)
24. show (exhibit)
25. fondness (weakness)

ASSESSMENT 20

1. c) weak and weary
2. a) final performance
3. b) a box
4. a) warn someone
5. c) cut closely
6. a) flat land
7. b) keep from
8. c) courageous
9. b) plenty
10. a) stretch tight
11. b) imaginary line
12. a) wooden stick
13. b) dirt path
14. a) defect or fault
15. b) look short time
16. c) bar of music
17. b) include
18. a) to free
19. b) make ineligible
20. b) to rely on
21. a) make shine
22. c) stare steadily
23. c) performance
24. a) to urge
25. b) a show

Word Index

Admire, Wk 19, 20
Advice, Wk 9
Aggressive, Wk 16
Alert, Wk 18, 20
Approach, Wk 1
Arena, Wk 18
Attic, Wk 14

Bare-waisted, Wk 6
Basement, Wk 6, 10
Beater, Wk 2
Bend, Wk 1
Billboard, Wk 8
Bleachers, Wk 19
Boardinghouse, Wk 1
Boisterous, Wk 11
Booming, Wk 2
Borrow, Wk 1
Bountiful, Wk 18, 20
Boutique, Wk 8
Bow, Wk 19, 20
Braided, Wk 4
Branch, Wk 4, 5
Britches, Wk 6
Buff, Wk 19, 20

Canvas, Wk 9, 10
Cartwheel, Wk 4
Catalog, Wk 4, 5
Cautious, Wk 1
Caveman, Wk 3
Challenge, Wk 16
Clammy, Wk 12, 15
Clutter, Wk 17
Collect, Wk 8
Collection, Wk 4, 5
Common, Wk 14, 15
Complain, Wk 12, 15
Compromise, Wk 11, 15
Concentrate, Wk 9, 10
Congress, Wk 6
Counter, Wk 2, 5
Crack, Wk 2
Crate, Wk 18, 20
Crater, Wk 2, 5
Creek, Wk 7, 10
Cuddle, Wk 8
Cure, Wk 14, 15

Dangling, Wk 17
Dare, Wk 18, 20
Decent, Wk 6

Decide, Wk 3, 5
Decision, Wk 9
Definitive, Wk 9
Delight, Wk 11
Demonstration, Wk 14, 15
Depend, Wk 17, 20
Depression, Wk 6, 10
Desert, Wk 12
Desperate, Wk 6
Dilemma, Wk 9
Diplomacy, Wk 11
Disappear, Wk 7, 10
Discovery, Wk 8, 10
Disposition, Wk 17
Disqualify, Wk 18, 20
Donate, Wk 14, 15
Downstream, Wk 6
Dresser, Wk 7

Either, Wk 3
Engineer, Wk 12
Establish, Wk 14
Even, Wk 2, 5
Events, Wk 18
Exchange, Wk 11
Exhausted, Wk 16, 20
Exhibit, Wk 18, 20
Experiment, Wk 16
Extraterrestrial, Wk 8, 10

Factory, Wk 13, 15
Fancy, Wk 6
Fasten, Wk 4
Festival, Wk 18
Fever, Wk 14, 15
Field, Wk 4, 5
Figure, Wk 12, 15
File, Wk 9, 10
Finished, Wk 13
Firm, Wk 9, 10
Frail, Wk 7, 10
Freight, Wk 7, 10
Furnace, Wk 6, 10

Gather, Wk 9
Gaze, Wk 17, 20
Giggle, Wk 4
Glance, Wk 16, 20
Ground, Wk 16, 20
Gruff, Wk 11
Grunt, Wk 3, 5
Guard, Wk 2, 5

Harvest, Wk 14, 15
Hassock, Wk 11
Herd, Wk 17
Hieroglyphics, Wk 8
Hire, Wk 13, 15
Horizon, Wk 17, 20

Ignore, Wk 1, 5
Imagine, Wk 17
Impatient, Wk 6, 10
Industry, Wk 13
Ingredients, Wk 14
Inspection, Wk 17
Inspire, Wk 19, 20
Integrate, Wk 19, 20
Interruption, Wk 9
Inventor, Wk 13
Irritable, Wk 7, 10

Knot, Wk 4

Laboratory, Wk 14
League, Wk 19
Leave, Wk 2, 5
Leisure, Wk 11
Link, Wk 17
Loosen, Wk 2, 5
Lounge, Wk 11

Mahogany, Wk 7, 10
Mare, Wk 18
Massage, Wk 19
Master, Wk 1
Mastodon, Wk 3, 5
Measure, Wk 19, 20
Metal, Wk 13
Method, Wk 3, 5
Mica, Wk 12
Mimic, Wk 16
Miner, Wk 12
Mixture, Wk 14, 15
Model, Wk 13
Murmur, Wk 7
Mustache, Wk 4

Nutrition, Wk 8, 10

Object, Wk 14
Operator, Wk 13